The Death of Judeo-Christianity

Religious Aggression and Systemic Evil in the Modern World

The Death of Judeo-Christianity

Religious Aggression and Systemic Evil in the Modern World

Lawrence Swaim

Winchester, UK
Washington, USA

First published by Circle Books, 2012
Circle Books is an imprint of John Hunt Publishing Ltd., Laurel House, Station Approach,
Alresford, Hants, SO24 9JH, UK
office1@jhpbooks.net
www.johnhuntpublishing.com
www.circle-books.com

For distributor details and how to order please visit the 'Ordering' section on our website.

ISBN: 978 1 78099 299 0

A CIP catalogue record for this book is available from the British Library.

Design: Stuart Davies

Printed in the USA by Edwards Brothers Malloy

We operate a distinctive and ethical publishing philosophy in all areas of our business, from our global network of authors to production and worldwide distribution.

CONTENTS

Part One: The Death of Christianity

"Claire Boothe Luce is said by the novelist Herbert Gold to have complained to a Jewish friend that she found all the talk about the Holocaust insufferably boring. Her friend said he knew just what she was talking about. 'In fact," Gold writes, "he had the same sense of repetitiousness and fatigue, hearing so often about the crucifixion.'"[1]

1

There is at the heart of Christianity a disturbing doctrine that has the uncanny ability to overwhelm cognition—and when internalized by the believer, it has the ability to traumatize. I refer to the belief, held by most Christians, that Jesus Christ, the central figure of Christianity, was tortured to death in public to redeem the world, so that God could be reconciled to his creation. Many observers have commented on the cruelty of this central event at the heart of Christianity, but this writer aims to make a different point than simply to note its violent nature. *That point is this*: that the doctrine of salvation through the violence of Jesus' crucifixion is radically different, incomprehensively different, from the God of love and forgiveness as taught by Jesus—so different, in fact, that it poses an unsolvable and irreducible moral problem at the heart of Christianity. The extreme sense of paradox created by Jesus' message of love, on the one hand, and the supposedly redemptive nature of the crucifixion's violence on the other, can traumatize the believer over a period of time, especially when disturbing images, narratives and beliefs concerning the crucifixion are constantly reiterated. This reiteration can create a trauma bond that bonds the believer to Christianity; but it does so by causing the Christian to internalize *as redemptive* the aggression of the crucifixion. Because of this, a profound identification with aggression tends to be the fundamental emotional orientation of institutional Christianity.

Christian theologians most commonly call this key belief of Christianity—that God caused Jesus to die on the cross for the sins of the world—substitutionary atonement. It has also been referred to as blood redemption or blood atonement—by dying on the cross, Jesus *atones* for the sins of humankind, and *redeems* sinners in the process. Some will object at the outset that it was humanity, and not God, that crucified Jesus. God, however, gave the crucifixion its redemptive power, according to almost all Christian theology in the West, because grace and salvation can only come from God. For that reason, and because only God can grant eternal life to the believer, the crucifixion of Jesus was at the heart of God's plan of redemption for humanity.

In other words, God colluded with the procurator of the Roman Empire, a specialist in imperial cruelty, to arrive at redemption for you and me, the redemption arising not just because of the sacrifice of Jesus (there are lots of other ways to sacrifice oneself) but specifically through the brutality and agony of public torture. God, in this scenario, is little more than a cosmic Mafia boss whose specialty is ritualized human sacrifice, and whose preferred method of redemption is public torture of dissenters. If you do not "accept Jesus as your personal savior" (that is, if you don't internalize the aggression of blood redemption as a part of a conversion experience), most American evangelicals will be happy to inform you that you will be going to hell, and that you're going to be tortured for all eternity. (Interestingly, this was also the imposed social contract involved in the use of the Inquisition as an instrument of social repression. If you were suspected of not accepting the torture of Jesus as redemptive, you could be tortured yourself as a kind of prelude to the eternity of torture that awaited you.)

So whatever else it may do, the doctrine of blood atonement *does* send a message that violence can be redemptive. This message came to be, over a period of time, the very heart and soul of Christianity. I am not talking about Jesus' life, the Beatitudes, the Sermon on the Mount or the parables. I am talking about the idea that God made a human sacrifice out of Jesus as a scapegoat for the sins of humanity. This belief in blood redemption is, I submit, the most violent idea ever devised by the human mind, with the single exception of eternal torment for temporal sins. And the belief in Jesus' blood atonement, far from being some unexamined bit of theology in the dank margins of religious exotica, is the foundational theological concept of almost *all* institutional Protestant and Catholic Christianity, the world's majority religion.

This doctrine is constantly reiterated in liturgy, hymns, sermons and homilies, in theology and in popular literature. Jesus' violent death on the cross (the central dynamic of salvation) is *constantly* referred to by Christian clergy as being of supreme importance, from the primitive church through the Middle Ages right up to, and very much including, today's conservative Catholics and Protestant evangelicals. It is constantly referred to because of its ability to traumatize and overwhelm the believer, who must inevitably internalize its implicit aggression. Please note that substitutionary atonement is also a central belief in the liberal mainstream Protestant denominations (Presbyterians, Methodists, Episcopalians and Lutherans). Even to those who do not understand or accept the doctrine of blood redemption, it is so disturbing it cannot be easily forgotten or dismissed, which means that most people who contemplate it must to some extent internalize the aggression it represents. (For an example of the cross as a deeply influential culture icon, see Chaim Potok's *My Name is Asher Lev*, the story of a Hasidic Jewish boy who is so obsessed by the crucifixion that he paints endless pictures of it, including one of his mother being crucified.)

Liberal Christians see the Garden-of-Eden story as an allegory for the growth of evil in human consciousness, and tend also to see Judgment Day—correctly, I think—as a remnant of the apocalyptical thinking of Jesus' time. But even the most liberal Christians, usually so adept at discerning the metaphorical nature of religious language, generally do not denounce (or at least do not make any very strong objection to) the idea that the execution of Jesus by the Roman Empire two thousand years ago was God's way of redeeming humankind. They, too, have generally internalized this central idea to such an extent that they can no longer see it for what it is: an attempt to redeem the psychic effects of aggression by accommodating, idealizing, and internalizing it, standard mechanisms of trauma bonding.

This particular form of trauma bonding has resulted in a generalized Christian obsession with crucifixion and the cross. This obsession with the violence of the crucifixion is associated with the worst and most obscurantist aspects of Christianity, at least partly because the emphasis on Jesus' death can be used to downplay and repress the importance of Jesus' life and teachings. But the primitive nature of the doctrine of blood redemption is especially conducive to—and tends to encourage—social practices of extreme brutality, when it is internalized by enough people. It shouldn't surprise anyone, for example, that a religion that embraces the doctrine of blood atonement should once have believed that Jews killed Christians in order to put their blood in matzo balls. In fact, Christianity's most violent and pathological obsessions (loathing of women, war in the name of Jesus, and flagrant anti-Semitism, to name just three) waxed and waned in roughly the same proportion as the Christian obsession with Jesus' death on the cross, and the accompanying belief in blood redemption.

It continues today in the recurring—and frequently nauseating—emphasis on Jesus' blood in evangelical sermons, hymns and literature, not to mention the Eucharist in the liturgical churches that culminates in the symbolic drinking of Jesus' blood and eating of his flesh. The anti-Semitism is still often there, too, although in a disguised form. The current Pope has again made possible the reading of prayers for the conversion of Jews during Easter Week, a clear reference to the idea of inherited Jewish guilt for Jesus' death. In many conservative evangelical churches, people long for the End Time (or End of Days), which means the end of the world, which many of them believe will result in the forced conversion of the Jews. For those Jews who *don't* convert to Christianity at the End Time—well, the final solution for *them* will be genocide. God, the same psychopathic God who needed a human sacrifice to be reconciled to the world he created, will murder all the Jews who refuse to convert to Christianity, thereby finishing the job that Hitler started at Auschwitz.

2

Blood redemption, the central doctrine of Christianity, is the train wreck of western civilization. You want to stop looking at Jesus up there on the cross, but you can't, because images and reminders of Jesus' death are everywhere. And even when there are no images, there is every imaginable kind of music about it, from Bach to bluegrass. Western classical music started in the church, and the blues, the *Quell* of American popular music, is a first cousin to gospel. Nowadays, when a good 70 to 80 percent of American Christians are evangelicals or conservative Catholics, wherever there is church music, there is probably going to be constant references to the crucifixion, and to blood atonement. It is the pain and horror and the *blood* of the crucifixion that evangelicals are obsessed with—that is their preoccupation, and that is what they think about and preach about. Nothing, you see, is quite as dramatic as murder—which is why cop shows on TV are so popular; and there is no murder with as much over-the-top, pulse-pounding excitement as the murder of God, especially when the listener can be denounced as an accomplice.

Driving through huge sections of the Middle West and the South, there is often nothing on the radio but the so-called Christian radio stations; and even the AM stations that aren't technically evangelical carry evangelical preaching, full of constant references to the blood and gore of the crucifixion. But all this evangelical hooting and hollering, all the fundamentalist sermons and declarations of faith and gospel-quoting and various country-style preachments—all these come to the same thing, namely, Jesus suffered on the cross for *you*, for *your* sins, because *you* are a sinner for whom Jesus had to suffer interminably and shed his blood; and you are complicit in all that suffering, simply by breathing the air and driving along in your car listening to your radio.

The frenzied *style* of modern radio evangelicalism and televangelism have deep roots in America, going back to the extremism of the seventeenth-century British Puritans who settled in Massachusetts (a splinter group of a splinter group, addicted to theological drama), certain ongoing forms of pietism, and the First and Second Great Awakenings. The excited style of American evangelical preaching evokes—and is intended to evoke—the intensity of a conflicted soul in crisis. Interestingly, though, modern televangelists and evangelical preachers on AM Radio use images and metaphors not all that different from those used by preachers in the First Great Awakening in 1735. Nor are they that different from ideas expressed by Bernard of Clairvaux in the twelfth century or the church bishops at the Council of Constantinople in 381. Jesus died for the sins of the world; and that's your only hope for salvation, which becomes yours not by denouncing his crucifixion as a particularly disgusting example of systemic evil—which it most assuredly was—but embracing it as your ticket to the New Earth.

Not only must you accept the primacy of blood redemption, you must accept the redemption originating in Jesus' suffering *by accepting his blood itself,* right up to the point of imagining yourself as being physically bathed in it. Of course, the image of being bathed, washed or covered in blood, *anybody's* blood, is intrinsically disgusting—but that's exactly why it is so powerful. All such imagines, which have at their root the idea that torture can be redemptive, are essentially traumatizing.

The mind rejects the images and the doctrine behind it every time they are reiterated, but there they are again and again, as one drives through Wyoming and Kansas and Louisiana and North Carolina, images of Jesus' blood washing over the sinners of the world, until finally the very loathsomeness of the images, not to mention the images themselves, find a home in the unconscious mind. Hearing again and again about the blood of Jesus, and the redemptive effects of being bathed in it, one must to *some* extent internalize the images and the seething aggression that is animating those imagines, simply to maintain enough cognitive focus to keep from driving off the road.

Accompanying AM Christian radio is its natural counterpart, the political and social fulminations of AM Hate Radio, a phenomenon that probably began with Russ Limbaugh, but which now includes up to a hundred and fifty talk show "hosts," all saying the same thing: the UN wants to take away your guns; the government is socialist; people who are different should be hated; and immigrants, liberals and Muslims are enemies of the state. (AM Hate Radio has had to tone down their rhetoric against gays, because the LGBTQ people are now organized enough to stage boycotts, file lawsuits, and in general defend themselves.) But immigrants and Muslims don't have enough clout to fight back effectively yet, so that makes them targets of opportunity. And that's what these radio hate-fests are really about: a chance to hate, and perhaps hurt, people who are different, and who don't have the political clout to fight back. (People who hate on the basis of group identity are usually sadists, to some extent, but also cowards, so they fear a fair fight.)

The underlying emotional dynamic of AM Hate Radio isn't just sadism. Hate Radio is seething with resentment toward people who are perceived as having more education, more money, more cultural literacy, more intelligence, or more *pleasure* than oneself; and it is also shot through with hostility against people who belong to different races and religions. Many listeners to AM Hate Radio feel offended by the civil rights movement and emasculated by the women's movement. These are overwhelmingly, in other words, angry white men whose skin color and gender no longer guarantee them a modicum of deference. Hate Radio is, in other words, aimed at all the poor *schleps* that got left behind, angry white guys who are sinking every day into deeper economic, emotional and spiritual blight, but who lack the intelligence or curiosity to figure out what's pulling them down; and are therefore clueless about how to stop it. Such people are ripe to discharge their frustration on handy scapegoats, as long as the scapegoat is in no position to retaliate.

Christian evangelicalism and AM Hate Radio not only go together very well, they represent two connected phenomena that have been interacting for well over sixteen hundred years. The first is the belief in the crucifixion of Jesus as the basis for human redemption, central to most Christian teaching. The second is the worship of aggression in the form of state power. The two validate and drive each other forward, and have done so since the time of Constantine in the early fourth century, and for this reason are intertwined in Western society. Blood atonement and the worship of state aggression don't appeal to those who already have power, but to people who feel powerless, clueless and without a coherent strategy for their lives.

In America, such people often have little insight into their own deficits, and therefore can't understand the source of their own pain. Instead of self-improvement—going to a night class, joining a union, or improving themselves in some way—they must be angry at the world and at other people, posturing themselves as righteous victims who are going to get even someday, in some unspecified but probably apocalyptic manner. It is that powerful identification with aggression as potentially redemptive that makes Christian evangelical radio and AM Hate Radio ideological twins. In the Christian evangelical and fundamentalist movements, it is blood atonement that redeems. In AM Hate Radio the redemption comes from hating—and fantasies about hurting—human beings who are different and who probably cannot retaliate. Either way, it is always about redemption through aggression, experienced through a constant stream of violent words and images. Politically, it tends to express itself as support for war, torture and repression.

I know there are progressive Christian evangelicals, and there are also a few progressive AM talk shows. But I've never heard

Christian radio that isn't in-your-face evangelical. That means that for hundreds and even thousands of miles, if you're driving through America and you listen to the radio, it's mainly AM Hate and evangelical Blood-of-the-Lamb, washed-in-the-blood Christianity. (In many markets, the Rush Limbaugh program is actually given *free* to radio stations, with pre-selected advertisers. We have Limbaugh's corporate sponsors to thank for that sweetheart deal.) And the unconscious message, on the level of the emotions, is identification with aggression, identification with the ecstasy of victim-hood, and redemption through violence. It's a long, hard drive through the great rural maw of flyover America, if you listen to the radio. You'd be well-advised to bring along some good CDs.

This obsession that Jesus *had* to die on the cross for your sins, and that *only* by accepting this can you avoid damnation, didn't start yesterday. It didn't start with Billy Sunday or Billy Graham, or even the great Puritan preachers like Jonathon Edwards. It started in 381 when the belief in blood redemption was institutionalized at the Council of Constantinople, and in the twelfth century was extended to confer salvation to those who killed Muslims on crusade, or were killed by them. All the violence—all the killing of Jews, Muslims, women and heretics—can be traced back to the belief that Jesus suffered publicly on the cross for the sins of the world, and in so doing redeemed the world. That established Christianity as an *exclusive* religion: only those who believe in blood atonement, who believe that Jesus died on the cross for their sins, can spend eternity in the New Earth. The rest of us must be punished—that is the basic message. But it did not start out that way.

3

Nobody knows exactly why he did so, but at the age of thirty, a man named Jesus, from the small, slightly disreputable town of Nazareth, in Galilee, began to roam across the country speaking to large crowds, talking to them about a new kind of relationship with God. In gospel accounts, we discover that this prophet or teacher believed that the end of the world was near, and sought to prepare his followers for it. The best preparation was to create a new relationship with God, Jesus believed, and he explained how that could be done, using the vernacular Aramaic language of his time, employing earthy, hard-hitting parables and metaphors that the people of his time understood.

He encouraged his followers not just to follow the law, but to internalize it, because only then could it change behavior. To accomplish that, Jesus taught them to pray to God for help, using a new prayer that Jesus taught as part of his spiritual discipline. If they prayed with all their heart, God would change their personalities in such a way that people would feel the same kind of love that people feel for their children, parents, siblings and best friends. As their relationship to God changed, so would their relationships with each other. You had to ask for help from God, and your ability to receive God's love would change how you see the world, and bond you to other people who were going through the same process. Jesus' beliefs included charity toward all people, a determination not to judge others, and an ever-present willingness humbly to ask God for guidance.

Supposedly, this would create a new "kingdom" of believers, psychologically bonded together by a new personal relationship with God, but also animated by God's law when it was internalized, when it was embedded in one's personality. That was the process. But Jesus was also concerned about aggression, and had some startlingly new ideas about how to deal with it. One idea was so counter-intuitive and so radical that it probably struck some listeners as a form of insanity: Jesus said that people should pray for their enemies, and even love them. Not kill them, not retaliate against them, but pray for them and love them. Of course, you had to pray to God a lot to get into that kind of mental and emotional state, but Jesus said it was possible. This was something people hadn't heard before.

Most of Jesus' teachings were inspired adaptations of Pharisaical and other concepts current in Judaism, but Jesus was selective about the themes he pursued, and expressed them in charismatic and exciting ways. Although Jesus was close to the Pharisees in both theology and temperament, he was different in one huge way: Jesus apparently believed that Jewish law couldn't become a part of one's personality until it was internalized, and that the Pharisees wouldn't, or couldn't, internalize the emotional implications of their own law. To Jesus, this meant that the Pharisees weren't practicing what they preached. The Pharisees were mainly interested in measuring social behavior against the law, whereas Jesus, although a shrewd observer of behavior, was concerned about the way people experienced God, morality and each other psychologically.

Jesus was a powerful speaker, skilled at reducing profound ideas to jokes, stories and parables, and was apparently one of those rare people for whom others feel an almost immediate attraction. He was, in other words, the consummate itinerant preacher, and one with a natural sense of comic timing. He was extremely quick on his feet, regularly turning the tables on those who tried to entrap him with trick questions. In the course of his ministry, Jesus challenged many prevailing cultural belief-systems of his time, especially attitudes toward women—in fact, he constantly deferred to women in ways his followers found sacrilegious. Jesus sought a spiritual revolution, and made it clear that he wasn't preaching violent revolution like the Zealots. (After all, Jesus believed that God was coming soon to set up a kingdom of the righteous, so a human rebellion wasn't necessary.)

Although Jesus judged religion by its effect on behavior, he was unique in the emphasis he put on the interior rather than public dimensions of religion. This fascination with a personal relationship with God, when combined with the insistence on praying for one's enemies, was, in a sense, a way of pleading with God to change humanity from the inside out. It was certainly a new way of dealing with human evil. Of course, Hillel and other great rabbis of that time were working along similar lines—Hillel, in particular, possessed an uncommon greatness. But in Jesus' case, the moral precepts he taught were intended not just for achieving a good life or a just society, but as preparation for the imminent end of the world. Perhaps partly because of this, his sermons had a searing psychological intensity that made Jesus special, especially to the poor, the rejected and the socially marginalized.

For most Jews of Jesus' time, righteousness tended to come from the laws Yahweh had created, just as later in rabbinical Judaism it would come from debating the various interpretations of those laws. For Jesus, righteousness could paradoxically arise from forgiving the obnoxious or homicidal behavior of others. Much of the drama of the New Testament arises from the irony—and pathos—of the difference between what Jesus was saying, and what his disciples wanted to hear. It was a time of religious enthusiasm, during which Jerusalem and its environs were thronged with would-be messiahs, secret Zealots, apocalyptic preachers, shamans and itinerant wonder-working magi of every description. Jesus' disciples very early formed an idea that Jesus was a Messiah, and quite naturally expected him to overthrow the Romans, because that's what a Messiah was supposed to do—the Messiah was supposed to rescue the Hebrew-speaking people from their oppressors. They fully expected that Jesus would use his special powers to get rid of the cruel Roman

Procurator Pontius Pilate, along with his disrespectful and sadistic troops.

But when Jesus was arrested and hauled in front of Pilate, the Procurator of Judea, he was scorned by the Pharisees, scourged by the Roman soldiers, and crucified by the imperial state. The messianic dreams of his disciples were smashed. Their teacher, their rabbi, their Messiah, their Jesus of Nazareth, the charismatic, tireless leader that they had accompanied in their itinerant wanderings throughout the country, was tortured in public by crucifixion, which was the special punishment reserved for the worst enemies of the state and the most despicable criminals. Throughout this, Jesus lifted not a finger to save himself. There was nothing even remotely messianic about his last hours. Why didn't Jesus use his spiritual powers to stop the Roman soldiers in their tracks? After all, he'd already used those powers to heal the sick, to raise the dead and to turn water into wine. But when the crunch time came, he did nothing, meekly allowing himself to be tortured to death before his followers' eyes.

For Jesus' disciples, it was a crushing experience that overturned everything they knew about the messianic vocation. The synoptic gospels make it unmistakably clear that Jesus' disciples had discerned an opportunity to improve themselves personally by getting in on the ground floor of the new kingdom they thought Jesus was about to set up. This is a recurring comic premise that is responsible for much of the humor in the synoptic gospels, seen clearly in the way the disciples keep arguing over the future power they're all going to wield. One smiles at the self-serving naivety of their ambition, but it's easy to understand why they would have seen Jesus as a political revolutionary as well as a religious one. To the Aramaic-speaking Jews of that time and place, religion *was* politics. God had made laws for society, righteousness came from following those laws, and the Messiah would come to defeat the enemies who threatened their religious system. It was natural for Jesus' disciples to believe that he would kick out the Romans and set up a new regime, and that they would share in his power.

But for Jesus, righteousness was a state in which laws were followed out of love rather than duty, and arose from a person's relationship to God. Jesus insisted that the right relationship with God came not from the endless parsing of law against public behavior, but from a private, inner attitude based on the willingness to humble oneself. When Jesus taught people to pray for a new kingdom ("thy will be done, thy kingdom come, on earth as it is in heaven"), the words refer not to a worldly kingdom, but to a spiritual one, in which he and his followers would strive not for power, but to change the *nature* of power.

They would accomplish this through radical love and forgiveness, which Jesus believed was God's will, and which he thought God could, if asked, help people to achieve.

Jesus' disciples never really got it. Jesus used metaphoric and analogical language in a way that was consistently taken literally, first by his followers and then by his enemies, with tragic results for all concerned. (Interestingly, modern evangelicals who believe in the literal inerrancy of the Bible are direct ideological descendants of those disciples who misunderstood the nature of Jesus' message.) Imagine, then, how shocked Jesus' disciples must have been when Jesus was crucified. Instead of calling down God's wrath on the Romans, Jesus went to his death like tens of thousands of other heretics, rebels and Jewish nationalists who had been similarly crucified. His followers went from being confreres of a Messiah to being hunted criminals.

They were not only traumatized, but psychologically crushed. Thus it should be no surprise to us that after his death his disciples began suddenly to see him in various places, under unusual and mysterious circumstances—after all, Jesus was a man with so much personal charisma that many of them had dropped everything (that is, they had actually walked off their jobs) to follow him. They loved him as they had loved no one else. So his frightened and dispersed disciples began to see him after he was dead, and they saw him in strange and unexpected places.

The hysterical character of these encounters is easily discerned from scriptural accounts. The disciples walk for many miles on a road with a stranger, and even eat supper with him, without realizing until later that he is Jesus. Of course, it makes no logical sense that the disciples could have walked or eaten with Jesus, a man with whom they'd spent so much time, without recognizing him immediately; but this should not be seen as literal truth but as a psychological phenomenon with great metaphoric value. Among other things, it meant that Jesus *could be anybody,* that kindness to strangers was actually kindness to Jesus—that feeding any hungry person was feeding Jesus. The disciples' sightings of Jesus after his death amounted to a *psychological* defeat of death.

As for the historical Jesus, the story of Jesus' body being interred in a cemetery is surely an invention, because the Romans would never have allowed one of their condemned prisoners to be so honored. Most likely, his remains were eaten by the packs of wild dogs that roamed Jerusalem, as John Dominic Crossan has suggested. The real Jesus disappeared from history after his death, along with his earthly remains. But his disciples saw him repeatedly, or apparitions they thought were him, and in so doing, were comforted in their loss. But in being so comforted, they turned the trauma on its head. Jesus hadn't been killed by the Romans after all. *Jesus had risen! The Romans had been defeated!* If Jesus returned to life after being dead for three days, that would enable the early Jesus movement to erase the stigma of the crucifixion by representing Jesus as so powerful that he could beat the rap, so to speak, outsmarting the Roman Empire at their own game. Even the Romans, with all their power, could not kill Jesus, because he had risen victorious from the grave!

It was a giddy, life-affirming victory, but the belief in Jesus' resurrection already contained a negative tendency. It took people one small step away from Jesus' message, putting the emphasis on Jesus' supernatural powers rather than the radical nature of his teachings. But it was not yet a big step, because the early church had no reason to suppress or dissimulate Jesus' radical teachings. The revolutionary nature of Jesus' ideas was not yet threatening because the Jesus movement had no political clout. They were merely another group of semi-indigent religious fanatics in Jerusalem, one of many such messianic groups, and probably one of the least attractive. It was easy for them to talk about loving their enemies, because they did not yet have the power to retaliate against them.

4

The second great trauma of Christianity was the mind-boggling experience of Paul of Tarsus. Paul was a Roman citizen, a tent-maker by trade, and a Hellenized Jew. Although his Judaism was fundamental and exacting, he was deeply influenced by Greek ways of thinking, and was quick to demand the rights that came with being a Roman citizen. He was, in other words, a highly civilized and active man of his time and place, and like many seminal thinkers was influenced by more than one culture. But his profound Jewish faith caused him to regard with horror certain practices that were thought harmless by the Greeks, including homosexuality—with tragic consequences for homosexuals over the next two thousand years. He was immensely conscientious, even fanatical; he possessed great physical courage; and he fearlessly examined his own life, framing his conclusions in the apocalyptic religious language of his time. He assumed others would benefit from doing the same, with a little mentoring from him. He was an incredible *yenta*, forever meddling and nagging his friends in his epistles, but without ever losing the big picture.

Paul's story began inauspiciously. He was what we would call today a security police officer, in the secret police of the ever-suspicious Roman Procurator (or Prefect), tasked with rounding up and eliminating various groups that his Roman bosses found subversive. This put him in league with the conservative Pharisees who had made their peace with the occupying Romans, and who didn't want radical groups rocking the boat. One of Paul's tasks was rounding up followers of Jesus of Nazareth, who were apparently meeting regularly to celebrate the rumored resurrection of their Messiah. That was enough to make them considered enemies of the state—that is, enemies of the Roman Procurator and the Roman Empire.

This kind of Gestapo-type job must have been tremendously stressful for Paul, and it probably generated no small amount of guilt, since he was largely engaged in persecuting his own kind. The people he apprehended and sent to their deaths were fellow Jews who had joined a new sectarian group, fanatical and possibly schismatic types to be sure; but Paul had to know that they were probably harmless to the Roman Empire, since they weren't interested in armed revolution or political power. As unpleasant as the job was, Paul characteristically threw all his energies into it, and from all accounts, including his own, he was very effective at rounding up the scattered remnants of the Jesus movement.

These early Christians probably met death stoically, which may have impressed Paul.

Paul was so good at getting rid of the Jesus people that he was sent to do the same thing in Damascus. Here he would continue his work of ridding the world of the followers of the crucified Jesus of Nazareth. But before he could even start rounding up the usual suspects, something astonishing happened, something that would change his life—and also change history.

On the road to Damascus, all the guilt and stress of running a gritty police operation against his own people caught up with Paul. As he was riding along, the sky was suddenly filled with light, so bright that Paul was totally blinded.

Paul heard a voice from above, "Paul, Paul, why do you persecute me?"

Paul fell from his horse and lay blinded on the ground.

"Who are you?" he managed to say.

"I am Jesus, the man that you persecute."

It was the voice of the very man whose followers he was tracking down and executing. Here was payback, here was Jesus confronting him, accusing him in broad daylight, right there on the main road to Damascus. Paul wrote of "meeting" Jesus at that moment, so it is reasonable to assume that he had a visual hallucination of Jesus as well as an auditory hallucination of his voice.

Whatever it was, it changed everything.

Paul lay immobile on the ground, unable to see, until someone took pity on him and led him back to Jerusalem. He was blind for three days—the same amount of time that Jesus had been dead in the tomb before his resurrection. Most ironic of all, his blindness was actually cured, and his sight restored, by the healing touch of a Jesus-follower, a man who belonged to the underground sect he'd been rounding up. Providentially and somewhat eerily, Paul was during this difficult time apparently befriended by several followers of Jesus, the very group he'd been ruthlessly persecuting. He spent the next two years studying the sayings and stories associated with Jesus' ministry, perhaps trying to figure out why Jesus had appeared to him on the road to Damascus, what it all meant, and what he should do about it.

During that two-year period, Paul found the answer. He became himself a follower of Jesus. Believing in Jesus' resurrection was no problem for him, because he had been accosted by Jesus in the desert; and now he prepared himself to be an activist with the new Jesus movement. With typical Pauline chutzpa, he decided to set off on a missionary trek to visit other Jesus groups, accompanied by a man named Barnabas. Their goal—which remained Paul's goal later, as he gradually became the most important leader in the movement—was to set up cells of Jesus-followers throughout the Greek-speaking world, believers who would promulgate the new faith whose adherents he had formerly persecuted.

This inevitably changed the Jesus message, because Paul and Jesus were two very different people. To begin with, Jesus saw himself as a Jew speaking to other Jews. True, many of his parables dealt with Samaritans and other outsiders, but he apparently aimed at changing Jewish attitudes, not founding a world religion. (In his recurring referrals to Samaritans, Jesus was an early and heroic adherent of what we would today call religious pluralism, an approach his followers would mainly ignore.) But Paul discerned an opportunity for a new faith community throughout the Greek-speaking areas of his time and place. Paul seemed at first to see the Jesus movement as a radical new form of Judaism, but as Jews showed few signs of converting in large numbers, he pragmatically opened the door to non-Jews. He would spend the rest of his life as an unpaid organizer of the early Jesus movement, checking up on the new Jesus groups and exhorting them to proper behavior, as well as bravely proselytizing for the new movement in synagogues and other semi-public places.

Paul referred to Jesus' teachings, but even more to Jesus' resurrection. It would be fair to say that Paul was obsessed by Jesus' resurrection—he had, after all, personally experienced the living Jesus on the road to Damascus, and it was the central event of his life. In being resurrected from the tomb, Jesus had demonstrated the power to defeat death, and Paul believed that Jesus' followers would likewise be able to defeat death, and have eternal life with Jesus in heaven. He was constantly exhorting people in his epistles to die with Jesus, so they could be born again—that is, resurrected—as new people who would live forever.

Paul and his followers developed a baptism ritual for new converts, and in this ritual the resurrection was simulated —the convert would be immersed in water, during which he "died" along with Jesus, but then rose up out of the water, "resurrected" as a new person. Only by dying with Jesus, then, could the convert be resurrected with him—not just resurrected to this life as a new person, but resurrected to *eternal* life, to live for all time in the New Earth that Jesus would create when he returned in glory to earth. This idea occurs constantly in the epistles of Paul, often accompanied by complicated metaphoric language about water and its supposedly miraculous and even curative powers.

In these passages, Paul was clearly referring to water as a medium of baptism, which was therefore a symbol of Jesus' resurrection from death after three days in the tomb; and when he wrote of the resurrection he also probably had in mind the three days of blindness he had suffered after being confronted by Jesus on the road to Damascus, and the miraculous return of his sight.

Mixed in amongst these references to the resurrection was another idea— Jesus had died to redeem the world from the original sin of Adam in the Garden of Eden. Or put another way, Paul suggested that Jesus had died as a blood sacrifice, just as the Jewish people had often sacrificed animals to propitiate God. (Paul even compares Jesus to the Passover lamb, whose blood redeemed the Jews in Egypt.) By offering himself as a human sacrifice, Jesus accepts God's punishment in our place. It is a wildly primitive idea that keeps bubbling up in the interstices between the other ideas that Paul is trying to impart, and never completely goes away.

But while Paul mentions this idea, he clearly gives it much less importance than the emphasis on Jesus' resurrection. The resurrection defeats the evil designs of the Romans in a most satisfying way, and prefigures the eternal life of the believer—and in the process reveals God to be a loving, healing, restorative father. The blood redemption idea was a different story. As Paul may have realized even then, allowing Jesus to suffer God's wrath for the sins of the people suggests an entirely different cosmological atmosphere, making God seem more like a vengeful, murderous tribal chieftain than a loving father. In any case, Paul puts much more emphasis on Jesus' resurrection than his crucifixion as redemptive and life-giving. Here is a typical passage from Paul—or somebody writing in Paul's name—discussing Jesus' resurrection and its power to defeat death.

"For what I received, I passed on to you as of first importance;

> that Christ died for our sins according to the Scripture, that he was buried, that he was raised on the third day according to the Scriptures, and that he appeared to Peter, and then to the Twelve. After that, he appeared to more than five hundred of the brothers at the same time, most of whom are living, though some have fallen asleep. Then he appeared to James, then to all the apostles, and last of all, he appeared to me. *And if Christ has not been raised, our preaching is useless and so is your faith.* Then those who have fallen asleep in Christ are lost. If only for this life we have hope in Christ, we are to be pitied more than are all men." (Italics added.)

This comes across almost as a reckless, Pascal-like tavern wager, rather than a spiritual revelation. Paul is putting all his eggs in one basket, the basket of Jesus' resurrection from the dead—for him, it is first and foremost Jesus' rising from the tomb that guarantees eternal life for the believer. Only the short second clause of the first sentence refers to Jesus dying on the cross for humanity's sins, and that is mentioned mainly in passing. This idea of blood redemption influenced the early Jesus followers, but the second—the resurrection of Jesus as the guarantor of eternal life—was clearly the most important to Paul, and therefore the most important to the early Christians who read his exhortations. This would not be changed definitively until 381 CE, when the Council of Constantinople would reverse the importance of the two ideas, and establish blood atonement as the guarantor of eternal salvation rather than the resurrection.

Paul's thoughts were written in the form of extremely pithy letters to small groups, and the letters were copied by hand, widely distributed and saved. Paul's letters were practical guides to organizing a new religious sect, so he wanted the letters to be circulated to as many believers as possible. This meant that he got more of a hearing than anyone else in the early days of the Jesus movement—in fact, Paul's epistles were circulating among believers long before written accounts of Jesus' life. Although there was probably a compilation of Jesus' sayings in circulation (scholars refer to it as *Q)*, the Jesus-followers probably didn't think it was necessary to have a written version of his life, because he was coming back soon anyway. It wasn't until after Paul wrote his epistles that anyone thought to write a chronological narrative of Jesus' life. By that time the politics of that historical period, not to mention the wildly inexact exigencies of time and memory, resulted in a particular kind of story which in certain respects—especially regarding Jesus' death—was almost certainly more fiction than fact.

Besides offering practical organizing advice, the central idea of Paul's letters is that Jesus was executed and then came back to life. Therefore, salvation for believers comes not from Jesus' death, but from his resurrection—and Paul, having seen the risen Jesus himself, is both witness to that miracle and a grateful recipient of its power. It is Jesus' *resurrection*, and not Jesus' *death*, that redeems the world from sin and guarantees eternal life to the believer. This idea would be the central and guiding concept of Christian faith until almost four centuries later, when it became an imperial religion.

5

The third big paradigm shift in Christianity occurred in 312 of the Common Era, and it, too, was traumatic. (If you're seeing a pattern here, it's not your imagination—Christian beliefs tended to develop in response to unexpected and violent crises, almost invariably involving organized aggression.) In the three centuries after Paul wrote his widely-circulated letters to the young churches of the Greek-speaking world, there arose within Christianity a theological free-for-all of astonishing energy and variety. What happened was the rise of many Christianities, with every group, it seemed, embracing its own belief-system, many of which were quite exotic, and all of which were somewhat different from each other. Most of them did not resemble what we would call Christianity today. This variety was not necessarily a bad thing—as a result, it was impossible for one theological group to impose its beliefs on all the other groups; and the resulting lack of unity prevented the church from becoming a temporal worldly power, with all the corruption that political power would inevitably entail. The problem was that all these different Christianities claimed to be right, and thought everybody else wrong. Jesus' admonitions about the essential humanity of different faith communities (using the Samaritans as his prime example) were forgotten, in favor of a dangerous emphasis on theological purity.

At the beginning of the fourth century, this chaotic situation changed. The man responsible for it was an ambitious Roman general named Constantine. He gave nominal fealty to the traditional gods of the Romans; but he also wanted a more dynamic state religion that could operate as an adhesive to bind together his disintegrating empire, which had become a collection of vastly different ethnicities. Christianity as it stood couldn't do that, because of the many variations of Christian belief—unless some powerful individual imposed a single brand of Christianity on the young church. For that to work, one brand of Christianity would have to become the state religion, and the others would have to be banned. Christianity would not necessarily replace the older gods, but if it became a state religion, it would be given a certain ascendancy over the older pagan beliefs that would increase with time.

This revolution in the fortunes of humanity occurred—or was set in motion—by the events of a single day in 312 CE. Constantine, who had ruled the Roman Empire's western dominions with a combination of brutality and strategic acuity, was preparing to go into battle against Maxentius, a rival Roman general. The evening before the battle, as he lingered at Milvian Bridge near the River Tiber outside Rome, Constantine saw a cross in the sky above the words *In Hoc Signo Vinces* ("In This Sign, Conquer"), which he decided was a sign from the Christian God. That night he had a similar dream. His interpretation, not surprisingly, was that the Christian God approved of him personally, and also his imperial ambitions; and according to his own later accounts (and those of his hagiographer) he used this inspirational vision—and the cross as a lucky talisman—to rally his troops, who soundly defeated Maxentius. He probably would have won this battle anyway, but the wily Constantine had good reason for wanting the support of Christians, because they had grown quite numerous in Rome.

The words *In Hoc Signo* later become a popular motto of the church, the letters IHS even appearing on communion wafers in the liturgical churches. (They were said to represent the first three Greek letters of Jesus' name, but the other connotation—of defeating an enemy in battle—was widely understood to be the real meaning.) Although Constantine was an exceptionally clever and ruthless tactician, there was nothing just or noble about his cause—his bid for personal power was merely one of many that were ongoing in the Roman Empire.

The thing that really made Constantine different was his defeat of his foe on that day in 312 CE, which resulted—along with his testimony about the fortuitous vision—in his becoming the first Christian emperor. That, in turn, made him the *de facto* leader of Christianity. Constantine had his rival's head carried through the streets of Rome on a pike, something that must have horrified his wife, Fausta, since the unlucky Maxentius was her brother. But Constantine was not one to consider his wife's sensibilities when presented with an opportunity to advertise his brutality. The days of Christianity as a mainly non-violent religious movement were coming to an end.

From now on, Roman Emperors would increasingly wage war or conduct affairs of state in the name of the Christian God, because they saw themselves as acting out God's will on earth. Christianity would no longer be led by idealistic, scruffy schismatic types living on the fringes of society—Christianity had become the official religion of the Roman Empire. That transformed it overnight from a movement of the lower classes into a defender of privilege and government repression. The bloodier the violence committed in the name of Christianity, the more violent its imperial theology would become.

"In a way, this is the second-greatest story ever told," author James Carroll has written, "at least concerning what we think of as western civilization. After the death and Resurrection of Jesus, the conversion of Constantine may have been the most implication-laden event in Western history. If we rarely think so, that is because we take utterly for granted the structures of culture, mind, politics, spirituality, and even calendar (Sunday as holiday) to which it led." Empire and church interacted upon each other, but clearly, it was the church that changed most. "When the power of the empire became joined to the ideology of the church, the empire was immediately recast and reenergized, and the Church became an entity so different from what had preceded it as to be almost unrecognizable."[2]

Consider, for example, that up to this time Christians had mainly been pacifists. When Christians had been persecuted, they tended to accept it without complaining, since by suffering martyrdom they were able to die in the same manner as Jesus. And no single brand of Christianity had been suppressed by any other, because no single group had been powerful enough to do so. Now, however, ascendant members of the church hierarchy saw the opportunity to consolidate their theological power in the same way that Constantine sought to consolidate his temporal power. The church would use its new political clout to impose theological uniformity upon the loose amalgamation of hundreds of different sects, traditions and beliefs that constituted Christianity. Constantine, the Emperor of Rome, did not simply orchestrate this movement toward theological uniformity—he was the originator, revelator and operational director of it.

He saw, even sooner and more clearly than many church leaders, how theological uniformity could reinforce his own political and military uniformity. He wanted to create a state church that could reinforce his own power, by promulgating a state theology enforced by the sword—all he needed was a hierarchy of Christians whose lust for power matched his own. The more conservative clergy had a theological agenda that matched Constantine's imperial agenda, which included blood redemption—that is, salvation of humanity by Jesus' death on the cross. Working together, the newly powerful church leaders and Constantine proceeded to set in motion a symbiotic relationship between the conservative clerical obsession with the cross, on the one hand, and organized aggression by the state on the other.

Soon the cross was to be found on the shields of the Roman legions, who considered it good luck. (It probably reminded Germanic and Celtic soldiers of the sacred tree of their indigenous religions, which may have been one reason why Constantine liked it more than other Christian symbols such as the fish.) The belief in blood redemption, which had been steadily growing within the church hierarchy, fit well with the brutality of imperial rule, and was especially popular with Roman soldiers, whose worship of Mithras revolved around the sacrifice of a sacred bull. Indeed, the whole idea of blood atonement was perceived by people of that time as a variation on the associated themes of human sacrifice, ritual murder, sacred burial and divine resurrection that were popular with many Mediterranean people at that time, as well as with many of the conquered peoples who were being absorbed into the Roman legions and into the empire. It reminded many of the legend of Isis, and it was not unlike certain indigenous Greek and Roman myths, the pagan worship of which had already influenced Christianity, and vice versa.

There were also a number of fantastic mystery cults at the time, most of them predicated on the theme of blood, death, sacrifice and renewal. The slaughter of gladiators in the arena was but a secular manifestation of this. In retrospect, it seems almost as though there was a kind of competition to see which version of human or animal sacrifice would become institutionalized most powerfully. Christian leaders no doubt saw the value of blood atonement as a centralizing theological belief partly because of the popularity of this theme in so many other religions in that time and place. And it accurately reflected the aggression of the new situation in which Christianity found itself. Even as the doctrine of blood atonement was promoted with increasing fervor by church fathers, there was a marked synchronicity between the doctrine and the brutal military behavior of Rome.

Nowhere would this become more monstrous than in Christianity's treatment of Jews, which is important for two reasons. First, anti-Semitism was without question the most violent of all Christian obsessions, lasting for more than sixteen hundred years and finally culminating in the murder of six million Jews in the twentieth century. Secondly, the growth of anti-Semitism became *a reliable indicator of the corruption, aggression and brutality that now began to characterize organized Christianity*. When anti-Semitism was at its height, it was then that the church engaged in unnecessary wars, state repression, loathing of women, obscurantism in ritual and belief, and sadistic cruelty on every level of government, whether imperial or monarchical. Furthermore, it was when Christian preoccupation with the crucifixion was at its height that there were most likely to be outbreaks of anti-Semitic violence. There was, in other words, a powerful relativity between the Christian understanding of blood atonement, and the likelihood of Christian violence against Jews.

The best and most honest account of this is probably James Carroll's *Constantine's Sword—the Church and the Jews*. Carroll's book leaves little doubt that anti-Semitism waxed and waned in general conformity with other excesses, almost invariably tending to be associated with the growing obsession of Christians with the crucifixion of Jesus, and also with the doctrine of blood redemption as being promoted by church hard-liners. The cross was becoming a central preoccupation of the church, and since "the Jews" were popularly thought to have been responsible for Jesus' death, they began increasingly to be seen as embodying the evil that Jesus supposedly died to redeem. And the evil of "the Jews" was particularly heinous because they rejected Jesus' gift of redemption.

Christianity went from being around 10 percent of the Roman Empire to being the majority religion, and began to see Jews not as co-religionists, but as threatening competitors. How could the church convince the pagans to convert to Christianity, when Judaism—whose sacred prophecies Christianity was supposed to fulfill—repudiated Jesus? Out of this tension arose the poison of anti-Jewish hatred, roughly paralleling the church's adoption of aggression and deceit as a method for ensuring its continued domination over the people in the Roman Empire. In 315, only three years after Constantine's adoption of Christianity, proselytizing Judaism became a crime. Over the next hundred years, Christianity would develop an antagonism toward Judaism that would result in the first all-out pogrom against Jews, early in the fifth century.

There was another way that the doctrine of blood redemption would, in an indirect and unconscious way, predispose Christians to anti-Semitism. If violence could redeem, and one person could suffer for all humanity's sins, why couldn't a single group of people be similarly made into a scapegoat for the sins of the world? The idea of the scapegoat, an animal that embodied the sins of the tribe, had of course preceded Christianity, but it now took on an unexpected and diabolical human dimension. The magical thinking involved in this aspect of emergent Christian theology would, on an unconscious level, prefigure the Augustinian idea that the Jews must suffer, to demonstrate God's disapproval of their unwillingness to become Christians. If Jesus could embody all the sins of the world when he was crucified, and redeem the world through his suffering, why could not a single people—the Jews—similarly embody all the evil in the world, and perhaps experience redemption at the hands of violent Christians?

In fact, it *was* argued that suffering could redeem them, because it would motivate them to "accept" Jesus—and his crucifixion as redemptive—by converting to Christianity. (Justifying violence and oppression against Jews became something of a growth industry among Christian theologians in the fourth and fifth centuries.) And let us not forget the *realpolitik* involved in these self-serving theological summersaults. Constantine wanted both religious and political uniformity in his Empire; and many people probably didn't care that much about theology as long as there was stability. Under pressure from Constantine, and to differentiate themselves from Jews, Christians would change their day of worship from Saturday, the Jewish Sabbath, to

Sunday, which became the new Sabbath of Christianity as a state church.

Constantine set about to repress many major religious tendencies within Christianity, in order to unify all Christians under him as their God-appointed leader. He gave temporary religious liberty to non-Christians with the Edict of Milan in 313, but moved quickly to suppress the Donatists, a sect of Christians whose rigid practices were giving him some political headaches. Significantly, Constantine wrote that he felt compelled to move against beliefs that were displeasing to God, because if he didn't move against false doctrines, God might move against *him*. The Christian obsession with rooting out and murdering heretics had begun; Constantine's assertion that his power derived from God—that his soldiers were acting out God's will—would continue to be a staple of European power politics until modern times. Constantine's assumption of power over Christianity, and the church's elevation to the state religion of the Roman Empire, led to a reversal, in practice, of almost everything that Jesus of Nazareth had believed and tried to teach his followers.

6

The fourth and most important trauma of Christianity was the logical culmination of the third. It began in 325 CE, at the Council of Nicaea, but went on for about fifty years, until 381 CE. The Council of Nicaea was accompanied by elements of butchery so gratuitous that for generations people were afraid even to talk about it. It was Constantine who convened the Council of Nicaea, because he wanted a formal venue to impose the uniformity that he thought, as head of both church and empire, was necessary for military, political and cultural unification. He dictated doctrines, as many later Popes would do, by identifying and punishing heresies. The most pressing issue was to determine the nature of Jesus, the Christ on whom the imperial church would be built. A majority of Christians probably continued to see Jesus as a prophetic figure in whose personality were combined both human and divine attributes.

Another view was rapidly gaining favor among church hard-liners, however, as well as with Constantine himself, as both sought to increase their own power. These conservative elements promoted the radical notion that Jesus wasn't just sent by God, or the son of God—they promulgated the notion that Jesus *was* God. He was God who came down to earth, and when people crucified him, they were crucifying God. But how could God come down to be crucified, when God was supposed to be in heaven? It didn't make a lot of sense, which is one reason why even the Council of Nicaea had difficulty accepting it.

But the church leaders, supported by Constantine, were adamant—they were determined to promote Jesus from being merely a prophet and a teacher, to being God himself. Their idea was that Jesus, God and the Holy Spirit were supposedly three parts of the same entity. Jesus was God, and God was God, and something called the Holy Spirit was God—they were *all* God, coexisting in a kind of celestial ménage-a-trois, adroitly presenting as three different persons when the need arose, and operating differently in different circumstances.

It was a hard sell. Most Christians believed that Jesus was special, but saying that he was God was hard for people to get their heads around. The Trinity was an interesting formula, but didn't make all that much sense. The church recognized this, and dealt with it by advising people not to think about it too much. "It's a mystery," the church said, "and is designed specifically by God to *be* a mystery, and for just that reason God *wants* you to be baffled by it." It wasn't so mysterious that God couldn't understand it, of course, and apparently so could a few highly-educated clergy—but everybody else was better off not even *trying* to understand it. Meanwhile, the Roman Empire was falling into disrepair, and most people didn't worry too much about the Trinity because they didn't understand it very well anyway, perhaps didn't believe what they heard, or didn't care one way or the other. Anyway, it was gradually becoming clear that Constantine was going to impose it whether people liked it or not.

So the Trinity prevailed. If the reader thinks about it a bit, it should be obvious why the doctrine appealed to the ambitious church hierarchy, and to Constantine. By quoting the words of Jesus (or whatever they said were the words of Jesus), they were now quoting not just a prophet or a Rabbi, but God Almighty—and it was blasphemy to contradict God. Constantine and his toadies within the church wanted Jesus to be God *because it gave them more power*. If Jesus was a human being like everybody else, you could agree with some things he said, and maybe disagree with others. But if Jesus was God, you *had* to believe what he said (and the church was there to enforce whatever they claimed that Jesus said). If Jesus hadn't been particularly clear about certain things, the church would be happy to interpret what he meant, and you could be sure it would add to the power of the clergy in some way.

Constantine and the imperial church were God's co-regents explaining—and enforcing—God's plan for human history. It was a major power grab by the Trinitarians, the hard-liners within the church hierarchy, and by Constantine. In 325 CE, at the Council of Nicaea, the power-seekers won their battle—it was declared that Jesus was "of the same substance" as God; and from this time on it became Christian orthodoxy, preserved in the Nicene Creed. Most Christians—in the liturgical churches, but also in many mainstream Protestant churches—are still required to repeat the Nicene Creed during church services, just to make sure that nobody gets any heretical ideas about Jesus not being the same thing as God.

The real losers at Nicaea were the Arians, who thought that Jesus had godly qualities, but was certainly not "of the same substance" as God. They were often people at some remove from imperial Rome, and generally less enamored of imperial power. And they were people who believed in a more moderate form of Christianity than the Trinitarians, with beliefs not unlike those of the original Jesus movement. But they and the other non-Trinitarians would now be completely suppressed. The triumphant Trinitarians went on to focus on the importance of proselytizing, because if Jesus was God it would be necessary for *everybody in the world* to accept Jesus' ideas, not to mention the primacy of the church as the Mafia enforcer of those ideas. And that kind of enforced conformity was theoretically possible, now that the church had the military clout of the Roman Empire behind it. The totalitarian implications of this idea, and the lasting nature of it, can be demonstrated by the fact that this computer on which I write, in Times New Roman script, automatically capitalizes the 'T' of Trinitarian, whether I want it to or not—and I definitely don't want it to. Such were the far-reaching consequences of the Council of Nicaea in the West in 325 of the Common Era.

This theological about-face was burned into the collective memory of Christianity by a traumatic series of events that arose out of the violent nature of Constantine's imperial world. Constantine cold-bloodedly murdered his wife and son in the year after the Council, and the horrific details leaked out even as the promulgations of the Council were put into effect in 326. In June of that year, Constantine had his oldest son Crispus, the son of an early lover, seized and put to death by "cold poison" in what is now Pula, Croatia. He also had his wife Fausta seized, and had her suffocated in an overheated bath. Both were assumed to be involved in a violent intrigue, whether sexual or imperial no one was quite sure; but in Constantine's court, *nothing*, not even a sexual liaison, could be entirely without some implication of imperial power-struggle.

Crispus was the son of another woman, so it is possible that he simply had a sexual relationship with Constantine's wife, Fausta. Or the two of them may have been plotting some kind of coup. Many historians believe that Fausta wanted her own blood children to succeed the throne after Constantine's death, and for that reason, she may have approached Crispus with a sexual proposition. In this scenario, Crispus, like Joseph in the Old Testament, contemptuously refused Fausta's offer. Furious, Fausta then approached Constantine's mother, Helena, and claimed she had been raped by Crispus. Then the hot-blooded Constantine flew into a rage and had his son murdered.

Afterwards Helena looked into the matter at length and decided Fausta was lying, at which point Constantine, overcome by guilt and anger, completed the circle of tragedy and intrigue by having Fausta murdered. But Helena was far from objective: in fact, she had a built-in motive for arriving at this version of events. Helena, the mother of Constantine, had been thrown out of court by Constantine's father to make a political marriage; she now assumed the dominant position at court, and proceeded to reinvent herself as a Christian saint. "Helena, with Constantine," observes James Carroll sarcastically, "was seen to preside over a version of the Holy Family, the amity of which was a sacrament of the unity of the empire."[3] It was one of the first high-profile uses of family values to promote Christianity, but not the last time such rosy public images would conceal crippling and sometimes murderous pathologies.

People associated in any way with imperial power in the Roman Empire used cruelty not simply as an expedient, but frequently developed a taste for it, tending ultimately to view sadism as a form of entertainment for the powerful. It is quite likely that Fausta must have harbored some residual anger toward her husband—he had, after all, personally murdered her father and two brothers in various wars for power. (Let us remember that after the battle at Milvian Bridge, Constantine had her brother's head carried about in the town on a pike.) She must have been concerned that none of her own sons by Constantine would succeed him, and was jealous of Crispus, a son by another woman. But whatever the exact alignment of victims and executioners, what one takes away from the situation is a sense of the murderous depravity of Constantine's court. And it was in this court that the future of Christianity was determined.

In fact, the murders actually served the cause of religious uniformity, in their own way, by bonding Christians to the kind of aggression necessary to empire. But it must have been a sobering time for church fathers, because by now they must have realized that they were encumbered—as details of the imperial slaughter began to come out—with the necessity of rationalizing such mayhem, with all the theological acrobatics that would require. And they knew very well they'd better not to make any missteps themselves, or they might end up like Fausta or Crispus. In short, they had to accommodate themselves to, and become the spokespersons for, an extraordinarily brutal empire. Nothing can bond a group to aggression more powerfully than the shared memory of a secret crime, committed with impunity and un-expiated by any sense of guilt, recompense or closure.

What we are presented with, in Constantine's cabinet of horrors, is the ultimate dysfunctional family—but all too typical, too, of what Christianity was becoming, as James Carroll has pointed out: "In all of this, the family of Constantine was an authentic sacrament of the true state of the empire he had created—not in the holy concord of the legend but in its unleashed murderous violence."[4] And this murderous violence was to continue as long as Constantine was alive. It was, as Carroll points out, a "pathological culture of holy violence."

The evolving theology of the new imperial church reflected that same pathological culture of holy violence, because the second great doctrine discussed at the Council of Nicaea was blood redemption. Jesus, said the proponents of this idea, had died on the cross for the sins of humanity, in order to redeem those sins and guarantee eternal life to believers. But the doctrine was not adopted definitively until 381. It was quite a leap to go from the familiar Christ whose power came from the Incarnation and the Resurrection to one person of the Trinity dying on the cross for all humankind. It seemed a bit much for many Christians, but for others it perfectly reflected the imperial ethos into which Christianity was being co-opted.

"It was a ruthless time," writes James Carroll. "We have already seen how, in his ascent, Constantine had not hesitated to dispatch a pair of rivals who were also his brothers-in-law. But a son! A father who slays a son! A father who slays his son in righteousness! It is impossible to consider the hidden tragedy of 326 apart from the glories of that year. Constantine's embrace of the ethos of the cross was already firm by then, but one needn't be a Freudian to sense the new power that they myth of the cross would have had over him. Evoking the binding of Isaac as it does, the story of the all-powerful father forced to put to death his beloved son—but for a redemptive purpose—must have obsessed the emperor at that moment. If God can kill his Son, so can God's co-regent."[5]

Throughout the next fifty years during which blood redemption was being debated, right up until 381 CE when it was finally accepted as an unalterable doctrine, the imperial familial violence continued. As James Carroll has noted, by the time of Constantine's death, only two males out of more than a dozen members of Constantine's household were left alive. (Not counting three sons, who—true to form—later fought and murdered each other.) And none of this takes into account the slaughter taking place elsewhere, on the battlefields of the empire, as the great Roman families jockeyed for power. The death-worship that accompanied the power-struggle between the top families in the empire, not to mention the everyday cruelty used to keep the average Roman citizen in line, would inevitably affect views of Jesus' purpose on earth, because "the emotional appeal of the crucifixion would have outweighed the glories of the Resurrection," as James Carroll puts it. Not only was cruelty a daily reality on all levels of empire; the ruling classes even sought to provide the less powerful with the addictive pleasures of *witnessing* cruelty, in the games in which spectators sometimes watched hundreds of gladiators perish in a single afternoon. It is natural that people in that world would identify more with the crucifixion that the Resurrection. It was in 326 of the Common Era, the year after he murdered his wife and son, that Constantine began construction work on the greatest church to be built up until that time, which he called the Martyrium. Should we be surprised that this church "was decidedly not a token of new life but of death?"[6]

In 381 CE the issue was decided, James Carroll tells us: "Finally, the creedal statement, as reflected in the text we know, put the crucifixion at the center of faith and the death of Jesus at the heart of redemption. That this is a mid-fourth-century innovation is emphatically revealed by the fact that the first

Nicene formulation, in mentioning neither death nor crucifixion, had, in line with the constant tradition of the Church, left the emphasis on Incarnation and Resurrection. This change means that the Son of God became man not to be one of us, nor to take on the human condition—which includes suffering but is not defined by it—and not, for that matter, to undergo the Resurrection, as the affirmation of the Father's covenantal faithfulness to the Son. Instead, according to the theological shift reflected in the amended creed, the Son of God became man in order to be crucified. The crucifixion takes the place of the Resurrection as the saving event, and Christ the victim takes the place of Christ the victor as the symbol of God's love for the world."[7]

Making Christ the victim—that is how the church would make Jesus a retrospective Messiah, able to save humankind not through his revolutionary teachings but through his violent death. Blood redemption now takes center stage, and in this paradigm, Jesus' power would no longer be *transformative*, with a strategy for transforming personality and behavior, but *redemptive*, able only to redeem sin retroactively. His power no longer resided in his teachings or even in his triumph over death. Now his power resided solely in his death. Even more, his power would now reside in the *manner* of his death, in the fact that it was painful and public, rather than quick and private.

It was a perfect fit with the values of the Roman Empire. As James Carroll has noticed, even the cross itself was "the perfect emblem of Constantine's program, with its joining of horizontal and vertical axes and with its evoking of the four directions: north, south, east, west. The cross of the compass unites the globe; a hand-held globe surmounted by a cross would be, with the crown and scepter, a symbol of the Christian king."[8] Constantine himself apparently made the connection; and—expert manipulator of symbols that he was—banned crucifixion in his empire, while retaining other forms of state execution.

(Constantine may have suspected that public crucifixions might cause the ordinary Roman to wonder about the nature of a Christian God who demanded such a horrible sacrifice; and it might also remind people too concretely of the real source of power in the Roman Empire, which was organized brutality.) It might also suggest, to the very intuitive, that both were driven by the same emotional orientation.

Both intertwined and appositional, blood atonement and state brutality supported and energized each other, their symbiotic relationship locked into an ongoing—and largely unconscious—tension. The belief in blood redemption as the source of eternal life, and the concomitant authority of the Emperor, were alternating pulsations in a powerful current that would ultimately drive all of European society: the king or emperor whose power was based on brute force, but who claimed divine rights, who was supported by a people animated by a vision of state cruelty as the ultimate agent of salvation. Overt brutality and an addiction to aggression were inevitable outcomes of the excesses of imperial Rome, on the one hand, but they were undoubtedly supported by Christianity's dark vision of human sacrifice on the other. Neither would be challenged until the eighteenth century; nor was their connection ever fully understood even then.

Out of the combustion of these two forces, one political and one psychological, came the archetype of the Christian prince, driven to avenge the murder of Jesus, his vocation to kill all who threatened the medieval order—and in so doing to endlessly replicate the crucifixion of Jesus, in psychological terms, by murdering others. The worship of state power and the rise of imperial Christianity quickly institutionalized war as humanity's highest and most heroic activity, with unquestioning loyalty to emperor or monarch running it a close second. War as a sacrament to achieve eternal life was not *theologically* institutionalized until the eleventh century; but by that time, the disruption of armed conflict had become such a commonplace to Europeans that it was but a short step for the papacy to introduce the idea of Holy War.

7

In the late eleventh century, a robust and expanding Islamic empire threatened Christian Europe. The *deification* of armed conflict, and the redemptive nature of religious war, now had to be made explicit. Killing people, or being killed by them, was now to be transformed into a means for salvation. Instead of a necessary evil, killing Muslims would become a sacred act—and you also received eternal life if the Muslim you were fighting killed *you*. Slaughtering Muslims (and also Jews, it turned out) became the ultimate Christian sacrament of the warrior. This occurred because the Pope wished to initiate the Crusades, a series of bloody, astonishingly ill-advised military campaigns to "take back" Jerusalem, a city for which Christians had cared not one whit before the rise of Islam. Jerusalem and its environs now became known somewhat lugubriously in the West as the "Holy Lands." What this all really meant was that European Christians were going to invade Jerusalem and dispossess those who had lived there for centuries, with the entire murderous (and ultimately unsuccessful) attempt to invade and permanently colonize Jerusalem starting with the First Crusade of 1095. The intent was to confront Islam militarily in the field while at the same time giving this power-play a grand religious motive, the individual religious reward being eternal life.

That same year, Pope Urban II granted "immediate recession of their sins" to those who died in the First Crusade to take Jerusalem. In other words, he promised those participating in the Crusades instant salvation if they died in the process—certainly that was the way it was understood by most Christians. During the following year, in 1096, Urban II again addressed this subject, specifying that violence in the service of the church (that is, killing Muslims) was a sacred act. Religious war as a way to get into heaven was just the latest and most egregious betrayal of

Jesus' original message, but it was also the logical culmination of the psychology of blood atonement adopted in 381 CE. The Christian knight would now be able—and to some extent obligated, as a good Christian seeking eternal life—to kill anybody who did not accept the gift of Jesus' sacrifice. Since Jesus died on the cross to redeem the sinner, according to the doctrine of blood atonement, and since Jesus was God, it followed that Muslims would similarly have to perish in the cause of redemption. Holy war, and the sanctification of religious murder, was the logical and final outcome of the Christian obsession with the cross. But the unhealthy, volatile aggression unleashed by the obsession would not be limited to Muslims, as we will see.

As the crusades were introduced to Europe, the obsession with blood redemption spiked. Just three years after the First Crusade began in 1095—right on schedule—Anselm of Canterbury finished writing and began to circulate *Cur Deus Homo*, a seminal work that maintained that the *only* reason God became man and came to earth was to die. Before Anselm's *Cur Deus Homo* in 1098, the partisans of blood redemption had at least given Jesus credit for saying a few interesting things on his way to Golgotha (the Beatitudes, the parables, the Sermon on the Mount, things like that); but now *the only value of Jesus' existence was to die on the cross*. This went beyond putting blood atonement at the center of Christianity. It effectively got rid of everything in Christianity *except* blood atonement.

This death-worship was acted out on a mass basis during the Crusades. There have been periodic attempts by modern historians—invariably Christian—to rehabilitate the Crusades, some arguing that perhaps they were not as bad as they have traditionally been represented. In fact, they were a great deal worse. Muslims and Jews were subjected to the most brutal forms of religiously-motivated terrorism, with tactics including mass executions, the mutilation and exhibition of corpses, the throwing of severed heads over the walls of besieged cities, and even a fair amount of cannibalism, as in the Seige of Maarat. Once in the field, Christian armies fought horrific battles with each other for booty and territorial advantage. (Was a Christian guaranteed instant salvation for killing another Christian while on Crusade? The papacy was silent on that possibility.)

All this mayhem gave the powerful ruling families of Europe a chance to confront their new Islamic rivals on their own turf, and it was very good practice for the kind of imperialism that Europe would impose on the developing world in the future. It also distracted people from the misery of their daily lives with promises of instant salvation, while making the lives of many much more miserable than they might have been. Most importantly, it unremittingly insinuated the trauma and horror of systemic evil into the heart of Christianity, promising people eternal life for some of the most revolting and systematic brutality that civilization had yet seen. This included not just war directed against Muslims, but recurring pogroms against Jews.

On their way to the "Holy Lands," Christian knights in the First Crusade took up the bloody practice of attacking entire Jewish communities. The crusaders apparently couldn't wait to get to Jerusalem to kill non-Christians, but decided to murder European non-Christians on the way. In both 1095 and 1096 there were attacks on Jewish communities in Germany and France, and the attacks spread to Speyer and Worms and ultimately Bohemia, with the largest massacre at Mainz. A few Bishops tried to stop the massacres; but others extorted money from Jewish communities in return for protecting them, as did Godfrey of Bouillon from Jews in Cologne and Mainz. It was a time of terror and insecurity for Jews in Europe and in the Rhineland especially, and the beginning of the violent pogroms that would periodically devastate their communities throughout the next nine hundred years.

In 1099, the siege of Jerusalem began, and within the year, the city fell to the invading Christians. Jews and Muslims living in

Jerusalem fought to keep the Europeans out, because they knew only too well what would befall them if the Christians breached the walls. Finally, however, the walls *were* breached—exactly how is disputed—and the inevitable killing of civilians began, with one contemporary account representing the blood of Jerusalem's defenders running up to the ankles of the mounted Frankish knights. The exact number of people killed in this massacre is disputed, with some Christian historians offering as mitigation that fact that after all, the crusaders massacred the inhabitants of *other* cities too. I am aware of no historian, however, who refers to the Christian treatment of civilians after the capture of Jerusalem in 1099 as anything but a massacre. Men, women and children were laboriously chased down and chopped into pieces, their dead bodies put into piles and burned over a period of several days.

In the classic manner of trauma bonding, European Christians would repeatedly return to this scene of mass murder, as one crusade followed another, in what seems to have been a futile attempt to confront and redeem the internalized doubts, demons and disillusionment generated by the First Crusade. Instead, it led to more killing, with successive crusades becoming major exercises in state aggression. Church-sanctioned crusades actually continued right up until the late eighteenth century; and the slaughter of innocent civilians was directed not only against Muslims, but also against Christians who had the wrong theology—the Albigenses and the Waldenses, for example. Usually, however, it was directed against non-Christians, who refused to accept the redemptive power of Jesus' death on the cross, which refusal had to be redeemed—logically enough—with *their* death.

At every point in the successive bloodbaths that were the crusades, from the 1095 First Crusade up until the last one in 1798, the toxic poison of blood atonement worked its way deeper into the psyche of Christianity. Blood redemption and mass murder had the inevitable effect of reinforcing each other. Saint Anselm's *Cur Deus Homo* is the consummate argument for redemptive violence. God is infinite, Anselm said, so human sin is infinitely insulting to God. But *that* meant that only an infinite being could be punished for infinite sin. God, therefore, had to die on the cross to *assuage his own anger.* Clearly, the inherent violence of this idea contributed, however unconsciously, to the new belief in Holy War as an agency of salvation: the surest method for salvation was to kill the enemies of the church, or risk being killed by them, or simply die in battle. Then one could be sure of getting to heaven.

The most notorious formulation of the new salvation-by-killing doctrine was by Bernard of Clairvaux in 1128, written as part of the rules for the Knights Templar at the Council of Troyes. *"I say that the soldier of Christ kills in safety and dies in greater safety. He profits himself when he dies and he profits Christ when he kills...Truly when he kills a criminal, he commits not homicide, but as I would call it, malicide."* Blood atonement had come full cycle. Redemption was no longer retrospective—the church's doctrine of salvation-through-murder could offer salvation proactively, far into the future, wherever Christian men were needed to fight for European interests.

Anselm's doctrine (that the *only* reason Jesus came to earth was to die) became the central dynamic of both Catholicism and Protestantism. John Calvin made a fetish of it; Jesus' crucifixion—and the grace that supposedly accompanied it—would become the core idea of Christian evangelicalism, and it still is. Interestingly, history records only one person of that time who seriously objected to Anselm's death-worship, and that person was Peter Abelard, who believed that Jesus' function was not to pay a blood debt but to inspire people by serving as an example—albeit a bloody one—of God's love for humanity. Abelard was dealt with in the manner that organized Christianity of the twelfth century reserved for those who had heretical ideas. He was castrated by church thugs for his passionate liaison with the nun Eloise, and in 1141 Bernard of Clairvaux succeeded in getting Abelard condemned as a heretic at the Council of Sens.

The Protestant Reformation did nothing to change this—if anything, it strengthened blood atonement, which became the central doctrine of Protestantism. Almost all Protestants, Calvinist and non-Calvinist alike, fervently supported the idea that humanity's only hope was renewed faith in the redemptive nature of Jesus' death on the cross. The only difference, according to the Protestants, was that Protestantism was supposedly a better vehicle to invoke God's grace than Catholicism. Luther above all believed fanatically in blood redemption, and he was particularly fanatical about getting Jews to accept this idea, in order to convert them to his brand of Christianity. When they did not take him up on his generous offer, Luther wrote "The Jews and Their Lies," which became the foundational document of German anti-Semitism. Luther's hatred of Jews was expressed with an appalling and unheard-of ferocity, and would deeply influence the political anti-Semitism of nineteenth-century pan-German nationalists, a particularly rabid form of religious and racial hatred that would find its ultimate expression in Hitler's Holocaust.

8

In 1144, a popular outcry arose against the Jews of England, who were accused by Christians of the ritual murder of a Christian child. This preposterous "blood libel," a paranoid fantasy of Christian Jew-haters, would be replicated innumerable times in all the countries of Europe. The mass hysteria generated by this anti-Semitic delusion would cause bloody pogroms—attacks by Christians on Jewish communities—for the next eight hundred years. Untold numbers of innocent people were murdered in these attacks, which gradually took on a ritualized and somewhat systemic aspect. The extent to which the "blood libel" delusion affected the English people in the Middle Ages can be gauged by the fact that it became the subject for a popular British ballad, "Sir Hugh, or, the Jew's Daughter."

This ballad was ultimately collected by the folklorist Francis James Child, who included it in his 10-volume collection of ballads in 1898, from which the following material is taken. The supposed story of Hugh of Lincoln appears in the Annals of Waverley for the year 1255, apparently written by a contemporary. It makes painfully clear the extent to which Christians were obsessed by the crucifixion of Jesus, and its connection to their hatred of Jews; and how violent, detailed and pathological their delusions arising from these twin obsessions were becoming.

A boy named Hugh was supposed crucified by Jews after having been tortured by them. After failing to throw the body of their victim into running water or bury it in the ground, the culprits throw it into a well. *"Thereupon the whole place was filed with so brilliant a light and so sweet an odor that it was clear to everybody that there must be something holy and prodigious in the well. The body was seen floating on the water, and, upon its being drawn up, the hands and feet were found to be pierced, the head, had, as it were, a crown of bloody points, and there were various other wounds: from all which it was plain that this was the work of the Jews."*

Why the Jews? Because the people who heard the story or sung the balled believed that a crucifixion had taken place, so who else could it be? Many miracles occurred and the sick were healed, mute testimony to the redemptive nature of crucifixion (including a blind woman who received her sight after touching the bier on which the martyr's corpse was carried); and the entire event ended with the hanging of eighteen Jews who supposedly confessed to the crime, under what duress we can well imagine.

Child's first version of the ballad, which appears to include elements from Chaucer's Prioresses Tale, has Hugh of Lincoln, no doubt a well-born lad, playing ball with his "four and twenty bonny boys," when the ball is lost, and Hugh goes to retrieve it.

He's doen him to the Jew's castell,
And walkd it round about;
And there he saw the Jew's daughter,
At the window looking out.

'Throw down the ba, ye Jew's daughter,
Throw down the ba to me!'
'Never a bit,' says the Jew's daughter,
'till up to me come ye.'

She entices the unsuspecting Hugh into the castle (with an *apple*), and kills him "like a swine" to get his blood. All versions of the song make a big deal out of the blood that comes gushing out of the unfortunate Hugh when she stabs him.

And first came out the thick, thick blood,
And syne came out the thin,
And syne came out the bonny heart's blood;
There was nae mair within.

She's rowd him in a cake o' lead,
Bade him lie still and sleep;
She's thrown him in Our Lady's draw-well,
Was fifty fathom deep.

Although Professor Child collected this ballad, he was no anti-Semite, in fact quite the opposite. In his notes for this ballad he denounced—with consummate Victorian contempt—the entire blood libel fantasy. The idea that Jews killed Christians was a malignant lie, Child wrote, as was the belief that Jews drank their victims' blood. "Murders like that of Hugh of Lincoln have been imputed to the Jews for at least seven hundred and fifty years, and the charge, which there is reason to suppose may still from time to time be renewed, has brought upon the accused every calamity that the hand of man can inflict, pillage, confiscation, banishment, torture, and death, and this in huge proportions. *The process of these murders has often been described as a parody of the crucifixion of Jesus.* The motive most commonly alleged, in addition to the contempt for Christianity, has been the obtaining of blood for use in the Paschal rites—a most unhappily devised slander, in stark contradiction with Jewish precept and practice." (Italics added.) Child continues with a powerful denunciation of anti-Semitism: "And these pretended child-murderers, with their horrible consequences, are only a part of a persecution which, with all moderation, may be rubricated as the most disgraceful chapter in the history of the human race."[9]

Child compares the "blood libel" accusation to the frequent charge that Jews poisoned the wells, and spread the Black Death—those were the three accusations, historians agree, that were most capable of igniting mass hysteria that led to pogroms. Above all, Child sees how the obsession with Jesus' crucifixion contributes to the Christian belief, common in the Middle Ages, that Jews are likely to torture, kill and crucify any Christians they could entrap. He also makes a connection between the

Eucharist and the common belief that Jews desecrated communion wafers in order symbolically to crucify Jesus, and the hysterical belief that Jews wanted to drink—and did often drink—the blood of Christians. (Clearly Christians who drank the transubstantiated blood of Jesus during the Eucharist in order to achieve eternal life would be more likely to believe that Jews would greatly enjoy drinking *their* blood.)

That this ballad circulated for eight hundred years in Britain demonstrates how deep the blood libel delusion ran in Christian societies. Child's awareness of the toxic nature of these beliefs is also significant, because it demonstrates that by the late nineteenth century some Christians—not many, but some—had begun to realize how dangerous these fantasies were, and that they threatened Christians as well as Jews. The belief that Jews drank the blood of Christians appeared in some form in every Christian-majority country in the world, and it was on such pathological beliefs that the spread of nineteenth-century political anti-Semitism depended—and that set the stage for twentieth-century fascism. Anti-Semitism would be at the heart of the madness that would reduce Europe to rubble.

Professor Child accurately points out that the blood libel of Jews was based on a "parody of the crucifixion of Jesus," a process that we would today identify as an unconscious projection, compounded by guilt by association. The process may be imagined as operating in the following manner: First, Jews were generally seen as villains who had murdered Jesus and had *inherited the guilt from that act*; second, Christians identified with the crucifixion and the blood of Jesus as redemptive; third, Christians drank (or believed they drank) the blood of Jesus every Sunday when they celebrated the Eucharist; finally, in a last fandango of self-exculpatory paranoia, Christians believed that Jews wanted to crucify *them* and drink *their* blood. And so they inflicted upon the Jews the "pillage, confiscation, banishment, torture, and death" that they believed the Jews wanted to inflict on *them*.

Greatly simplified, the process went like this:

1 Jesus was murdered by "the Jews";
2 The shedding of his blood is the source of redemption for humanity;
3 Christians drink Jesus' blood during the Eucharist;
4 *Therefore,* every good Christian knows that "the Jews" want to crucify and torture Christians to drink *their* blood.

The projection—not to mention the circularity—inherent in these ideas should be obvious. And it all begins with Jesus' bloody suffering on the cross, and its supposedly redemptive nature. It starts, in other words, with blood atonement—containing within it the belief that cruelty can redeem, on the one hand, presenting on the other hand the irresolvable dilemma of a God who demands the death of his own son. Tragically, over the centuries the violence of blood atonement became linked to another pernicious idea, the supposed blood guilt of all Jews. Christians were taught that Jews inherited the guilt of Jesus' death—and in times of crisis and mass hysteria assumed that therefore Jews wanted to kill any Christian they could get their hands on.

It was all psychological projection, and spectacularly paranoid projection at that, generated by the unfathomable dilemma of a violent God who sanctifies his own blood for human redemption. The idea that aggression can redeem, combined with the belief in inherited Jewish guilt, was the emotional and social dynamic that drove the horrific pogroms through which Christian communities in Europe sought to cleanse and redeem themselves. Never in human history have two ideas had such evil effects on a single people, as the Christian belief in blood atonement and inherited guilt has had on European Jewry.

9

Historians use the word *pogrom* to retroactively describe violence against Jews as early as the fourth century, but the actual word did not come into use until the 1820s (it is Russian, and means to 'wreak havoc'). Why had Christian Europe not devised a word to describe what happened in the eleventh century, and for so many centuries after that, when Christians practiced mass murder against Jews? Because Christendom did not care to give names to the monsters it had created, and which it fed, year after year, with the belief in redemptive violence that was so much a part of institutional Christianity. From 1096 on, violence against Jews frequently involved a recurring scenario: A violent rumor would begin to circulate about Jews, usually that they were supposedly kidnapping, hurting or crucifying Christians, and then drinking their blood. (The most horrific charge was that Jews kidnapped Christian children and murdered them, putting their blood in various kinds of food, including matzo balls.) As we've already seen, two other common charges were that they poisoned wells, or were spreading the plague. Mobs would gather when such rumors circulated, and then the violence would begin, sometimes taking hundreds of lives, sometimes thousands. These terrifying outbursts of hysterical Christian blood-letting sometimes happened with very little warning.

We have seen that large-scale attacks against Jewish communities were recorded at the time of the First Crusade in 1096, although there were large-scale massacres of Jews in York and elsewhere in Britain in 1189-90. It did not stop as the momentum of the first crusades slowed down, but actually seemed to accelerate. In 1348, to mention just one famous example, Jews were accused of spreading the Black Plague, and were massacred in Basle, Chillon, Stuttgart, Ulm, Speyer, Dresden, Strasbourg and—once again—in Mainz, in the Rhineland. In 1543, Martin Luther published "On the Jews and Their Lies," in which he urged Germans to burn Jewish synagogues and schools, destroy their prayer books, silence their rabbis, demolish their homes, and confiscate their property. Far too many Germans followed his call for violence, not all of them Protestants by any means. Pogroms were disruptive and traumatic, they were not uncommon, and Jews knew that once the madness got underway there was little they could do about it.

There were pogroms by Cossacks in the Ukraine in the seventeenth century, and in the eighteenth century, there were successive outbreaks in Russia. Large-scale pogroms were carried out in the nineteenth century, usually by Russian peasants who were encouraged to do so by Czarist authorities. (If peasants could be encouraged to attack Jews, perhaps they wouldn't be so interested in attacking the Czar's government—that was the thinking of the Czar's men.) In the late nineteenth century, in France, anti-Semitism kept Captain Dreyfus in prison, although he was innocent of the treasonous activities with which he'd been charged. French society divided into two hostile camps, the Dreyfusards and the anti-Dreyfusards, driving further splits into republicans and nationalists.

A new kind of anti-Semitism was arising, a political anti-Semitism—in addition to being Christ-killers, Judaism was also blamed for the introduction of new ideas into Christian society. In fact Jews often *were* advocates of new ideas, almost invariably ones that benefited humanity—democracy, social and economic justice, and religious liberty among them. Jews were the great champions of secular democracy because they saw that it offered them, a marginalized group, more opportunities than any other system—and the West greatly benefited from this, because democracy also gave everybody else more opportunities to improve themselves.

There were also exclusions, expulsions of entire communities, theft of property and other devices of the Christian authorities used against Jews, not to mention prohibitions against Jews working in most trades and professions, unfair rules and protocols that forced them into marginal occupations. When the Russian Revolution broke out, so did the intensity of Russian anti-Semitism, and pogroms flared up across the country. Somewhere between 100,000 and 250,000 Jews were killed by these outbreaks. Anti-Jewish pogroms also spread to other lands. During the Greek War of Independence, Jews were massacred by the thousands; there was even a pogrom in Argentina in 1919.

During the Holocaust, the Nazis encouraged pogroms by local governments and citizens in every county of Eastern Europe. Hitler's Final Solution can best be seen as the application of the industrial method to mass murder, but despite that the Nazis also encouraged less technologically-sophisticated weapons for pogroms as well: automatic weapons, pistols, old rifles, virtually anything would do. Mass murder was, as the Nazis knew, an important method for bonding various nationalist and rightwing groups together, so that they could serve as militias and auxiliary paramilitary groups.

Furthermore, once they had participated in the mass murder of Jews, individual Lithuanians, Romanians and Ukrainians would be fully committed, because they were no longer merely soldiers but were now war criminals, and irrevocably bonded to the Nazi enterprise. Ukrainian nationalists organized two pogroms in 1941 in Lviv, which reportedly took 6,000 Jewish lives; more than 13,000 were apparently killed by Romanian authorities during the Iasi pogrom, in Romania. Lithuanian nationalists killed almost 4,000 Jews in 1941. (All of these pogroms were encouraged by top Nazis.)

Why did these things happen in Europe in the twentieth century? Because Christians had believed for a thousand years, and had been taught as part of their theology, that Jews had inherited the guilt of murdering Jesus, because they were the blood descendants of the original Jews, and *because they refused to convert to Christianity*. By refusing to convert, were they not still rejecting Jesus? Of course none of this would have made any difference if the church hadn't given the crucifixion so much importance—if Christianity had focused less on Jesus' death, there would have been no need to find some group to blame for it.

Political anti-Semitism picked up where traditional Christian anti-Semitism left off. Christians believed in the Middle Ages that Jews threatened Christendom's hegemony, that Jews physically attacked and crucified Christians, and threatened the health of the community. Political anti-Semitism built on these delusions, which had become archetypes within the collective Christian unconscious. The ideologists of the new anti-Semitism taught that Jews threatened the hegemony of Europe by introducing democratic ideas, weakened national spirit by supporting internationalism, and compromised the mental health of societies with new-fangled ideas in science, politics, and the arts. The main text used by the new political anti-Semites was *The Protocols of the Elders of Zion*, a Czarist confabulation that represented Jews as ruthlessly plotting to take over the world. But none of it would have stuck had not it been preceded by Christian anti-Semitism, which had predisposed Christians to makes scapegoats out of Jews for whatever aroused their guilt, hate or fear.

It is a mistake to think that European Jewish life from 1096 CE until the Holocaust was nothing but one long pogrom—such a view ignores the evolving richness of rabbinical Judaism, and it trivializes the historical complexity of particular individual experiences. And it does not take into account the remarkable example of the *convivencia* in Spain, in which Christians, Jews and Muslims thrived together. But it is also an undeniable fact that pogroms, banishment, loss of property, and institutional discrimination in all its guises were often visited on Jews by their Christian neighbors. The uncanny emotional insecurity that arose from the ever-present reality of anti-Semitism drove Jews to mysticism and introspection and to the disastrous acceptance of various charlatans and False Messiahs, but also to the adoption of Enlightenment ideas and secular democracy as a way out of the ghetto; whereas anti-Semitism bonded Christians more tightly to the baseline of aggression at the heart of blood redemption. Jews lived with the knowledge that if Christians wanted to kill them, discriminate against them, or hate them, the archetype of the sneering, Christ-killing Jew was too deep in the collective unconscious of Christendom for Jews to overcome it, at least in the short term, with law, reason or common sense.

Is it any wonder, then, that Jews did not want to convert to Christianity, except for the most pragmatic reasons of self-advancement? Given the way Christians treated Jews, the most truly and undeniably heroic thing that European Jews managed to do was *not* convert to Christianity, because they could see all too well that it was based on the worship of ritualized violence. Still, the pressure to identify with the oppressor must have been enormous; and it is the supreme victory of European Judaism that it had the spiritual integrity to resist that pressure for so long. Did a great many Jews unconsciously internalize imperial violence when they adopted Zionism, finally identifying with the redemptive violence of Christianity that had for so long oppressed them? Yes, inevitably so; but they did so unconsciously, as a psychological response to the aggression of the pogroms, culminating in the Holocaust. Jews who went to Palestine may have embarked upon one of the gravest and most spectacular mistakes a people ever made, but let us remember that they did not leave Europe for their health. If Jews internalized redemptive violence, let us remember that it did not originate with them.

The great D'Israeli once remarked that if Christians really believed that Jesus died to redeem the world, and thought the Jews were responsible for his death, then Christians should go out of their way to be nice to them, because they'd done the world a big favor. But Christians were not likely to accept such a witticism gracefully. Despite their insistence that Jesus' crucifixion had redeemed the world from sin, they still had to find some group to blame for it, indicating that at bottom they knew there was something wrong with their claim. Ultimately, despite all the talk of the cross as redemptive, Christians felt obligated to find an external enemy to blame ("the Jews") for the horror of Jesus' suffering. Without the *deus ex machina* of the perfidious Jew, the believer would have to acknowledge that the whole gruesome spectacle was really set in motion by God himself, and that therefore Jesus' suffering had to be blamed on the Almighty. But most believing Christians could sooner fly to the moon than allow that thought to reach their conscious minds.

It was always, always about the centrality of the crucifixion to Christendom, which in turn drove the Christian delusions of ritual murder by Jews. Indeed, the great Pope John XXIII explicitly and expertly made the connection between Jesus' crucifixion and Christian violence against Jews, when praying for forgiveness for the church's anti-Semitism with these remarkable words: "Forgive us Lord, for the curse we falsely attributed to their name as Jews. *Forgive us for crucifying Thee a second time in their flesh,* for we knew not what we did." (Italics added.) The astonishing reality of Christian-Jewish relationships is that "the Jews" didn't kill Jesus, but Christians *did* kill hundreds of thousands (and finally millions) of Jews, symbolically crucifying them because of their own Christian obsession with a God who demands redemption through violence. And most Christians still do not see Christian theology as in any way complicit with genocide against the Jews, even as a fair number of them still believe in inherited Jewish guilt. If evil is aggression plus deceit, including self-deceit, this is evil on a prodigious scale.

10

The Crusades were extremely important—so important, in fact, that one historian calls them *meta-historical,* which means a series of events so big its effects can't be measured. It prepared the Christian West for the rise of imperialism and the world wars of the twentieth century; and it reduced Christianity to one ideological element in the growing European worship of militarism, power and profit. This worship of aggression and profit would become, along with technological superiority, the main determinant of Western history. Associated with this brutal new trend in the West were two malignant ideas that developed opportunistically, as the pursuit of power and profit led to more violence. One was the idea that people with white skins had the right to exploit and tyrannize over darker-skinned people. The second was that since aggression by the Christian knight was now a sacred act, social privilege based on force might itself be the will of God. The divine right of kings, a subtle re-framing of the divinity of the Roman Caesar, was an extension of this. The nobles, the priestly classes, the rising merchant classes, all had power *because God wanted them to have it.* If all existing power relationships were exactly as God wanted them to be, the Christian should never try to resist systemic evil in society, and should on the contrary support even the most brutal government measures as God's will.

Because of the obsession with the crucifixion of Jesus, a ghastly, fetishistic cult of death and sadism grew up within Christendom during the dark ages, lasting almost until the Reformation. Part celebration of aggression, part expiation of guilt arising from it, it was also sadomasochistic catharsis of the organized violence inherent in the new order, in which the cult of the cross was the principle cultural reference point. Self-flagellation and mortification of the flesh (in which Christians were given the supreme "privilege" of experiencing the pain that Jesus experienced on the cross) arose from a heightened identification with the suffering of the crucifixion (enhanced by the suffering of everyday life), and almost every aspect of it became subject to various kinds of unhealthy beliefs. The height of this generalized identification with redemptive violence was realized in the supremely pathological figure of the stigmatic, the person on whose body the actual wounds of Christ appeared. The morbidity of Christianity can be clearly grasped by understanding that the stigmatic was greatly admired, and thought to be especially beloved of God, not in spite of but because of his or her wretched state.

Easter Week became by far the most important time in the Christian calendar. Ask most modern Christian theologians what Easter Week is all about, and they'll probably say that it is about Jesus rising from the grave. *But where are the visual representations of Jesus rising from the grave?* They were nowhere to be seen in medieval Europe, and they are nowhere to be seen today. What you *do* see is endless replications of the cross, often with Jesus hanging on the cross in his death agony, which is what Easter Week is really all about, and what Christianity is really all about. Nothing could more clearly demonstrate the truth of this than the millions, perhaps billions, of representations of Jesus on the cross that appear in every imaginable venue around the world, and not only in Christian-majority countries.

The cross, a symbol of the sensual brutality that had once ruled the Mediterranean world, now ruled the mind of medieval Europe, and symbolized the brutality and misery suffered by ordinary people on a daily basis. In so doing, it bonded people to a worldview in which cruelty was the highest good, the most persuasive truth, and the most authentic religious experience. This bonding with the implements of death served the organizational ends and purposes both of the church and of the monarchy. Of course, the Christian doctrine concerning the bloody death of Jesus is that it supposedly leads to redemption, but in terms of power relations in the real world, that is a lie—identification with brutality leads to more brutality.

Why was this Christian brutality so compelling to so many people? Partly because it created a trauma bond that bonded believers to the religion. But there was another reason as well. *Christianity recognized the existence of evil, and put the problem of evil at the center of its preoccupations.* And if people in Europe experienced anything, it was the omnipresence of evil. Violence by the monarch determined power in society, and to a great extent, it determined the nature of human relationships. The cult of the cross simply recognized this fact, and put the most obvious symbol of state terrorism at the center of the Christian religion. This process resulted in more aggression in the world, but at least it *did* recognize that evil existed. Christianity over-emphasized the helplessness of human beings in the grip of sin, and with their florid language (and their obsession with sex), they managed to make evil seem attractive. (Although Baudelaire's paltry sins were nothing compared to twentieth-century evil, *Les Fleurs du Mal* was a consummate expression of the idea of evil as compelling and attractive.) Still, what made Christianity durable and important was its understanding that evil exists, that it is everywhere, and that everybody is vulnerable.

The danger of *not* recognizing the existence of evil can be seen clearly in the late nineteenth century, embedded in certain of the experiences and attitudes of Americans, British and Europeans who felt that humankind was poised on the edge of an enlightened and more progressive world. People all over the world, in fact, were excited by the many breakthroughs of science, and thought that a new world was at hand. Many of these brave and idealistic people were active in social movements for more education, better housing, better wages and working conditions, and similar improvements in the lives of the American people. And these improvements did make a huge difference in the quality of life. Because so many of these changes were positive, the progressive activists of the late nineteenth century did not acknowledge the existence of evil, largely because they did not see it in themselves.

Thus they paid almost no attention to nationalism, militarism, or racism, nor did they think very much about imperialism. They did not grasp how slavery and racial segregation and the destruction of the tribal people of North America predisposed men and women to lust for empire, to worship warfare as the greatest human adventure, and look for opportunities to oppress non-white people. Above all, they did not look at the way power operates in the world, how it traumatizes oppressed and oppressor alike, and how it bonds them to aggression as the standard for social behavior. Therefore they were completely unprepared for the outpouring of slaughter and hatred that engulfed the nations during and after World War I, and the manner in which Versailles led to Hitler, and Hitler to Auschwitz. Because they could not see evil in themselves, or in the middle-class world in which so many of them lived, they could not comprehend why and how it had suddenly become so overpowering in the world.

In the twentieth century, this outpouring of evil resulted in multiple crises within organized religion throughout Western society. Liberal Christians had no answer to the problem of evil, because they were unable to acknowledge its existence. (The same thing was often true of political liberals and both the social-democratic and Marxist Left.) Institutional Christianity really had no answer to the problem of evil except to fall back on the doctrine of blood redemption, which American Protestantism had been on the verge of abandoning. This led to the fantastic explosion of fundamentalist and evangelical Christianity in America, which if nothing else once again placed evil at the center of Christian concerns. But that revealed for all time the utter bankruptcy of substitutionary atonement as a methodology for dealing with evil.

Most secular philosophies have seemingly given up on the problem of human good and evil. (Marxism and Freudianism, to name just two, were spectacularly unsuccessful in dealing with it.) To no one is this default more obvious than to the ordinary people of this world. People know that the denial of evil is a lie, because they see evil all around them, sometimes in their relationships to people closest to them. People do not want to be aggressors, and yet they are. People struggle to be neither victims nor aggressors, yet end up being both. The people of the world sense a slow drift toward destruction, and nobody has answers that can reveal how evil replicates itself in the world, nor can they explain why aggression is so powerful. This creates a vacuum; and evangelical and fundamentalist Christianity have come rushing in to fill that vacuum.

But their proposed solution simply makes things worse. It fact the solution of institutional Christianity to the problem of evil really hasn't worked that well since the fourth century, when blood atonement was embraced as a doctrine. What it does is to re-direct the aggression that the believer has internalized, and encourages the believer to act it out in the service of the imperial state. It encourages him to re-direct his aggression by hurting other people, preferably people who are not like him and who lack the ability to fight back. When the Roman Empire co-opted Christianity, it showed Christians how to redirect their hostility and aggression toward people who questioned the authority of the church hierarchy and imperial Rome. Medieval Christianity showed believers how to re-direct their aggression (and project their guilt, fear and anger) against Jews and Muslims, not to mention women, heretics and each other. With the coming of the Enlightenment, institutional Christianity generally re-directed its aggression against those who believed in democracy, social justice and religious pluralism.

Today's Christian evangelicals, overwhelmingly rightwing in

their social, theological and political outlook, re-direct their internalized aggression toward Muslims, immigrants, gays and "secular humanists." Furthermore, like the Christians in the Middle Ages, they tend overwhelmingly to identify with state torture against their religious rivals. As a survey by the Pew Research Center recently revealed, *six out of ten white Christian evangelicals* believe in torture of Muslim detainees, whereas only four in ten people unaffiliated with religion support it. The big difference between Constantine's Christians and American evangelicals in the early twenty-first century is that they sublimate their aggression into support for Republicans that will have the state torture non-Christians on their behalf, rather than torturing them personally. But in other ways the whole degrading process is very much the same. *Plus ça change, plus c'est la même chose.*

To be sure, Christian evangelicalism offers the believer a sense that he is engaging evil on its own turf, but in reality it can only redirect the believer's aggression onto some new victim, making the world more dangerous and the believer more hypocritical. Christian evangelicalism almost invariably increases oppression, obscurantism and exploitation in every area of life, political, social and cultural; ultimately it aims at the most brutal kind of theocracy. Identifying with one's own evil—that is, one's own internalized aggression—as a form of spiritual power creates a sense of moral ascendancy that is pleasurable in the short term; but it constitutes a dangerous form of religious narcissism, and the easy answers it offers can be lethal to emotional growth.

The single asset of today's evangelicalism (and of institutional Christianity historically) is that it acknowledges the reality of evil in the world. Its overwhelming deficit is that it deflects the evil onto a new set of victims, thus continuing the cycle of aggression in which we're all caught. The cult of the cross cannot defeat evil—it can only make it worse, by encouraging the most repressive kind of social and political behavior. Anyone who wonders about this has only to look at the way Mel Gibson's film *The Passion of the Christ* was marketed to, and was used to strengthen, the most depraved aspects of American cultural and political life.

12

The single greatest modern expression of conservative Christianity in popular art has been *The Passion of the Christ*, produced and directed by the actor Mel Gibson and released in 2004. The impact of this film on Christian evangelicals and conservative Catholics, currently the overwhelmingly dominant forces within organized Christianity in America, has been incalculable. Its impact on secular America, although harder to gauge, was likewise considerable. *The Passion* is based on a literal interpretation of the fourteen Stations of the Cross, some thirteenth-century devotional material, and the visions of the stigmatic German nun Anne Catherine Emmerich (1774-1824); but mainly it follows the story line of a late-medieval 'Passion Play' that focuses almost completely on the death of Jesus. The film's relentless demonizing of the Jewish Sanhedrin is one obvious example of its cultural roots in the Middle Ages, but the central thematic and moral problem of *The Passion* centers around another equally disgusting medieval idea—the belief that the crucifixion of Jesus is redemptive *because* of its brutality, the assumption being that the effectiveness of redemptive violence increases according to the amount of pain it causes, and is thus the standard by which religious authenticity is measured.

Gibson's movie—and his life, work and religious beliefs—clearly demonstrate the connection between Christian evangelicals, their obsession with the crucifixion, and authoritarian rightwing elements in the US political class. Gibson marketed *The Passion* to the Religious Right, and sought the help and advice of rightwing celebrities and intellectuals in promoting it. They, in turn, used the film to promote their "values"—glorification of an unnecessary war, justification of torture, and an assault on the US Constitution. *The Passion of the Christ* is, in other words, simply the latest example of a process that began when Christianity, after being co-opted by Constantine, embraced the imperial doctrine of blood redemption. Sixteen hundred years later, the obsession with redemptive violence is still being used to generate war, repression and torture.

Mel Gibson was born in the US, but was taken when young to Australia because Hutton Gibson, Mel's father, did not want him to be drafted for the Vietnam War. Mel received theatre training in Australia and picked up an Australian accent, which he later managed to lose. Although his mother's relatives were Australian, Mel was influenced more by his father than anybody else, and that influence continues today: both Hutton Gibson and his son Mel belong to an ultra-conservative group associated with the extreme right wing of Traditional Catholicism, a religious offshoot of Catholicism that rejects the liberalized teachings of Vatican II. It also rejects one of the most important documents arising from Vatican II, *Nostra Aetate*, which absolves Jews of inherited guilt for the death of Jesus.

In other words, Mel Gibson's church believes that *all* Jews are guilty of the crucifixion of Jesus. (After Vatican II, the vast majority of Catholics were no longer required to believe this.) Hutton and his son Mel celebrate only the Tridentine, or Latin, Mass, and worship in a church they built with their own money. Hutton Gibson believes that the current Pope is a clever (and perhaps surgically-altered) imposter who was somehow foisted off on the Holy See by conspirators, some of whom he believes to be part of a world-wide plot. Hutton Gibson has made a number of statements about Jews that any fair-minded person would quickly recognize as standard anti-Semitic paranoia. (He stated in a radio interview, for example, that the planes that blew up the World Trade Center in New York City on 9/11 were really drones operated by a shadowy conspiracy of Jews and Freemasons.)

Mel Gibson does not make public statements about his father, but has clearly been influenced by him in religion and in other ways. Mel's lifelong struggle with alcoholism and drug addiction probably also have something to do with his father, and his father's beliefs, as we will see later. His work as a film artist is probably to some extent an attempt to act out (and exorcise) the painful contradictions in what is clearly a complicated and highly enmeshed relationship.

Mel received formal theatrical training as a young man, but made a huge and immediate impact in *Mad Max,* his first important film role, in 1979. *Mad Max* is set in a violent dystopia in a post-apocalyptic Australia after a nuclear war, in which the weirdly-named protagonist, Max Rockatansky, is a cop attempting to maintain order amidst the general chaos. This film tells the back story of the Rockatansky character, which sets up the entire Mad Max franchise: besides being a protagonist with an inherently unbelievable name, Max Rockatansky is traumatized by the violent murder of his wife, child *and* best friend; and is thereby motivated to Wreak a Horrible Revenge on the guilty parties—or anybody who gets in his way. Max lights out for the territories, as the American cultural paradigm would have it, to live the life of a haunted, restless, semi-indigent vigilante in a world in ruin.

In *Mad Max: the Road Warrior,* and *Mad Max: Beyond Thunderdome,* Gibson's character is even more violent. He is still an unconventional guerilla warrior, but his character is now a homicidal Christ-figure, forever being violated and emotionally traumatized (in the *Road Warrior,* one of the bad guys even kills his dog, the one creature he is able to love). Mad Max's power as a protagonist comes not from scoring knockouts, but in his ability to take a punch, repeatedly, and in a variety of venues: Max Rocketansky, like Gibson's other popular characters, is a man you can torture, torment and very nearly kill, but he keeps coming back.

"Ever since his star began to rise after the 1979 Australian thriller *Mad Max,*" David Edelstein has written, "Mel Gibson hasn't seemed fully alive on screen unless he's being tortured and mutilated." (Another writer refers to Gibson's 'martyr complex'.) But what at first seems to be one man's version of the anti-hero is really an explication of the classic victim-aggressor: people do vile things to *him*, and therefore he is obligated to do vile things to *them*. (His victim status, in other words, redeems in advance the violence he is about to commit.) Gibson developed early in his career a clever *shtick* of keeping his eyes slightly but permanently widened, which suggests a man stuck in a private moment of trauma. Gibson uses it often, because his characters tend to be obsessed, compulsive and delusional men who are radioactive with internalized trauma and homicidal fury.

In 1987 and 1988 *Lethal Weapon* and *Lethal Weapon 2* came out, in which Gibson plays Sergeant Martin Riggs, an honest cop who has been driven mad by a bad divorce. Gibson is still a crazed warrior in these films, in the guise of a contemporary urban cop, but he and his detective partner (Danny Glover) mine a dark vein of black humor, the joke arising from the tension between the suicidal Riggs, who is forever trying to get himself killed, and his partner, who has no desire to check out yet. There were four films in the *Lethal Weapon* franchise, their popularity arising in part from its gleeful satirizing of the cop-buddy movie genre, but also from Gibson's emerging gifts as an actor: using his permanently widened eyes to telegraph unresolved conflict and suppressed psychosis, Gibson played Riggs as a misfit who is dangerously self-indulgent but oddly comical, and also interesting to watch because of his unpredictability. Gibson's Martin Riggs is the insane detective of *The French Connection* and *48 Hours*, but purged of all agendas, hidden or otherwise. Riggs has no Dr. Moriarty to pursue; his arch-enemy is himself.

Tequila Sunrise, Air America, Gallipoli, Attack Force Z, Ransom, Payback and *The Patriot* were all meditations on men as warriors, engaged in both conventional and unconventional war. *The Year of Living Dangerously* used violence as deep background to a passionate love affair that suggests the alienation of the trained observer in the midst of systemic evil. In *What Women Want,* one of his best films, Gibson skillfully employs his widened eyes to suggest the pleasure of reading somebody else's mind (mind-reading, a favorite delusion of psychotics, is given an intriguing feminist twist); in *Conspiracy Theory* he is an unpleasant but mainly harmless conspiracy nutcase not unlike his father, Hutton Gibson, in real life. The paranoia of the protagonist in *Conspiracy Theory* is eventually explained, close to the end of the film, as being the result of government manipulation of his brain (another common psychotic delusion). In *Braveheart,* Gibson is again the crazed warrior, driven mad by injustice—his wife is raped and he is tortured to death, but he survives long enough to scream *"Freedom!"* as he is being drawn and quartered at the film's apocalyptic end. Mel Gibson's personal recovery from severe addictions, as well as his deepening faith in radical Catholic traditionalism, had lead him out of recurring depressions, and given him a terrifying but coherent worldview that many of his action films have been trending toward. The battered warrior must be tortured, and the trauma must be piled on; but in *Braveheart* the redemptive nature of violence is more explicit than ever before, because it serves the transcendent cause of patriarchal Scottish nationalism.

What was driving this worldview of violence as redemptive? Clearly, it was to a large extent Gibson's intense identification with the blood atonement of Jesus Christ as he had assimilated it through the teachings, imagery and rituals of his extreme branch of Traditional Catholicism—he has said so himself in interviews. It dominated Gibson's psychological profile, his politics and his film art, first as an actor, and later as director and producer of *The Passion of the Christ*. At some point it become apparent to Mel Gibson that it was time for him to make the classic modern film narrative of Christ's crucifixion. The theme that had been driving him all his life—the connection between violence and redemption—could now be made explicit in a great religious work of popular art. It would have enormous emotional power, because it would put on the screen a story *in which the connection between violence and redemption was already internalized and understood by the audience.*

He would, in other words, cinematically relate the archetypical story of redemptive violence in the West, the story of Jesus' last hours—his arrest, torture, trial and crucifixion—the story that had, in other words, changed and redeemed Gibson's life, and which continued to drive his values. Sadly, it also animated his homophobia, his patriarchal idealization of the traumatized warrior, and his conservative worship of state power. It is not too much to say that Gibson's cultural and political conservatism revolved around—and was expressed through—his far-right brand of Catholic Traditionalism, including his belief in inherited Jewish guilt. Included in these beliefs was his rejection of Vatican II, on the one hand; and on the other, an obsessive identification with Jesus' crucifixion-as-redemptive-violence. And now Mel Gibson had the resources to put his apocalyptic vision on the screen.

13

The Passion of the Christ is not a great work of art, but it has an uncanny, harsh, and potentially traumatizing effect on the viewer, partly because it tells a story everybody knows, and partly because of its repeated, prolonged use of extreme violence. The Christian viewer is predisposed toward strong emotion while watching the violence of Jesus' suffering, because the Christian accepts—or is more likely to understand—the doctrine of blood redemption, and the idea that Jesus' suffering is redemptive. (In the West, even non-Christians are usually aware of the argument that Jesus' crucifixion is what gets the believer into heaven.) If the movie was simply of a man being tortured by criminals, repeated scenes of torture might cause the audience to riot. (This actually happened at early previews of *Marathon Man,* when director John Schlesinger included nine minutes of Dustin Hoffman being tortured with a dentist drill.) One *expects* violence to be directed toward Jesus, because that is simply part of the crucifixion story.

But it quickly becomes clear that the extreme brutality of the whipping, scourging and crucifixion scenes is not intended to tell a story. These scenes have the power to disgust, overwhelm and traumatize because of their repetition and duration, and that is clearly the film's intent.

In almost all films that tell a story, action is foreshortened or communicated through "establishing" shots, and the passage of time is indicated in a variety of ways. That is how the visual grammar of cinema works; and—for that matter—it is through such devices that the passage of time is indicated in virtually all narrative art. In *The Passion,* the scenes of Jesus' torture and crucifixion are mainly shown in real time. The intent of these long, brutal scenes of torture is clearly to overwhelm the viewer with violence. Ultimately the purpose of the film—exactly like the medieval Passion Plays upon which it is based—is to ignite an intense emotional response during which the viewer internalizes the recurring aggression he sees happening before his eyes.

Some critics have commented that the film's use of light and darkness reminds them of Caravaggio and El Greco, but *The Passion* depends much more on standard Hollywood idioms. The movie borrows stylistically from science fiction and horror films, and reminds one of attempts to portray evil in such films as *Rosemary's Baby, The Exorcist* and the *Omen* franchise. It is completely different, however, from previous mainstream Hollywood treatments of Jesus, such as *God-spell, King of Kings*, or *Jesus Christ, Superstar.* These films were of interest to non-Christians as well as Christians, because they were attempts to dramatize a life. *The Passion* is solely, darkly and obsessively about experiencing Jesus' death; it assumes, as most Christianity has come to assume, that Jesus' death is more important than his life.

The Passion is basically a propaganda film with both a political and religion message. It is not just about aggression but specifically about state aggression, and in that way is much like Leni Riefenstahl's *Triumph of the Will.* The two films are similar in another way: both films are almost entirely concerned with expressing, in a systematic and sometimes lurid way, the physical attraction of organized aggression; and both films seek to develop a deliberate aesthetic of violence. Both Riefenstahl and Gibson use religious images, both project the idea that violence can be visually stunning, and both are obsessed by the redemptive nature of state violence. *Triumph of the Will* and *The Passion* both want the viewer to internalize the organized aggression on the screen—but there are big differences in how they go about it.

Unlike Riefenstahl's work of evil genius, *The Passion of the Christ* is not a great film, but is a well-made Hollywood movie with great production values, and one that happens to be a skillful work of propaganda. *Triumph of the Will* presents National Socialism as a secular religion and Hitler as a secular Messiah, using carefully choreographed movement of massed human beings to suggest the ecstasy of *Gleichschaltung* (willed participation in societal regimentation) and also the futility of resistance to the Nazi state. Mel Gibson, on the other hand, is not so subtle—he hits the viewer over the head with one scene of violence after the other. He makes no argument for blood redemption, because blood redemption does not enter the personality through syllogistic reasoning. Instead he seeks to penetrate the viewer's subconscious mind with seemingly endless violent images that can bond him to the subject matter unconsciously, rather than win him over with consistency or logic. Both films want the viewer to internalize the state aggression played out on the screen, but whereas *Triumph of the Will* seeks to seduce, *The Passion of the Christ* aims, openly and systematically, to traumatize.

14

The Passion of the Christ begins with Jesus (Jim Caviezel) praying in the Garden of Gethsemane. He is tempted by Satan, while his disciples sleep. Much has been written about Gibson's conception of an androgynous Satan (Rosalinda Celentano), one who seems to combine the least savory aspects of both male and female genders; but her Beelzebub does not frighten. We already know that Jesus will be crucified, so Satan has nothing to do—evil is already there, in the daily brutalities of the Roman Empire and their indigenous toadies. So why have Satan tempt Jesus? To provide a little Deep Background, it seems, because Gibson's Satan hissily tells Jesus that it's "too much" for one person to die for the sins of humanity, because "no one can take on the sins of the world." (So *that's* what's going on!) Given the harm that the doctrine of blood redemption has done in the world, it seems appropriate that Gibson gives Satan the job of explaining it to the viewer.

The film cuts to Judas, who receives his 30 pieces of silver. Jesus is taken by the High Priest's men, who appear to be the private security police of the Sanhedrin, the Jewish council. This is the first opportunity for various groups of sadists to start beating Jesus to a pulp—which they all do so well, and so repeatedly, and by such a lengthy process, that by the time he arrives in the court of Caiaphas (Mattia Sbragia), the High Priest, one eye is completely closed, causing more than one reviewer to compare Gibson's Jesus to Rocky Balboa. By this time the viewer is starting to wonder why the beatings are so graphic, and take so long to happen. Wouldn't a minute or two do, to establish what's going on?

Jesus' mother Mary and Mary Magdalene are told that Jesus has been taken, but not before Mary murmurs, "Why is this night different from all other nights?" This line probably wasn't used at

Passover for another couple of centuries at least, but Gibson isn't interested in authenticity—he's interested in a movie that *seems* authentic, at least to people who don't know that much about the subject matter.

At this point a couple of Roman soldiers ask the Sanhedrin what's going on—apparently the soldiers of the Roman Proconsul are so uninterested in Jesus, that they don't even know he's already been busted. We are led to believe that it's the High Priest Caiaphas and the Sanhedrin, the Jewish council, who want him dead. Most modern scholars have concluded that it was probably the other way around: it was Pilate or his imperial representative who wanted Jesus dead, because Pilate was a homicidal maniac who murdered anyone he could get his hands on. The villainy of Caiaphas might have been real enough, but he didn't have anywhere near the political or military clout that Pilate had. The presentation of Caiaphas as the main antagonist of Jesus was almost surely invented by later Christians who wanted to demonize Jews, with whom they had begun to compete for converts.

More proof of the supposed "authenticity" of Gibson's film is that characters in *The Passion* speak Aramaic and Latin *just like they did back in the days of Jesus*. Some characters in *The Passion* do speak in Aramaic, an ancient language that influenced both Hebrew and Arabic; but according to Oxford professor Geza Vermes, writing in the *Guardian*, the translation is done poorly, suffering from a tendency to fall back on "unnecessary Hebraisms." One of those unnecessary Hebraisms appears to be the compound word *Yitstalev*, which means *crucify him!* in Aramaic and Hebrew.[10] Thus the Hebrew-speaking customer in New York or Tel Aviv would hear the mob in *The Passion* screaming *in Hebrew* for Jesus to be crucified. Using a Hebrew cognate instead of a different Aramaic word is, to say the very least, in spectacularly bad taste. Given the beliefs of Gibson's church about Jewish deicide, it probably wasn't just an oversight.

Two members of the Sanhedrin object to the proceedings, and are ejected. Having gotten rid of the opposition, Caiaphas begins to question Jesus about his identity—and Jesus says, "I AM." Since this is what God says in the Torah, this is enough for a charge of blasphemy. (The film doesn't quite make up its mind what Jesus is being charged with, but the small crowd watching Jesus and the Sanhedrin seem certain that death would be an appropriate punishment.) The crowd starts to bleat for Jesus' death, and members of the Sanhedrin initiate a new beating, rushing in to strike Jesus with their hands and fists. Peter, who is watching at a distance, is asked about Jesus, and denies him three times. Meanwhile Judas is tormented by demons in the shape of children (looking very much like they stepped out of *Omen II*), and wisely chooses to hang himself.

The movie now cuts to a scene far from the madding crowd clamoring to have Jesus executed, to focus on a beautiful couple as different from everybody else in this rather grubby venue as night and day. They are Pontius Pilate, the Roman procurator (Hristo Naumov Shopov), and his wife Claudia (the beautiful Claudia Gerini). This live in a startlingly clean, if not spacious, imperial compound of some sort, and they are as thoughtful and sensitive as everybody else is crazed and unkempt.

> Claudia pleads with Pilate not to kill Jesus. "He's holy," she explains.
>
> Pilate goes outside to look at Jesus. He is shocked, shocked to discover that the Sanhedrin's men have been beating him. "Do you always punish your prisoners before you sentence them?" he asks disapprovingly. "What accusations do you bring against this man?"
>
> A priest says, "He has violated our Sabbath, Proconsul."
>
> "He has seduced the people…taught foul, disgusting doctrines," says another.
>
> "He claims he is the Messiah."

One clever-looking chap says, "He has forbidden his followers to pay tribute to Caesar, Proconsul."

Pilate takes Jesus up the steps, through the doors of his compound, and they stand in the anteroom. Here Pilate offers Jesus a drink, which Jesus declines.

Pilate: "Are you the king of the Jews?"

Jesus: "Does this question come from you? Or do you ask me this because others have told you that is what I am?"

Pilate: "Why would I ask you that? Am I a Jew? Your high priests, your own people delivered you up to me. They want me to have you executed. Why? What have you done?"

Gibson has Pilate and Jesus speaking in Latin. Now, there is no way that Jesus of Nazareth could have known Latin. To compound this whopper, Gibson has them using modern Italianate or church Latin, which is even crazier. If Jesus and Pilate ever spoke at all—they almost surely didn't—it would have been in Greek, the lingua franca of educated people at that time. (One suspects that the modern church Latin may have come from Gibson's love of the Tridentine Mass.) In any case, these mistakes are further evidence that this movie is "authentic" only in the sense that it accurately reflects Gibson's preoccupations.

"Are you a king?" Pilate is asking Jesus.

Jesus: "My kingdom is not of this world. If it were, do you think my followers would have let them hand me over?"

Pilate: "Then you are a king?"

Jesus: "That is why I was born. To give testimony to the truth. All men who hear the truth hear my voice."

Pilate: "Truth!" He steps closer to Jesus. "What is truth?"

Pilate apparently didn't hear the answer he wanted in this version of the truth, because he handles this latest political football by making a lateral move, sending Jesus to the court of Herod Antipas (Luca De Dominicis). Herod is portrayed as a hysterical drag queen, the exact temperamental opposite of the sulking Turkish Bey (Jose Ferrer) who gives Peter O'Toole the once-over in *Lawrence of Arabia*. Ensconced among his playful courtiers, Gibson's campy Herod pleadingly asks Jesus, "Will you work a little miracle for me?" When he gets no response, he concludes that Jesus is insane, and sends him away, in effect pardoning him. Despite it weird ambience, the scene is convincing, the only difficulty being that biblical accounts of Jesus' meeting with Herod are probably fictitious, concocted by later gospel writers who wanted to punch up the importance of their martyred leader. Gibson's piece is simply the latest addition to the tale, notable mainly for its parody of homosexuality.

Meanwhile, Pilate is having a remarkable conversation with his wife, Claudia. This conversation constitutes the dramatic, psychological and moral core of the film. It is not about the world of Jesus—nothing about this film has much to do with Jesus, who is merely required to suffer and die at great length—but about the Roman imperial machinery that is intent on having Jesus crucified. If salvation arises from Jesus' execution by the state, clearly it is the government *apparatchiks* that are important. That includes the highly-charged political and psychological world of Pontius Pilate and his wife, as Mel Gibson imagines them.

> "What is truth, Claudia?" Pilate asks his wife. "Do you hear it, recognize it, when it is spoken?"
>
> "Yes, I do. Don't you?"
>
> "How? Can you tell me?"
>
> "If you will not hear the truth, no one can tell you."
>
> "Truth…" Pilate murmurs.
>
> He looks up at her imploringly.
>
> "Do you want to know what my truth is, Claudia? I've been putting down rebellions in this rotten outpost for eleven

years. If I don't condemn this man, I know Caiaphas will start a rebellion. If I do condemn him, then his followers may. Either way, there will be bloodshed. Caesar has warned me, Claudia—warned me twice. He swore that the next time the blood would be mine."

He concludes despairingly: "That is my truth!"

This is a pretty good description of the cycle of aggression in which a Roman Proconsul like Pontius Pilate might get caught up in. Of course people like Pilate are rarely able to express their dilemma with such sensitivity—except in movies intended for modern evangelical audiences. Other details are similarly wrong: Jesus' followers were not likely to start a rebellion, and even Pilate would have known that. Claudia gives no clue as to how she discerns truth when she hears it, or why Jesus is "holy"—but arguably that is not important, because Jesus' personality doesn't matter in this film.

The biggest mistake of this scene is that the historical Pilate, a blood-thirsty psychopath if ever there was one, would never have said these words, because instead of being morally conflicted by having to kill people he would have relished it as a source of pleasure. But the dialogue directed by Pilate to Claudia in *The Passion* is dialogue by an *imagined* Pontius Pilate, and takes place in an imaginary world (that is, the world of Mel Gibson), and tells us mainly about what it means to live in Gibson's world.

So how does one escape this cycle of violence that Gibson's imaginary Pilate confronts us with? The answer is supplied by Gibson himself. We are to escape the cycle of violence, first, by submitting to it, just as his heroes in his action movies must constantly be beaten, pummeled, smashed, tortured, shot, stabbed, thrown from heights, or jump into raging fires or rivers. (It was Gibson himself who took the movie *Payback* away from the assigned director to add a scene in which the protagonist—played by Mel Gibson—has his toes smashed with a hammer.)

And why does Gibson's character in his movies have to suffer from all these different kinds of torture? *Because violence is redemptive.*

And once having experienced its redemptive effects, Gibson's protagonists bounce back as full-blown, ass-kicking warriors, fully traumatized but even more inclined to kill. It is like the common practice of torturers who are themselves subjected to torture before being loosed on their victims. This is what blood redemption produces; violence redeems by empowering the survivor to engage in more violence. It is that brutal process—the process of redemption through violence—that for Gibson creates the highest and most authentic reality (and the most exalted religious experience) to which mortals can aspire. So it is in *The Passion of the Christ* that Mel Gibson's Jesus, like Gibson's other protagonists, must submit to the entire panorama of sadomasochistic torments to fulfill his destiny.

First, however, Pilate tells the crowd in the courtyard of his compound: "Herod has found no cause [for punishment] in this man. Neither have I."

But "the Jews" will have none of it. The small and seemingly interchangeable crowd of about fifty people clamors for Jesus' blood, despite Pilate's desire to spare Jesus. Caiaphas is so anxious to see Jesus killed that he even hints at a possible destabilization of Pilate's administration.

> The conflicted Pilate tries to save Jesus: "What would you have me do with Jesus?"
>
> Caiaphas: "Crucify him!"
>
> Pilate glances at his wife, who watches from a nearby window. "No! I'll chastise him, and set him free."

There is a long scene in which Jesus is whipped with rods. The Roman soldiers shout out the number of each stroke as they beating goes on and on—clearly an attempt to create the illusion of a beating happening in real time. One should remember that the evangelical Christians who see this movie believe that it is *God* who is being whipped, and that each blow of the rod, however horrifying, actually guarantees their own triumphant entry into heaven. Therefore they must be forced to see in inexorable detail (and real time) the *horror* of the public torture that Jesus endure. The intent is clearly to overwhelm the viewer with the repetition of violence—but Gibson is also making a point about its redemptive nature. The brutality against Jesus redeems *because* it is hideous. (The instinctive resistance of the viewer to seeing violence only adds to its ability to traumatize, because the shame and disgust it generates cannot be rationally examined—after all, it's all *God's will.*).

In the middle of all this easy-to-internalize gore, Gibson's androgynous Satan strolls about among both Jews and Roman soldiers, clutching in her arms a small, unpleasantly-smirking midget with hair growing out of his back, perhaps another unconscious reference to *Rosemary's Baby* or the child in *Omen II.* Again, these androgynous figures, apparently designed to evoke a sense of ultimate horror, create almost no resonance whatsoever, because there is so much systemic evil clearly evident in the robotic behavior of the Roman soldiers. But for Gibson, systemic evil is not a so much a matter of behavior, as something that manifests itself visually—and must be manifested in film art—through generic visual representations (either from American movies or the New Testament) created to enhance the main story line, which now consists entirely of escalating scenes of violence against Jesus.

The film cuts to several close-ups of three people watching from a distance: Mary Magdalene; the disciple John; and Jesus' mother, Mary. From now on, they will never be very far from the main action, because the rest of the film, with the exception of one short scene with Pilate, is unambiguously a delivery system for the horror of Jesus' suffering—which can be evoked, first, by showing endless scenes of him being tortured and crucified; and two, by close-ups of the reactions of those who love him. But there is also an increasingly schematic feeling of the film—actors say their lines woodenly, there's not much cross-talk, and there's a rigidity that makes it seem like more of a ritual than real events. But it *is* a ritual, because we are watching a narrative that is embedded in the collective unconscious of the West.

At one point Mary asks despairingly, "My son…when, where, how…will you choose to be delivered of all this?"

Which telegraphs Gibson's premise, just in case the viewer has forgotten: that Jesus could stop the hideous charade at any point because he's divine, but *chooses* to die (and be beaten to a pulp) because it can redeem the world. This is not an itinerant preacher sentence to death because of his radical ideas, but cosmic thaumaturgy. And since the point of this story is redemption through violence, we should not be surprised that there is now more violence.

Having whipped him with rods, the Romans proceed to scourge him. A scourge was a multi-thong whip or lash, and was used to flay those who were about to be crucified. Here Gibson relies entirely on the account of Anne Catherine Emmerich, a stigmatic Roman Catholic nun (1174-1824) and hysterical anti-Semite. Emmerich had a highly-detailed and thoroughly repulsive visionary experience of the crucifixion, and all the events that led up to the crucifixion; in her vision the Jews of the Sanhedrin were, predictably, demonic criminals who gloat endlessly over Jesus' death. Her visions include a great deal of mayhem that is not in the synoptic gospels, but it is not surprising that Gibson used her material, because it makes the suffering of Jesus more horrible; and in any case Gibson does not feel himself bound by the New Testament. He was, after all, guided by the Holy Spirit, as he repeatedly pointed out during and after making the film.

After he is scourged, Jesus—who is now little more than a

bleeding carcass with a pulse—is again hauled up before Pilate. Pilate again tries to save him, even giving the crowd the option of freeing Jesus and instead crucifying Barabbas, a notorious thief; but the mob wants Jesus to die. Film critic David Edelstein references this deliberate falsification of history with a negative review worthy of the late Pauline Kael: "Pilate, whom historians identify as a surpassingly cruel ruler responsible for crucifying many thousands to maintain his authority, is portrayed as a sorrowful, even-tempered man whose wife shows acts of loving kindness toward Mary (Maia Morgenstern) and Mary Magdalene (Monica Belluci). Pilate is shocked by the Jews' brutality and by the determination of the priest Caiphas to see this so-called blasphemer executed. While Pilate wrinkles his forehead, searching his tender conscience, sundry Jews lean into the camera and hiss or keen through rotted teeth."[11]

Although I didn't notice that many bad teeth (Susannah Heschel pointed out this detail too, making me wonder what I was missing), there is no doubt whatsoever that *The Passion*, like all the medieval Passion plays upon which the script is based, portrays the Jewish mob as guilty of Jesus' death, not Pilate or the Roman Empire. All "the Jews" in Pilate's courtyard are dressed more or less alike, and you have to wonder what exactly brought them all there at the same time. And "the Jews" do indeed look like dodgy characters straight out of an Orientalist's nightmare of a North African Casbah (although one must say that the Roman soldiers are no prizes, either). Jesus, played by Jim Caviezel, looks like a German tourist who wandered away from the tour bus into the clutches of an inexplicably violent Middle Eastern lynch mob.

It had to be beyond infuriating for Jews to watch these scenes, because here was the same old pre-Vatican II nonsense of swarthy, shifty-eyed Jewish Christ-killers murdering a beautiful white European (that is, "Christian") Jesus. And "the Jews" weren't just a few High Priests trying to bump off a bothersome subversive, but—as the movie later makes clear—were representing the whole Jewish people engaged in willful, intentional deicide, taking on the guilt, in the process, of being responsible for all the other bad things that went on before, during and after the crucifixion. We know this because Gibson includes the spoken lines, in Aramaic, from Matthew 27:25, in which "the Jews" inexplicably demands that God to punish their descendants for willfully murdering Jesus. ("His blood be upon us and our children.")

Of course, as every reputable Biblical scholar knows, these words were almost surely added by Christians after the actual crucifixion of Jesus, the motive being to discredit Judaism, with which the early Jesus movement was in competition. (Why would pious Jews—or pious anybody—ask God to punish their descendants? Because it is a mean-spirited anti-Semitic Christian fantasy, pure and simple.) Furthermore, Christians were trying to ingratiate themselves with the Roman Empire, so they had a built-in incentive for playing down the brutality of Pontius Pilate. Gibson is very careful to perpetuate this historical libel by including the words from Matthew 27:25 in Aramaic, but without supplying a subtitle.

> Pilate receives his crown of thorns, and another beating. Pilate shows the crowd the battered Jesus while his wife Claudia watches in horror.
>
> "Isn't that enough? Look at him!"
>
> Caiaphas and the blood crazed mob in the courtyard: "Crucify him!"
>
> Pilate: "Shall I crucify your king?"
>
> "We have no king but Caesar!"
>
> Pilate turns to Jesus: "Speak to me. I have the power to crucify you, or else set you free."
>
> Jesus speaks:
>
> *"You have no power over me except what is given you from*

above. Therefore, it is he who delivered me to you who has the greater sin."

These lines, given to Jesus by Mel Gibson, are in fact the film's big declaration of blood redemption; and also the film's unmistakable declaration of Jewish deicide. Pilate exists to do God's will, and is not himself at fault. But the ones who deliver Jesus to Pilate—Caiaphas and the Jewish Council—*they're* the evil ones, because they delivered him to Pilate. (Remember that when Jesus was taken in Gethsemane, it was by the Sanhedrin's men.) Immediately upon hearing this, someone from the crowd says in Aramaic, "If you free him, Governor, you are no friend of Caesar's. You must crucify him."

The crowd becomes more unruly.

> "It is you who wants to crucify him, not I," a virtuous Pilate insists. "Look you to it. I am innocent of this man's blood."

Poor Pilate is forced against his will to do as "the Jews" say. The Jewish mob is so inflamed with hate that they are desperate to take the responsibility, inexplicably asking that God punish their descendants.

So Pilate turns Jesus over to the soldiers to be crucified.

Jesus carries his cross on the Via Dolorosa all the way to Calvary, with a little help from Simon of Cyrene. The rest of the film is basically one torment of Jesus after another, up to and including the crucifixion, which is accomplished with incredible cruelty. There are a couple of brief flashbacks, but they exist only to explain the purpose of the horror we are watching. Just in case the viewer still doesn't understand the mechanism of blood atonement, in one flashback Jesus says:

> *"I am the Good Sheppard. I lay down my life for my sheep. No one takes my life from me, but I lay it down of my own accord. I have*

> *the power to lay it down, and the power to take it up again. This command is from my father."*

Later, in a scene of mind-boggling vulgarity, a single tear-shaped drop falls from heaven, the implication being that God is weeping for the death of Jesus. (But if God loves Jesus so much, why did he make him suffer on the cross? The big tear feels like the self-pity of the sociopath, exquisitely aware of his own suffering but blind to the havoc he causes others.) At the end of his public execution, Jesus is lowered from the cross and embraced by his mother, who looks directly at the camera, creating in that tableau the image of the Pieta. It isn't done particularly badly, but it isn't particularly effective either, and we are back to that feeling of a cinematic chess game, rather like Peckinpah's approach to the American West: certain behaviors equal certain effects because all the paying customers know the rules of the game and accept the game's controlling metaphors.

Finally, in what is perhaps the most a-historical and gratuitously Judeo-phobic scenes ever to appear on film, God gets everybody's attention with an earthquake, during which the Temple in Jerusalem collapses on Caiaphas and the other Jewish plotters, presaging with one scene both the ultimate destruction of the Temple and Christianity's later doctrine that because "the Jews" rejected Jesus, they must be punished. (According to this reading, the Temple was destroyed as a judgment for rejecting Jesus, implying that whatever punishment they received from Christians later they deserved for the same reason.)

Later, three days later, Gibson cuts to Jesus in the tomb. In yet another spectacularly bad directorial choice, the winding sheet falls slack as Jesus comes back to life. Jesus has arisen, and is preparing to exit the tomb. As several reviewers have pointed out, the risen Jesus does not look at all happy, but like someone with revenge on his mind. Reviewer David Edelstein put it this way: "When Jesus is resurrected, his expression is hard, and, as he moves toward the entrance to his tomb, the camera lingers on a round hole in his hand that goes all the way through. Gibson's Jesus reminded me of the Terminator—he could be the Christianator—heading out into the world to spread the bloody news. Next stop: the Crusades." I think Edelstein's black humor is metaphorically on the mark. Torture by the state doesn't redeem, but leads to the internalization of violence—and then more violence. Aggression does not deliver humankind from aggression, but creates more aggression.

15

Mel Gibson's main contact within the Religious Right and the conservative establishment was Peggy Noonan, a speech-writer for Ronald Reagan and George Bush, and a clever Republican operative with strong ties to conservative Catholicism. In a conservative political tradition that boasts few good writers, Noonan excels. But she is also an opportunist, and has moved right as American conservatism has gone to the far right; and has an irritating tendency to fall back on a wide-eyed kind of moral vacuity when anything important comes up. "Some things in life have to be mysterious," she famously said about high-level approval of torture in the Bush administration. (*Translation*: She doesn't know anything, so don't ask about it.) In any case, she exhibits in all her writings the same moral autism, the same glaring blind spot, shared by almost all American conservatives, both religious and political: the flagrant worship of profit and power, especially state power in the service of militarism, patriarchy and nationalism.

Noonan saw early in the game that *The Passion of the Christ* was a seminal work of popular culture that would have great emotional appeal to the conservative coalition that supported George Bush; and saw also that its emphasis on blood redemption could bring together evangelical Christians and conservative Catholics. It would also shore up lagging support for the Iraq war. (Noonan does not shirk from using the grossest forms of Christian nationalism for conservative political purposes, as witnessed by her book *A Heart, a Cross and a Flag*, a pathetic tribute to power-worship published in the summer before Gibson's film came out.)

It was, in fact, during that summer of 2003 that Noonan was invited to a private July screening of *The Passion of the Christ*, organized for herself, Linda Chavez, Kate O'Beirne and some other rightwing operatives. Noonan was quick to see what the main problem with *The Passion* would be, and which groups would be likely to criticize it.

"This summer I was invited to a Washington screening of the film," Noonan wrote six months later. "I went with some trepidation: Could the charges of anti-Semitism be true? I didn't think that Mel Gibson would set out to create a deliberately anti-Semitic piece of work; that kind of movie would have been rejected by audiences and lambasted by critics. But people can do ignorant things and thoughtless things, and their work can be destructive. I didn't know what Mr. Gibson's film would be. So I watched, and found myself moved and inspired by the film, which isn't about hatred but love, and love's continuing war with evil."

So far, so good—she's entitled to her opinion. But there was more, much more. Noonan forgets to mention that the "Washington screening" was a private one limited to political operatives rather than film buffs or people of faith. The screening was a *political* event, not a cinematic or religious or even broadly cultural one. Nor did she mention that there was a fair amount of activity during this period aimed at getting Pope John Paul to see the film, in the hopes that he might say something supportive of it; nor did she explain that she was privy to this activity going on at the highest levels of the Catholic Church.

In December of that year, Noonan was contacted by Steve McEveety, the film's producer, who told Noonon that Pope John Paul had—after being repeatedly begged to do so—watched *The Passion of the Christ*. Pope John Paul is then said to have murmured, "It is as it was," an odd statement that could have referred either to the film, or the boorish behavior of the film's producer and assistant director, who had been relentlessly hounding everybody around the Pope to get him to view the film. The intent, of course, was to use whatever the Pope said to advertise the film. In any case, Noonan was able triumphantly to inform the world in her regular newspaper column in the Wall Street Journal that the Pope was apparently impressed with *The Passion*, although his actual words were noncommittal at best.

Thereupon there was an eruption of complicated interactions in which various people in the Vatican affirmed, denied or expressed consternation about the quote. This is standard Vatican procedure regarding the culture wars, the intent being to confuse everybody sufficiently that no one can determine what the Pope really said or thinks. "Believe me," Noonan wrote worriedly in the WSJ, "it is painful to be accused however implicitly of being the accessory to a lie." (But if she really believed it, how could she be complicit in lying?) Exactly what the Pope said isn't important. What is important is that the director of *The Passion of the Christ* wanted to break the news of the Pope's approval in the United States with a political columnist in the Wall Street Journal, and not a film critic. He did this because he realized that the major marketing opportunities would be with conservative Christian evangelicals generally, and the Religious Right specifically. In other words, this film, unlike most films, would succeed not on aesthetic grounds, or even as a religious entertainment, but on mainly political grounds, with the help of rightwing evangelicals and conservative Catholics close to the Bush presidency. It could not be otherwise, because Mel Gibson would need expert political help from established power-brokers, due to the film's overt demonizing of Jews and his own membership in a church that rejects Vatican II.

Unlike previous Hollywood movies such as *King of Kings* and *Jesus Christ Superstar*, which appealed to others besides rightwing Christians, its success would lay solely in its edgy, over-the-top attraction to audiences that identified with the extreme violence of Jesus' death, and who identified with the doctrine of blood atonement as the centerpiece of their faith. Those viewers would tend to be conservative evangelicals, whose political concerns overlapped with those of the Religious Right. In making such a marketing decision, Mel Gibson put himself at the disposal of the Religious Right's cultural, social and political apparatus, as well as seeking out the best way to promote his own conservative religious and political ideas.

During the autumn of 2003 Robert Novak, the rightwing commentator, was likewise invited to a private screening of Gibson's film. He, too, was ecstatic, and got right to the job at hand: reassuring everyone that there was nothing anti-Semitic about *The Passion*, as so many of "its detractors" had claimed. There had only been private showings up to that point, all in front of hand-picked conservative and Christian evangelical audiences, but Novak was apparently referring to the fact that Abraham Foxman of the Anti-Defamation League had somehow gotten hold of a script of *The Passion* some time before, and was trying to generate opposition to the film's depiction of the Jewish Sanhedrin. But Novak wrote that the real problem was that "secularists" were trying to find fault with Gibson's film; and took the opportunity to note that certain Democratic candidates were likewise far too secular, unlike the pious President George W. Bush, who prayed regularly.

This became a regular and growing chorus from conservatives during the election year of 2004, especially among neo-cons and leaders of the Religious Right, at first mainly in connection with Gibson's film; but later—often using *The Passion* as a point of departure—it became a generalized criticism, the idea being that civil libertarians, secular people in the arts and in society, and in the Democratic party generally, sought to suppress religion (that is, conservative Christianity) and drive it from the public square. Books were written about the attacks of "secularists" on *The Passion* (the truly masochistic should try reading Gary North's apocalyptic *The War on Mel Gibson*, which sees criticism of Gibson's film as part of a conspiracy led by Satan).

In the three years before the election of 2004 that would pit

George W. Bush against Democrat John Kerry, the US had become a torturing society. Recurring rumors of "enhanced interrogation" used against Muslim detainees had begun to appear in the media, and organizations motivated enough to search for evidence had become aware that those excesses in the treatment of US government detainees were occurring. There were three kinds of torture being used. There was the so-called extraordinary rendition of detainees to other countries, where they were tortured. There was the torture of so-called high-value detainees at the CIA black sites by the agency's case officers and contract employees. Finally there was the mass abuse of prisoners at Guantanamo Bay, Bagram Air Base in Afghanistan and Abu Ghraib prison in Baghdad.

The abuse in the last three facilities, some of which resulted in deaths, had little to do with getting actionable intelligence, because it usually didn't accompany anything one could call interrogation. Circumstantial evidence suggests it was done to create religion-specific forms of torture. In other words, Donald Rumsfeld, who was in daily contact with personnel at those sites, and who was managing the abuse, may have been looking for torture techniques that could be used specifically on Muslims in the future.

Given the manner in which the systemic use of torture can demoralize entire civilizations that use it, and the eventual reaction from the Muslim world to these excesses, the systematic use of torture was a moral and diplomatic catastrophe for the United States.

But George W. Bush knew he had nothing to fear from the rightwing evangelicals who were the most important part of his electoral coalition. In fact, a majority of Christian evangelicals in the US were actually in *favor* of torturing Muslim detainees, a fact that was to become painfully clear later in the decade; and they supported it much more than non-evangelicals. According to the results of a survey by the Pew Forum on Religion and Public Life released in early 2009, six out of ten white Christian evangelicals support torture as "often or sometimes" justified. Only four out of ten non-evangelicals supported torture.

Furthermore, the Pew poll discovered that the more a Christian evangelical attends church—that is, the better his or her attendance—the more likely he or she was to support torture. Since Christian evangelicals were the major constituency supporting George Bush, and since they were so politically engaged in their support of war, repression and torture, one is forced to conclude that they are one of the most aggressive and immoral groups in America. In fact, their support for torture, and the fact that it is so clearly based on religious sentiment and reasoning, when combined with the fact that they are such a large group, and so reliably involved in electoral politics, makes them more likely to support systemic evil than any other constituency in public life.

There are, of course, progressive evangelical groups, most notably the Jim Wallis *Sojourners* group. But if one reads their literature—including their magazine—it quickly becomes clear that the *Sojourners* people have found the psychological wherewithal to break free from the obsession with the crucifixion so typical of other evangelicals, and define their social and personal ideas in terms of Jesus' teachings. But the vast majority of Christian evangelicals and conservative Catholics cannot do that—in fact, their very identity depends on not doing that.

Should it surprise us that Christian evangelicals supported torture at a much higher rate than any other group? Not really, because many evangelicals believed that it was God's will that George Bush become President; and it would logically follow, then, that torturing Muslims—and when possible, killing them—was simply God's will. Such attitudes were not substantially different than those of the First Crusade in 1096. They consist, first of all, of the idea that Islam seeks to destroy Christianity, and is therefore a special enemy that must be destroyed at all costs. But it is also accompanied by a deeply internalized belief in redemptive violence. Anybody who has spent any time at all with evangelicals knows the extent to which they are focused on Jesus' crucifixion; such a believer invariably comes to believe that violence can redeem whenever God wants it to, which in turn predisposes the believer to the idea that torture by the state is not a bad thing, especially when practiced against Muslims. But institutional Christianity has always tended to support war and torture, for exactly those reasons.

The most well-known Jewish supporter of *The Passion* was probably the ubiquitous Michael Medved, a protégé of Daniel Lapin, who with Lapin is associated with the American Alliance of Jews and Christians (AAJC), a conservative advocacy group that Lapin helped to found with rightwing commentator Gary Bauer. The AAJC's advisory board included Dr. James Dobson, Chuck Colson, the late Jerry Falwell, Pat Robertson, Rick Scarborough, and Rabbis David Novak and Barry Freundel. Medved, like Noonan, is an opportunist—a liberal democrat who became an ecstatic Reaganite in 1980—and was one of the first of the conservative propagandists to denounce critics of Gibson's film as "secularists," portraying them as part of a larger movement to denigrate religion and destroy its influence.

For his part, Mel Gibson's attitude toward Jews, modern and ancient, can be understood only if one remembers that he belongs to the same radical off-shoot of Catholic Traditionalism as his father, Hutton Gibson. Mel Gibson's father is both anti-Semitic and a Holocaust-denier, and subscribes to a species of conspiracy theories often referred to by experts in the field as Judeo-Masonic. This appalling but fascinating form of anti-Semitism begins, as does most anti-Semitism, with a belief in inherited Jewish guilt for the death of Jesus, an idea that was firmly established by the fifth century of Christianity. According to various Judeo-Masonic conspiracy theories, at some point in history, the Jews made a deal with the Freemasons. The Jews agreed to finance and otherwise cooperate with their new Masonic allies in a joint project, which was to introduce subtly Enlightenment ideas into religion, politics and culture, in order to subvert Christianity in the name of secular beliefs and institutions.

According to Hutton Gibson, the Jews used the Masons to undermine Catholicism, gradually increasing their power until the Judeo-Masonic plotters eventually kidnapped the real Pope in 1957 and substituted a bogus look-alike Pope, who promptly started moving the church toward greater secularism. Thus Hutton Gibson's ideas recapitulate in a single lunatic belief-system the entire two thousand years of anti-Semitism, beginning with pure Christian Judeo-phobia and morphing seamlessly into a species of pure political anti-Semitism. It ends, appropriately, with the biggest and most apocalyptic caper of the twentieth century, the kidnapping of a pope and the hijacking of Catholicism. (Hutton Gibson believes that the astounding success of the Judeo-Masonic cabal in kidnapping the Pope without anybody noticing is strong circumstantial evidence that the end of the world is not far off.)

It is not surprising, then, that people wondered if Mel Gibson's attitude toward the Jews had been influenced by his father—after all, they both attended the same church, a church that believes in inherited Jewish guilt. But Mel Gibson's attitudes toward Jews were also influenced by his father in way most people wouldn't suspect. According to an article by Jean Cohen in the *Jerusalem Post* of March 12, 2004, Mel Gibson attempted at one time to convert to Judaism, but was forcibly prevented from doing so by his father. This incident is rarely mentioned, partly because Mel Gibson's so-called biographers aren't really interested in Mel Gibson as a person, but in Mel Gibson, the persona; and partly, apparently, because Gibson himself hasn't wanted to talk publicly about it.

In the summer of 1974, according to the *Jerusalem Post* article, Mel Gibson had a violent argument with his father. Shortly afterwards he flew from Australia to Israel. (This suggests that the younger Gibson's disagreement with his father might have had something to do with Judaism, or perhaps Mel simply needed at that time to rebel in a way that would particularly aggravate his father Hutton Gibson.) In any case, an idealistic eighteen-year-old Mel Gibson found himself at Kibbutz Degania in the Galilee, where over the next six months he became friends with at least two of the young people there, who later testified that he began to observe the Sabbath and attend services, ate only kosher food, and observed various traditional Jewish laws. He was soon taking conversational Hebrew classes, changed his name to the un-Christian-sounding Moishe, and informed his astonished family that he planned to become an Orthodox Jew.[12]

Hutton Gibson predictably saw this as the ultimate act of filial insubordination, swearing that his son would never be a "kike." The elder Gibson then flew to Israel where he confronted Mel about his recent choices. To trick Mel into returning home, Hutton told his son that his mother had been diagnosed with cancer, and insisted that Mel come home immediately to be with her. As soon as Mel got home, however, his father and his brothers locked him in his room and refused to let him out until he promised to give up his plan to convert to Judaism. Gibson reportedly held out for two and a half weeks before agreeing to return to Catholicism—that is, to his father's bizarre, extremely rightwing version of Catholic Traditionalism.

"Not long thereafter," write Timothy Kandler Beal and Tod Linafelt in *Mel Gibson's Bible: Religion, Popular Culture and The Passion of the Christ*, "Gibson began to denounce Jews and Judaism to anyone who would listen, although he later learned to be more discreet. His familial rebellion was at an end. The paterfamilias had restored his unquestioned authority."[13]

The traumatic effects of such an experience can only be guessed at. Despite the fact that Mel Gibson's emigration to Israel might have been ill-advised for any number of reasons—and was certainly provocative, given his father's beliefs—Hutton Gibson's actions effectively robbed his son of his freedom of choice, along with whatever individuality he had developed up to that time. It would be very hard for a son to recover from such a thing, unless he was willing to internalize the father's aggression in its entirety. There is no evidence that Mel Gibson did not love his father; but on the other hand, his father deliberately and with calculated deceit took away his son's identify as a free man. For Mel—a man who places such a high value on freedom—that would be close to being unforgivable.

While he was being held against his will by his father, it is likely that a primitive kind of 'Stockholm Syndrome' became the only way Mel Gibson's personality could survive, requiring, one might surmise, a total and complete identification with his father, and his father's ideas. To be released from the room in which he was locked, Mel not only had to give up his plans to become a Jew, but also had to wholly accept his father's cult-like religious offshoot of Traditional Catholicism—a process that strongly suggests the presence of a trauma bond in which Mel identified with and internalized the most brutal and patriarchal elements of his father's religion. Despite this powerful identification, there must have been a Vesuvius of suppressed anger inside the son against the father, anger that has been repressed over the years and could only have gotten more toxic and more emotionally impacted for just that reason. After all, he did not choose to identify with his father's religion—it was forced upon him during the traumatizing experience of being kidnapped and held hostage, which was not only violent but the ultimate betrayal since it was perpetuated by a parent he trusted.

In *The Passion of the Christ*, Mel pleads the case for his father's intense belief in redemption through Jesus' crucifixion, a belief that Mel also embraces; but at the same time, he seems to enhance the violence of the film in such a way that suggests a personal crisis—a howl of fury at having been forced to internalize such feelings in the first place. What seems clear at this point is that Mel Gibson believes many of the things his father believes, and is unable to disagree publicly with him. Mel Gibson's ability faithfully to portray conflicted, tormented men who cannot identify the source of their pain comes from a deep place in his own personality; and his fascination with violence—and the supposedly redemptive nature of that violence—comes from that same place.

Mel Gibson's ambivalent feeling toward Jews also comes through clearly in *The Passion of the Christ.* Gibson has consistently dealt with charges of anti-Semitism in *The Passion* not as a moral but as a public relations and political problem, aided and advised by the rightwing political and cultural leaders who had first helped him promote the film. The immediate political problem at one point predictably became Hutton Gibson's Holocaust denial; and Peggy Noonan was soon at the center of an effort to resolve this "problem." This Noonan accomplished through an interview with Gibson, although it appears to be carefully scripted and is more an example of damage control than a real interview. Noonan managed to place it in the March 2004 *Reader's Digest*, a good venue for a piece that was designed to calm conservative concerns about the film.

The interview gives Gibson an opportunity to reiterate some things he'd already said about the Holocaust. Since Hutton Gibson's Holocaust denial and anti-Semitism were by now widely known, as well as his church's belief in inherited Jewish guilt, the question of many people came down to this: How much was Mel influenced by his father, and what extent were his motives as a co-author of the script determined by the anti-Jewish attitudes of the church that he and his father attended?

Noonan's question about the Holocaust and Gibson's answer was as follows:

Noonan: "You're going to have to go on record. The Holocaust happened, right?"

Gibson: "I have friends and parents of friends who have numbers on their arms. The guy who taught me Spanish was a Holocaust survivor. He worked in a concentration camp in France. Yes, of course. Atrocities happened. War is horrible. The Second World War killed tens of millions of people. Some of them were Jews in concentration camps. Many people lost their lives. In the Ukraine, several million starved to death between 1932 and 1933. During the last century, 20 million people died in the Soviet Union."

Noonan: "So the point is that life is tragic and it is full of fighting and violence, mischief and malice."

Gibson: "Absolutely."

This is to some extent a restatement of what Gibson had previously said in his interview with Diane Sawyer. It is also, the reader will quickly see, a thoroughgoing evasion of the question. For one thing, Noonan's question was posed so that Gibson wouldn't have to answer "Yes" or "No." But there was something else. Gibson is being asked about a historically specific event, the Nazi Holocaust against the Jews in 1942-1945. And he refuses to reply to this question, instead engaging in empty generalizations about what a vicious place the world is—and Noonan jumps in and helpfully validates this evasion with her comment about all the "fighting and violence, mischief and malice" that goes on.

This is, of course, quite disingenuous. The world is a violent place, but the Holocaust consisted of a particular kind of violence, planned and executed by the Nazi state at a particular time in the twentieth century. Gibson, with Noonan's help, never lets on whether he believes the Holocaust happened or not—that is, he never says whether he believes that Adolph Hitler created something called the Final Solution, in which around six million Jewish civilians perished, most of them in gas chambers. In fact, Gibson's answer sounds like something carefully constructed to *sound* like he believes in the Holocaust, but which is sufficiently vague so that Mel Gibson never has to disagree openly with his father, Hutton.

This convenient managing of Gibson's 'Holocaust problem' by Peggy Noonan was essentially a *political* process, not a religious, cultural or moral process. Getting the heat off Mel Gibson had become an important goal for political conservatives, especially if *The Passion* was to continue as a successful project of the Religious Right, and a successful pop-culture accoutrement of Bush-era conservatives. Peggy Noonan had political clout and plausibility; and by providing a way for Gibson to tap-dance around the Holocaust in the middlebrow/lowbrow *Readers' Digest,* she demonstrated, if nothing else, how valuable Gibson was at that time to the Religious Right, as well as her own unique importance as a cultural facilitator. The Religious Right was promoting its various political interests, all of which were conservative (it would be more accurate to say rightwing), and most of which were oriented toward a particular political goal, the support of President George Bush and support for his policies, including the Iraq war.

The issue of anti-Semitism in Gibson's film *was* raised eventually by Abraham Foxman of the Anti-Defamation League; but Foxman managed to get it wrong in several important respects. Someone close to *The Passion of the Christ,* either acting alone or at Foxman's request, got hold of a script and sent it to him, who not surprisingly was alarmed by what he read. (It could have been one of Gibson's own public-relations people who gave the script to Foxman, with or without Gibson's knowledge. As they say in Hollywood, there's no such thing as bad publicity.) Foxman's first reaction was a good one—he contacted liberal and centrist Catholics who support Vatican II, and who had formed their own organization to prevent anti-Semitic images from being used in narratives of Jesus' crucifixion. They had a strong interest in opposing Gibson's over-the-top demonizing of the Jewish Sanhedrin, because they understood this to be an attack on Vatican II, which they were intent on defending at all cost. Gibson was their worst nightmare, so Foxman did a good thing in getting their help. In other ways, however, he both overplayed and underplayed his hand.

There was always the troubling issue of how the script got to Foxman, and the awkward position in which that put people who read it at Foxman's request. Some people, who read the script claimed later that they were shocked, shocked to learn that it might have been stolen. Suffice it to say that Foxman's behavior gave Mel Gibson the perfect opportunity to play the Christian martyr, a role at which he predictably excelled. Foxman could have made things easier for everybody by simply coming clean about how he got the script, saying something like this: "Yes, I received an unauthorized copy of the script, and I apologize for that. But any fair person should see that my offense is not as important as the inaccuracies in this film, which have been responsible for so much violence against Jews."

There was another problem with Foxman's advocacy, which was the same problem dogging several generations of Jewish intellectuals who have engaged in the benign American hypocrisy known as "interfaith dialogue," especially those who have in that process dealt, or tried to deal, with Christian anti-Semitism. The fact is, most Jews are afraid to say what they really think about it, because such an advocacy would involve a thoroughgoing critique of Christianity itself—which would necessarily include criticism of Christianity's mostly pathological fixation on the crucifixion.

The reason for this is simple. Institutional Christianity for a thousand years blamed a mysterious entity known as "the Jews" for killing Jesus Christ. So the natural tendency—especially among officials of Jewish interest groups—was not to directly confront Christians for their crazy tendency to believe in inherited Jewish guilt, but to rehabilitate the Jewish Sanhedrin of Jesus' time, to show that the Romans were *really* to blame, and the Jewish High Priests *really weren't so bad*. But what difference does it make who was to blame that long ago? The problem is not how good or bad certain Jews were then, or even last week—the problem has always been the idiotic and unacceptable Christian idea that guilt can be inherited at all.

But Abraham Foxman didn't point this out, nor did most Jews, because they were afraid of offending the Christians. To begin with, inherited Jewish guilt wouldn't be such a big deal if Christians weren't so obsessed with Jesus' crucifixion—but Jews did not want to be in the position of pointing this out. Secondly, even Christians who *don't* believe in inherited Jewish guilt often believe in *another* kind of inherited guilt—the inherited guilt of all humanity that supposedly originated in the Garden of Eden. *That* inherited human guilt is why, according to Christianity, people need blood atonement to redeem them. But the reality is that although all human beings inherit a disastrous capacity for aggression and deceit, either culturally or in their DNA, every person also inherits the cognitive ability to figure out ways to sublimate and eventually deconstruct whatever aggression they have internalized. (Whether they want to do so is a separate issue.) Inherited guilt *of any kind* is a primitive concept that needs to be tossed on the ash heap of history's most destructive ideas.

Thirdly and very importantly, most reputable historians now believe that the entire story of Pilate, Jesus and the Jewish Sanhedrin in the New Testament is a collective fabrication. If something is not true, it needs either to be thrown out, or separated from those parts of the narrative that may actually be true. The controversy about *The Passion of the Christ* would have been a perfect time for somebody to make this point in an especially uncompromising way, however harshly it would have jarred sensibilities in the established Christian denominations. Foxman did not do that, because although he is a powerful cultural figure he nonetheless knows very well that his bona fides are to some extent dependent on the approval of the Christians. Until very recently the only power Jews had to influence Christians in America was an emotional one, and if Foxman alienates too many Christians he will also lose his ability to influence them.

Fourth and finally—and perhaps most important of all—what was needed was someone to point out, systematically and coherently, that Christians have an unhealthy, morbid and thoroughly dangerous obsession with Jesus' death on the cross, and that this obsession minimizes the importance of Jesus' life and teachings. Attached to this obsession is the dangerous idea of redemptive violence—the belief that the violence of the cross redeems the world from sin. It should also have been pointed out that this belief in blood redemption, the idea that Jesus redeemed humanity by being crucified, has always been the cultural and emotional wheelhouse of Christian anti-Semitism. If redemption of the world depends on the suffering of Jesus on the cross, then people will focus on it—and if they focus on it, there will always be the niggling question of the role of "the Jews" in facilitating that death. But if Jesus' life and teachings can be seen as more important than his death, Christianity becomes kinder and wiser, and issue of Jewish guilt evaporates. It's a win-win for both Jews and Christians.

That is the root of the problem called Christian anti-Semitism. If Christians can start focusing on the life and teachings of Jesus, they will not only have a much more positive religion, but will also become aware that Jesus was above all a Jew, speaking to other Jews—and that he was a prophet in a prophetic tradition that starts with Abraham and ends with Mohammed. When Christians accept these things, the entire reason for Christian anti-Semitism disappears. But anyone who openly advocated these things would have been asking for a paradigm shift of fantastic proportions from the Christians. Abraham Foxman was not capable of doing this because, sadly enough, he is a cultural vigilante tasked with defending Israel, and as such he is focused on his own power, rather than the sacrifices and risk-taking necessary to make the thoroughgoing critique of Christianity that could defeat Christian anti-Semitism.

Maybe what was needed in this situation was not a power-obsessed enforcer like Foxman, but a public intellectual on the order of Norman Finkelstein, Noam Chomsky, or the late Hannah Arendt, someone who could have spoken authoritatively and without patronization to the Christians about their socio-religious pathologies. But such a person would surely have been obligated to point out that large sections of the New Testament are not true, and they also would also have to point out the connection between blood atonement and anti-Semitism, not to mention Islamophobia. *The Passion of the Christ* presented an opportunity for a free-ranging, no-holds-barred discussion about such things that have hitherto been off-limits for polite discussion. Sadly, however, people in the league of Finkelstein and Chomsky tend to be people who are concerned with the big, geo-political issues, and who are therefore instinctively hesitant to encourage Christians and Jews to think about themselves as tribal entities—but perhaps they should, if only to help the above-mentioned faith communities get over their tribalism.

The Passion of the Christ cried out for a no-holds-barred discussion of ways that Jews and Christians have defined themselves tribally *in the past*. Again, the big issues that Jews and Christians *should* have been discussing were Christianity's obsession with the crucifixion and the essentially fictional nature of certain parts of the New Testament. These are huge issues, which suggest that Christians ought to rewrite the New Testament and throw out most Christian theology since Constantine—and that, finally, is why Jewish leaders did not use the popularity of *The Passion* to make a thoroughly incisive critique of Christian anti-Semitism. Despite all the decades of warm and fuzzy interfaith dialogue, it was still too dangerous for Jewish leaders to make such a critique if it included foundational criticisms of Christianity. Having been accused of killing Christ for several centuries, established Jewish leaders did not care to be accused of trying to kill institutional Christianity. These difficult issues could only be raised by prophetic intellectuals within Christianity itself.

Realistically, however, one cannot divorce the social history of Christianity from that of Judaism, at least not for very long, because it is precisely the sixteen hundred years of anti-Jewish beliefs and behavior that proves the essential malevolence of Christianity, which is now the world's largest religion. (Jews know this dark side of Christianity best of all, even if they do not make a habit of verbalizing their knowledge of it.) In short, if behavior is the test of religion, one can only conclude from any study of Christianity that it is, judged solely by its own standards, a failed religion.

As for Mel Gibson, questions about his anti-Semitism were largely answered when he was stopped by a sheriff's deputy, on July 28, 2006, for drunk driving. Gibson launched into a drunken tirade against Jews, which naturally captured the interest of the officer, since he was Jewish. The officer made some fairly comprehensive notes of everything Gibson said, and although they were at first suppressed by the Sheriff's Department, they eventually made their way to the popular website *TMZ*. Gibson went into rehab, and also acknowledged that his anti-Semitic remarks while drunk had come from "a very deep place," announcing that he intended to work on the issue. Sadly, he and his long-suffering wife split up, and Mel took up with a beautiful young actress.

It was reported by various media on June 1, 2009, that Mel Gibson had, on a particular Sunday morning at the Traditional

Catholic church he had built with his father, gone on a long, rambling harangue against the other parishioners whilst pacing up and down in front of them—the subject of the rant, it was reported, was Gibson's feeling that he was being "judged" by people in his church, and perhaps by people in general. (By now everybody knew about his impending divorce, and the beautiful young actress that he was living with.) Given everything that he has done and been through, it is hard not to feel that Mel's harangue was against his father Hutton as much as anything else. Certainly that is where his anger, his deep identification with violence as redemptive, and his conflicted feeling about Jews began. It also did not surprise many who knew of Mel's struggles with his father, when Hutton Gibson closed down the church where they had both attended, and locked its doors.

One could hardly find a better example of the trauma bond (the internalization of aggression because of traumatic violence directed against the victim) than the youthful Mel Gibson being locked in his room for two and a half weeks in order to force him to give up his plan for converting to Judaism. The intention was clearly not just to make him give up Judaism, but also to accept his father's peculiar, cult-like brand of Catholicism. Mel Gibson did so, and in the process internalized Hutton Gibson's violence as well, with what ultimate discomfort we can only speculate about. In any case, the anger arising from these events has influenced everything Mel Gibson has done since. And he isn't alone, since every Christian in the world has to some extent internalized the same anger, in the story of a father who destroys his son to redeem the world.

16

So what happens to Christianity, if the doctrine of blood redemption is jettisoned? It is tempting to think that one could go back to the "original" Jesus, and recapture the innocence of the early (or "primitive") church, not least when considering how many ridiculous doctrines have been invented within Christianity, most of them for purely political purposes. As any historian of modern religion will tell you, the impulse to go back in time to recover the lost truth of a faith community is a central, driving motivation in the current religious revivals throughout the world. But is it possible to really see with modern eyes the historical Jesus, and understand what he was trying to do when he left Galilee and began to roam the countryside of Palestine? Albert Schweitzer conducted his own search, and concluded that the historical Jesus is caught in a cultural eclipse that makes him inaccessible to us—that the figure of Jesus has been freighted with too many cultural and tribal markers, had been imbued with too much emotion (especially aggression, one might think) for modern men and women to know him as he was in Galilee, on his own turf, before he was made into a deity and a dying god.

But there were other attempts to recover the basic spirit of Jesus' teachings that had a happier outcome. One such attempt happened on American soil. The generation of British Americans that made the American Revolution was engaged in just such a quest, because one of the goals of educated people of that time was to simplify religion, and make it into something that could be understood rationally, rather than solely as a matter of divine revelation. Of course, our modern Religious Right has tried to sell us on the idea that the Founding Fathers were all good evangelical Christians, but nothing could be further from the truth. In reality, the Founding Fathers of the Declaration of

Independence and the US Constitution and the Bill of Rights were mainly Deists and liberal Anglicans, often *extremely* liberal Anglicans. Neither Adams nor Jefferson believed in the divinity of Jesus, and both saw Jesus as a teacher or prophet whose moral system (or moral philosophy) could be understood by the average person.

It was for that reason that the astonishing "Jefferson Bible" was created by Thomas Jefferson himself, consisting simply of the King James New Testament, but with the crucifixion removed. It tells the story of Jesus of Galilee's life and teachings, but does not mention Jesus' death on the cross, which Thomas Jefferson snipped out as unimportant. What remains are the bare facts of Jesus' bittersweet life as a traveling itinerant preacher, with the Sermon on the Mount, the Beatitudes, and the parables preserved in full. Thomas Jefferson, the most important mind behind the US Constitution, the Bill of Rights and the Declaration of Independence, got rid of the one thing that institutional Christians over the centuries have been taught was the most important event in history—Jesus' death on the cross as a blood sacrifice for the sins of the world.

The present writer has on his desk a copy of the Jefferson Bible, on the inside cover of which is the coat-of-arms of Richard Evelyn Byrd, a liberal Anglican and clever self-promoter not unlike many in Jefferson's generation. The Jefferson Bible was once, astonishingly, given as a matter of course to everyone who was elected to the US Senate, which was probably how Admiral Byrd got his hands on it. The fact that it was given to newly elected Senators well into the twentieth century is interesting, because although the gift was thought to have cultural rather than religious significance, it offered mute evidence at that very late date of the importance to so many in Jefferson's generation of doing away for all time with the mumbo-jumbo of blood redemption.

Jefferson saw Jesus as a radical prophet or teacher with a

distinctive moral "system." One recurring dream of many in Jefferson's generation was to make of the New Testament a practical applied Christianity that could guide behavior and shape human institutions in a new society. To them, there was something sublime about Jesus' message, something that could infuse a burning love of justice into everyday human relationships, and probably also into human institutions. That, in turn, means taking out everything having to do with the trial, torture and crucifixion of Jesus. In what remains, therefore, there is no place for the doctrine of blood redemption, nor do the Jews of the Sanhedrin call down God's judgment on their descendants. Taking that part out removed, in one fell swoop, the motivation for Christian anti-Semitism—not a bad day's work, I would say, although that was not Jefferson's primary concern.

It is hard for us to realize today what an utterly sacrilegious, stunning work of cultural advocacy the Jefferson Bible really was—the first time since the invention of printing, perhaps the only time in human history, that an important political leader in Europe or the New World had actually concocted his own Bible *leaving out Jesus' crucifixion.*[14] Jefferson had his little Bible published; and then—in a colossal gesture of theological and cultural heresy—proceeded to distribute it to colleagues in government. By taking out the crucifixion, Jefferson's Bible aimed to overturn the old Christianity, and Jefferson himself (according to what he wrote) sought to reveal himself to his critics as a "real" Christian, rather than the atheist he'd been portrayed as being by the gutter press of his day. One implication of this radical stance, and of the Jefferson Bible, was that millions of Christians before him, in placing so much importance on the crucifixion, had been witting or unwitting frauds. It was an astounding performance. But by removing the crucifixion, he reframed the question of how to deal with good and evil. If Christians' sins could no longer be redeemed in the old way, how could they be redeemed? If Christianity was no longer about the crucifixion, what was it about?

Institutional Christianity had previously viewed human nature as fundamentally evil. This essentially negative view of human nature had been largely correct, but it did not consider the possibility of *changing* the human personality. It saw human evil as static because—or so they thought—God intended it to be that way; and it was Christianity's unique role to deliver redemption for the individual believer's inevitable sins. This unchanging redemptive strategy remained the prevailing cultural paradigm right through the Reformation, with the Protestants simply devising a different way than the Catholics of receiving the redemptive effects of the crucifixion; but by the time of the Enlightenment, people were beginning to challenge this paradigm in another way. *If people were essentially evil, as Christianity maintained, what made them that way?* Could human nature be changed, perhaps partly by changing society?

These were the questions that were asked by the Enlightenment thinkers; and those same questions informed the Declaration of Independence and the US Constitution. The Founding Fathers clearly understood the reality of human evil, or they would not have invested so much time and energy in creating a separation of political powers, to prevent tyrants from arising who would use American government for their own power or profit. But they also entertained the idea that the human personality could change, and that the way to accomplish this had something to do with producing more enlightened citizens, and with internalizing ideas of right and wrong. Many warned repeatedly of the dangers of pure democracy, in which "the mob" might run riot and create chaos; in their study of the religious wars of Europe, they had clearly discerned in the political affairs of humanity the operation of what this writer would call systemic evil. The Founders embraced, in other words, both a profound sense of the human capacity for evil, on the one hand, and an equally profound belief in personal transformation that was not unlike the kind that Jesus preached.

Could modern Christianity retain that understanding of human evil, and yet embrace the possibility of transforming human personality, in the same ways that the Founding Fathers sought to transform government? Not today, in 2010, because American Christianity has been hijacked by Christian evangelicals and conservative Catholics, both of whom base their worldview on the doctrine of blood redemption—and that has, as we've seen, made them a major force supporting torture, repression and war, because a belief in redemptive violence leads inevitably to the social ideology of aggression and power-worship. But can institutional Christianity survive *without* the belief that Jesus died on the cross to redeem humanity?

Taking the cross out of Christianity might, after all these centuries of identification with the crucifixion, be giving up the glue that has held it together—a negative kind of glue, to be sure, but nonetheless an emotional orientation capable of creating a powerful bond for people who are habituated to it. Without the trauma bond of an inexplicable and brutal God who sacrifices his son, the church would almost surely lose its mass base. It would become a radically smaller and less moneyed religion, and would probably result in a new church that, instead of offering redemption that ensures eternal life, would be aimed at changing personality and behavior right here on earth. That is hard work, even when prayer is a daily part of it. Most people who turn to Christianity are not looking for that kind of challenge, but rather seek forgiveness that will allow them to go on with their lives without making any changes. Such a new church, then, would be able to attract only a tiny fraction of the people it attracted before, because the trauma bond of the crucifixion would be removed.

Christianity is stuck, its best minds afraid of the next step—and that's easy to understand, because the next step is terrifying. The dream of Vatican II has given way to a much more authoritarian Roman Catholicism; liberal Protestantism cannot define evil, much less tell people how to deal with it. The Christian evangelicals and fundamentalists, having failed to achieve their political goals in the Religious Right, know that something is wrong, and seek frantically—good capitalists that they are—to re-brand and to re-issue a new and improved version of their faith, in the hopes of making it more palatable to the average religious consumer. But they are missing the point. Redemptive violence doesn't work in the long run—it creates personal frustration and bad societies. If blood redemption is not challenged, nothing will change. Interestingly, blood redemption *is* being challenged, most often by Christian feminists, but they are in a very small minority, and have been almost invariably ignored.

People in the pews can feel in their own lives the toxic aggression at the heart of modern Christianity, and they know in their gut that something is wrong. The cultural phenomenon of *The Passion of the Christ* has simply brought into focus the doubts that many Christians feel. Just as many evangelicals felt exalted and thrilled at *The Passion*, other Christians were disgusted, unsettled and angry—it was a life-changing experience for them, too. Christianity is at the hinge of its contemporary history, and *The Passion* simply brought into focus trends—ecstatic approval and extreme doubt—that were already present, but often suppressed. Christianity is in crisis, in an excited and unnatural state consisting of both opportunity and danger.

What happens to those who lose their faith when they lose the cross? At least blood redemption acknowledges the existence of evil—without it there will be a temptation either to give in to evil, or fashionably to deny its existence. What will Christians do, once they have lost the gut-wrenching metaphor of Christ's crucifixion as the central act of human history? How will they be able to imagine their own salvation, once they can no longer believe in human sacrifice? How will they imagine morality once the drama of deicide no longer provides the dark matter around which everything else revolves?

One thing is sure—Christianity without blood redemption cannot be worse than Christianity with it. It has been on the wrong side of almost every issue of enlightened thought for the last five hundred years. In the twentieth century it had no power to stop evil, or even say how evil operates. On aesthetic and common-sense grounds alone, the fact that a morbidly unhealthy movie like *The Passion of the Christ* could be considered profound and inspiring illustrates perfectly the moral crisis of modern Christianity. Evangelical Christianity in particular has, by virtue of its support for war and torture, revealed itself to be morally bankrupt.

Each believer must now decide what to do—to go forward in the quest for a new kind of Christianity, or declare Christianity null and void. Some will take the traditional path of least resistance, practicing Christianity only occasionally and ignoring it the rest of the time, settling for cultural religion. If for no other reason than its proclivity for creating and supporting systemic evil, Christianity cannot go on as it is. A few, a brave few, will attempt to devise a new faith based on Jesus' life, rather than his death, but whether anyone will pay any attention to them is anybody's guess.

The cross upon which Jesus was crucified is at the center of the debate, not just because it is the central icon of Christendom, but because for so many Christians it *is* Christianity, outweighing everything else. The Cross pulses in the living heart of Christendom's dream of the City of God, not to mention the American vision of a City on a Hill. But within that living heart resides also the tragic figures of the Christian prince, and the Christian warrior—and the brutal religious wars and the vicious anti-Semitism of which they were a part. There also is the Inquisition, the dread of women and the horror of the body, the nightmare of the Muslim as murderous exotic, and the heretical intellectual who must be hunted down and burned in public.

All of these things are animated by a belief in redemptive violence, ensconced most purely in the doctrine of blood redemption. For this reason, it is time we retire the cross and put it back in the world of imagination and narrative art, back in the troubled and traumatized collective unconscious of humankind from whence it came. It has had its sixteen hundred years of social and cultural ascendancy. It's time to put it aside.

Should Christianity die? Yes, if it cannot take the cross from the center of its theology, its culture, and its preoccupations, it should die. It would be worth it, if such a death could stop one homophobic assault, one Islamophobic foreign policy, one religious war. Most Christians know instinctively that something has been lost, something that was there before the theologians got to it, before the crusades, before the pogroms, before the centuries of religious war, before the witch-burning and Luther's hatred of Jews and intellectuals, before Auschwitz. Most Christians know that Christianity has, by its own standards, failed. Because of that, even many Christians would be willing to see Christianity die—but I think they would also like to meet, for one moment, the Jesus who walked in Galilee. But they will never meet him if Jesus' death continues to be more important to them than his life.

If the cross were removed from Christendom, what would be left? Would there be a big hole in the center of Western culture? With what symbol would people replace it? Perhaps the Book of Life that every person must write, or the Tree of Life that grows in every Promised Land; perhaps a democratic Faust-book, in which every person is their own Mephistopheles; perhaps a new Grail, filled with kindness rather than the strong drink of the hero; or perhaps it would be the tattered coat of Joseph, on each patch a dream, for such public dreams are the luminescent motley of the prophet, the poet and the fool. But these are symbols most people do not know—so we must find better and more universal symbols to go where the cross was before. I think I know what one symbol could be. It could be a woman holding a child. Behind her, a husband or father, perhaps, or a lover or grandparent or a friend, perhaps even Jesus himself, standing there— imagining together, imagining with her, the sacred dream of a safe place for a child. That would be a symbol I would want to internalize. That could be a symbol for life on this earth.

Part Two: The Death of Judaism

1

In 2002, when Jewish peace activist Cecilie Surasky went to the World Social Forum in Mumbai, India, she couldn't help but be a bit concerned—she had been warned that the Forum was a hotbed of anti-Semitism. At such a free-wheeling international meeting dedicated to social justice and human rights, she fully expected criticisms of the government of Israel, because Surasky herself, like an increasing number of American Jews, was sharply critical of Israel's rightwing government. As Communications Director of Jewish Voice for Peace, an American Jewish group that advocates peace between Israelis and Palestinians, she was familiar with the drama that tends to accompany any discussion of Israel/Palestine. What really stuck in her mind was that the Simon Wiesenthal Center, a Jewish advocacy organization located in Los Angeles, had described the previous year's Forum, held in Brazil, as being "anti-Jewish." That sounded more than a little ominous.

On her first day at the Forum in 2002, Surasky braced herself for the worst, but she encountered no anti-Semitism, and not even much criticism of the Israeli government. Out of 500 information stalls, only two represented Palestinian human rights groups, and of several thousand political posters, there was only one series related to Israel/Palestine. Except for the workshops, there was surprisingly little activity at the World Social Forum that had anything to do with Israelis and Palestinians, and certainly nothing anti-Semitic.

She was particularly impressed by the tone taken by people at the Israel/Palestine workshops. She writes here in the first person of her impressions of those workshops: "What I do not hear (or see) is anything I would consider anti-Semitic. In a global conference of 100,000 people, one expects to hear an enormous range of political perspectives, including the occasional extreme or intolerant remark. Given that I am prepared for the worst, I am shocked that the overwhelming majority of what is said in workshops critical of US and Israeli policies in the territories are milder than the articles and essays one can read in Israeli newspaper on any given day."

Surasky interviewed a Palestinian woman from Gaza, and the two women became friends. Both shared a vision of Israel/Palestine that would offer both Jews and Palestinians security. It occurred to Surasky that the World Social Forum could be used by peace activists as a venue for informal meetings between Palestinians and Israelis. She characterized the 2002 Forum as "a cacophony of anti-globalization/human rights activists from all over the globe. The roughly 100,000 participants represent every imaginable cause—from Indian 'untouchables' and Bhutanese refugees, to child trafficking and sexual minorities. They are seen in the hundreds of marches that seem to appear out of nowhere down the main thoroughfare, at the 500 information booths, in more than 1,000 workshops, and on the political posters filling every inch of available wall space."

Far from being anti-Semitic, Surasky found that Arabs, especially Palestinians, were hungry for contact with peace-oriented Jews. "In my own experience as a very 'out' Jew at the conference, I felt no hate. Instead, I met a number of Palestinians and Arabs who, on some fundamental level, expressed the pain of separation. 'I am Muslims, and we were raised to respect the Jewish tradition,' a Palestinian woman living in Jordan told me. 'We used to live next door to Jews, and we were friends.'"

"After I spoke at a session about suspending military aid to Israel until it ends its occupation, and identified myself as a member of Jewish Voice for Peace, a Palestinian woman thanked me and a distinguished Lebanese man from Jordan came up and gave me a huge hug and a kiss." Two of the Arab delegates who were most friendly to Surasky were environmental scientist Rania Masri and activist journalist Ahmed Shawki.

"Thirty minutes after meeting me for the first time at the Forum, Ahmed Shawki offered to loan me the new digital camera given to him by his wife," Surasky wrote. "He knew I was eager to take pictures and the airline had misplaced my luggage. Knowing nothing of my politics, only that I was from a Jewish peace group, he gave me his digital camera."

"The next day, the bag containing my passport, credit cards, and his camera was stolen. Our mutual friend and colleague from Lebanon, Rania Masri, handed me a hundred dollars from her wallet and absolutely insisted I take her ATM card and PIN number so I would have money for the rest of the trip. And Ahmed? To this day, Ahmed refuses to accept payment for the camera that was stolen."

"This is the real story of Jews, Arabs, and the World Social Forum that needs to be told; that is, the ways in which we so quickly and easily recognize each other's fundamental humanity." She quoted a young Arab-Israeli woman who spoke on the last night of the conference: "Yes, I experience discrimination in Israel. But my friendship with Jewish Israelis is proof that it is a lie when both sides tell us we can't live together. We can live together. You must not believe the lie."

Energized by these inspiring experiences, Cecilie Surasky was understandably anxious to share them, but back in the San Francisco Bay Area she received a shock. In Israel, the Jerusalem *Post* had come out with a lurid story about the World Social Forum entitled "Networking to Destroy Israel," written by none other than the Simon Wiesenthal Center, of Los Angeles, the Jewish advocacy organization that had previously maintained that the previous year's Forum had been "anti-Jewish." This article made the claim that the World Social Forum, which Surasky had just attended, had been totally taken over by anti-

Israel and anti-American forces.

Surasky was astounded. "The article claims that this year's World Social Forum was 'hijacked by anti-American and anti-Israeli forces' and leads me to wonder whether we attended the same conference. In this piece, and for the second year in a row, they strangely declare themselves the only Jewish NGO to attend the WSF." That in particular puzzled Surasky, since she had personally witnessed that fact that there were other Jewish groups there. "They go on to cite a litany of statements, including mine, as proof that the World Social Forum is a place where people who want to destroy Israel meet to plot and recruit. Employing a form of twisted logic that would make Donald Rumsfeld proud, they essentially claim that the absence of any blatant anti-Semitism is not proof that there was none, but merely an indication of a more 'sophisticated' kind of anti-Zionism (and therefore anti-Semitism) in which sympathetic Jews such as Jewish Voice for Peace play a starring role."

"The account is so riddled with errors—I am misquoted, JVP is described as 'campus-based,' all of my colleagues are given the wrong attributes, and quoted either inaccurately or out of context—that it is pointless to list them all. It contains bits of truth but strings together isolated statements to make them sound like a tidal wave of hatred and part of what they call an 'orchestrated' and 'insidious' campaign to destroy Israel."

The Wiesenthal piece in the Jerusalem *Post* piece was a particularly clumsy example of disinformation, and the most blatant claim of the Wiesenthal Center, that they were the only Jewish group there, was an out-and-out lie. In reality, there were a fair number of Jewish groups there, one of the best known being Brit Tzedek v'Shalom, an American Jewish human rights organization supporting a negotiated two-state resolution to the Israel/Palestine conflict. This was not a small group, claiming 50,000 supporters and as many as 1,000 rabbis in the US alone. Brit Tzedek has been one of the principal Jewish supporters of

President Barack Obama's peace efforts in the Middle East, and has since merged with J Street, another pro-peace Jewish organization in the United States.

Another Jewish group at the World Social Forum in 2002 was Yesh Gvul, a group of Israeli combat veterans who opposed the occupation of Palestinian territories. This veterans' group has inspired similar groups of Israeli veterans. And then there was Jewish Voice for Peace, whose name was clearly printed on the Forum program, and whose representative Cecilie Surasky was actually quoted in the Jerusalem *Post* article. There were other Jewish groups, too, in addition to the three named above, and there was no way that the Wiesenthal Center could not have been aware of that—yet their article claimed that there were no Jewish groups there except for themselves. That wasn't spin; it was a lie. But the Jerusalem *Post* didn't bother to fact-check it, nor did the mainstream media, which disseminated it as though it were the gospel truth.

Why did this happen? Why did a seemingly reputable Jewish organization report rampant anti-Semitism at the World Social Forum, when the opposite was true? Why did the Wiesenthal Center lie about being the only Jewish group present at the Forum? Most puzzling of all, why did the Wiesenthal Center portray the World Social Forum as bristling with hatred against anything Israeli, when it is clear that the Arabs at Mumbai were intensely interested in exploring peace with Israel?

2

The Simon Wiesenthal Center in Los Angeles, California, is named after the famed Austrian Nazi-hunter, Simon Wiesenthal, a connection that turns out to be appropriate in disturbing but unexpected ways. That is, both Simon Wiesenthal and the Center named after him have been accused of flagrant lying, exaggerations and half-truths. Simon Wiesenthal's confabulations were not generally discussed by mainstream scholars, and appear to have been mainly unknown until after his death. (Simon Wiesenthal died September 2005, at the age of 97.) In any case, it is now known that Wiesenthal, a born story-teller, rarely let the facts get in the way of a good story. In fact many of the things he claimed to have done were fabrications.

This recently came to light with the publication, in June of 2009, of *Hunting Evil*, by British Author Guy Walters, in which he characterizes Simon Wiesenthal as "a liar—and a bad one at that." Wiesenthal, he maintains, would "concoct outrageous stories about his war years and make false claims about his academic career." Walters found that there were "so many inconsistencies between his three main memoirs and between those memoirs and contemporaneous documents, that it is impossible to establish a reliable narrative from them. Wiesenthal's scant regard for the truth makes it possible to doubt everything he ever wrote or said."[15]

The Wiener Library, perhaps the world's oldest and most reputable institutions for the study of the Holocaust, has endorsed this revaluation of Wiesenthal. That is interesting because one assumes that they, like many others in the field of Holocaust Studies, may have been aware for some time that there were problems with Wiesenthal's resume. The Wiener Library's Director Ben Barkow concluded that "accepting that Wiesenthal was a showman and a braggart and, yes, even a liar, can live alongside acknowledging the contribution he made."

Daniel Finkelstein, grandson of the Wiener Library's founder, had this to say in an August 2009 article in the London *Times* about Guy Walters' *Hunting Evil*: "Walters's documentary evidence on Wiesenthal's inconsistencies and lies is impeccable. He shows how the Nazi hunter's accounts of his wartime experiences are contradictory and implausible. [Walters] demonstrates that he had no role, contrary to his own assertion, in the capture of Adolf Eichmann. He pitilessly dissects Wiesenthal's overblown claims about the number he brought to justice, suggesting it was not much more than a handful."[16]

So what is the truth about Simon Wiesenthal? Born in 1908 in Galicia, Wiesenthal attended the Czech Technical University in Prague in 1929, where he had a reputation as a gifted raconteur. (Walters says he appeared as "a stand-up comedian," which could be a British approximation of the cabaret theatre popular at that time.) Wiesenthal claimed to have graduated from Czech Technical, but records show that he didn't. He also maintained that he studied at Lviv Polytechnic in Galicia in 1935, but there is no record of him ever attending classes there. Wiesenthal likewise claimed to have operated his own architectural office and built elegant villas, but again Polish records do not support this. Instead he appears to have worked as a supervisor in a Lviv furniture factory from 1935 until 1939, a somewhat more mundane occupation, and one that Wiesenthal himself acknowledged before he became a famous celebrity in Vienna.

During the Second World War, Wiesenthal was apprehended by the Nazis, and was in at least six different Nazi camps. For reasons unknown, however, he claimed later to have been in 13 of them. This raises the question that must inevitably come up when contemplating Wiesenthal's stories about himself. Being in a *single* Nazi camp would clearly be a horrific, mind-blowing experience, much less being in six of them. (This writer cannot confirm which ones were death camps and which labor or concentration camps.) So why did Wiesenthal feel it necessary to inflate the number of camps he'd been in to 13, particularly since such claims were likely to be checked later?

Part of the answer seems to be that Wiesenthal was a natural-born confabulator and liar who had a powerful need to create the persona of a superhero. But that alone does not explain his behavior. The Holocaust raises questions about human nature, and because of that there is a craving for accounts that can explain, rationalize, and create a moral context for it. Wiesenthal offered people a plausible narrative with a moral framework: Nazis incarcerated him; he miraculously escaped; later he tracked them down. The systemic evil of the Holocaust was so huge and so threatening that it could be successfully addressed only by a superman whose capacity to survive evil and punish transgressors was larger than life. Wiesenthal was acutely aware of this; and his heart-stopping accounts of last-minutes escapes from the Nazis played to this anxiety. And the fact that he was bringing masses of Nazi war criminals to justice was the happy ending to the success story, the kind people wanted to hear; but as Walters demonstrates in *Hunting Evil,* at least one of Wiesenthal's accounts of last-minute escapes from the Nazis can be shown to be a fabrication, and others are questionable.

After the war, Wiesenthal founded two organizations that sought to collect and centralize information on Nazi war criminals at large. Sometimes these war criminals were "hiding in plain sight," in the sense that governments knew where they were but lacked the political will to arrest them. The main function of Wiesenthal's organizations, then, was to keep the issue current in the public eye—and he had the kind of personality, and the public relations skills, to do just that. This is the real reason for Wiesenthal's notoriety. The organizations set up by Wiesenthal were research organizations, and had no real investigative functions, such as law enforcement might have, and no power to arrest people. Guy Walters concludes (correctly, in my opinion) that the disinclination of western governments to hunt down Nazi criminals—not to mention the US and British government's mass hiring of them for Cold War purposes—was far more repugnant morally than Wiesenthal's experiments with the truth. That said, the fact that Wiesenthal told so many unnecessary lies, and that people who might have suspected this said nothing to challenge them, is one more example of the Holocaust's ability to corrupt.

Although Wiesenthal claimed to have brought over a thousand Nazi criminals to justice, he generated information leading to the arrest of less than a hundred at most. His most outrageous claim was that he participated in the tracking down of Adolf Eichmann. This was, and remains, a falsehood—the tracking and kidnapping of Eichmann was the work of Mossad, the Israeli intelligence service, and Wiesenthal's involvement was limited to passing on whatever information he had to them. This inconvenient reality was widely known—certainly it was known to Mossad, which despised and resented Wiesenthal's self-serving stories—but apparently few people were willing to question Wiesenthal's many claims.

Except in Austria, that is, where Wiesenthal was for a long time a controversial figure. It the 1970s, Wiesenthal publicly berated Austrian Prime Minister Bruno Kreisky for having so many ex-Nazis in his cabinet—and in this, Wiesenthal was undoubtedly right. The controversy he stirred up was especially important because Austrians had, up to that time, generally avoided much public discussion about their own responsibility for Nazi crimes; and Wiesenthal may have welcomed the opportunity to open up this issue when he made his sensational—but accurate—accusations about Kreisky's cabinet choices. Kreisky, a Jewish Social Democrat, hinted that Wiesenthal had survived the war only because he collaborated with the Gestapo; but Wiesenthal sued for libel and won. Wiesenthal also drew fire for emphasizing that others besides Jews died in the gas chambers, which brought him into conflict with Elie Wiesel, who took the view that the Holocaust should be seen as an exclusively Jewish event. Some of Wiesenthal's ideas were good ones—how ironic, then, that his ideas were given serious consideration only because of the rough-and-tumble public persona that Wiesenthal had invented for himself as part of his entrepreneurial and overly-imaginative self-promotion as a swashbuckling Nazi-hunter.

Wiesenthal received practically every honor known to the twentieth century, over 100 of them. Mainly because of his own self-promotion, Wiesenthal became much more than an author with some dubious and not particularly well-written books—he became a secular saint. But of what secular religion was Saint Wiesenthal the exemplar? The trouble with Wiesenthal was not his extraordinary efforts to focus public attention on Nazi criminals—the problem was, and is, that his accounts of his own experiences were never challenged by people who professed to have an interest in historical truth. His addiction to confabulation made him a prisoner of what Norman Finkelstein has called The Holocaust Industry, which may be described as the systematic use of the Holocaust for personal and organizational gain.

We are left with the sense that perhaps some who noticed discrepancies in Wiesenthal's books said nothing because they were afraid of being denounced as anti-Semites. Author Guy Walters refers to this in his July 2009 article in the Sunday *Times*. "Some may feel I am too harsh on [Wiesenthal] and that I run a professional danger in seemingly allying myself with a vile host of neo-Nazis, revisionists, Holocaust deniers and anti-Semites. I belong firmly outside any of these squalid camps and it is my intention to wrestle criticism of Wiesenthal away from their clutches. His figure is a complex and important one. If there was a motive for his duplicity, it may well have been rooted in good intentions." Guy Walters made this caveat a month after his book came out last summer; the fact that he made it at all indicates the sensitivity with which a professional historian must approach anything having to do with the Holocaust.

In fact, the appearance of Walters' book had some of the characteristics of a literary campaign, although not necessarily of pre-arrangement. Walters' *Hunting Evil* was published in Britain on June 18, 2009, at the beginning of last summer. A month later, in July, an article by Walters appeared in the Sunday *Times,* which set forth his reasons for revealing Wiesenthal's duplicities. (One might think that because something is true might be reason enough for a historian to reveal it.) In August 2009, a month later, Daniel Finkelstein's supportive review appears in the *Jewish Chronicle,* validating Walters' research. Finkelstein's review was pivotal, since—as the grandson of the founder of the world's oldest library on Holocaust history—he is assumed to speak with an authority that others lack, including perhaps Guy Walters himself.

That is not to say that the above was part of a coordinated campaign. Walters wrote on his website that he does not know Finkelstein, and based on internal evidence this writer believes that to be true. It simply indicates how complicated telling the truth can become when one writes about the Holocaust, and how carefully historians must consider the public-relations angle before revealing things that might make people uncomfortable. In Guy Walters' case, he received support for his findings from a man whose credentials in Holocaust Studies cannot be challenged.

On November 26, 2009, there appeared a sensational Associated Press report that 12 members of the 15 member international advisory board of the Vienna Wiesenthal Institute for Holocaust Studies have resigned, apparently after a hysterical uproar about the availability of research material to scholars. (The AP report gives as the reason for the international hullabaloo certain objections by scholars "that restrictions on access to files made independent research impossible.") Inevitably, one of those involved in the AP report warned that unrestricted access to the Institute's files might encourage "holocaust deniers." The opposite seems much more likely. The longer people hide the truth about Wiesenthal, the more doubts it will create about how objectively historians are able to write about the Holocaust.

Beginning with the publication in 1961 of Raul Hilberg's *The Destruction of the European Jews*, people on the Left, political and cultural progressives, and some psychologists sought to deconstruct the Holocaust so that they could learn how systemic evil operates. If the *Shoah* was history's greatest crime, why not try to understand how it happened, so such crimes could be thwarted in the future? That was the right approach to take, but it quickly led to a kind of truth that many people did not want to accept—that there is a Nazi in every person, and that any tribe, national group or country in the world could experience the same moral collapse as Germany experienced, given the right conditions. That was too threatening for many people, because they did not want to acknowledge how deep evil runs in human nature.

And it was, also, the ultimate threat to the neo-cons that were beginning to gain power in the US. If the same moral collapse that happened in Germany could happen elsewhere, such an analysis could be applied anywhere, which meant that the big neo-conservative foundations could not control discourse about the Holocaust. *An objective deconstruction of systemic evil in Weimer Germany could even serve as a guide to Israel's long slide to the extreme right.* The neo-cons could not allow that to happen, because of their position that Israel's government can never be criticized, at least publicly; and because the neo-conservatives did not want a truly objective deconstruction of the Holocaust that could teach people how to defeat systemic evil. On the contrary—they sought to create their own systemic evil in the US and in the Middle East, by using the Holocaust to browbeat people into accepting almost anything that Israel did. Their interest was building a power base for themselves, beginning with the Likud party of Israel, and ultimately by taking over the institutional leadership of the organized Jewish community in the US.

Invoking the Holocaust in social and political discourse became a way for the powerful neo-cons and the Israel Lobby to use the unresolved trauma of the Holocaust, in some cases to generate ideas and in other cases to suppress them. The use of the Holocaust to manipulate people and societies to uncritically support Israel depends on a particularization of the Holocaust—it insists, in other words, that Nazi evil cannot be compared to any other form of systemic evil. It insists that the causes of German moral collapse (violent nationalism, fanatical identification with victim status, deep feelings of inferiority, a longing for apocalyptic solutions) cannot be applied anywhere else. That is despicable nonsense.

Not only can the causes of German moral collapse be seen in other nations and situations; such an analysis *must* be applied to other nations and situations, if we are to learn anything about how systemic evil works. Neo-cons generally dislike that, because they wish to discuss the Holocaust only within a context of Jewish exceptionalism. But sadly, there's a Nazi in everybody—in fact, that's the most important thing that the Holocaust teaches us. As Avraham Burg writes, today's Israel feels a lot like Weimer, not because Israeli culture is so similar to central Europe's culture, but because the descent into evil always presents certain common characteristics wherever it occurs. How could Israel not look like Weimer, when so much of what passes for a national consciousness in Israel is simply trauma from the Holocaust, which people do not attempt to deconstruct along universal lines but around which they build their personal and national identities?

It was not until after Simon Wiesenthal died in 2005 that a popular British author was able to write frankly, in a historical book aimed at a popular audience, about the duplicity in Simon Wiesenthal's stories. Again I must ask, why did not the people who may have known about Wiesenthal's casual relationship with the truth speak up about it?[17] Predictably, the Simon Wiesenthal Center of Los Angeles, California, is in no hurry to accept this new historical appraisal of their namesake—their website, in fact, faithfully replicates many of Wiesenthal's lies and inaccuracies. But that should not surprise us, because the Simon Wiesenthal Center, like Simon Wiesenthal himself, is not interested in historical truth, nor is it committed to teaching about the history of the Holocaust in all its complexity. The Simon Wiesenthal Center is, rather, committed to using the Holocaust to raise money, and using the trauma associated with it to promote the Center's extremist political perspectives.

4

The Wiesenthal Center's deliberate inaccuracies regarding the World Social Forum in 2002 are typical of the way they work. The Center presents a worldview in which anti-Semitism lurks everywhere, any criticism of Israel is anti-Semitism, and a new Holocaust is right around the corner. If Arabs or Muslims are inconveniently inclined to seek peace with Israel, or if Christians fail to manifest the necessary anti-Semitism, something must be invented. This tendency to lie and embellish is uncannily similar to the methods of Simon Wiesenthal himself, but with a big difference—Simon Wiesenthal made things up mainly for reasons of self-aggrandizement, and to generate public awareness about Nazi war criminals still at large. That is something we can understand, even if we cannot approve of his lying, or the covering up of his lies by Holocaust scholars. The Simon Wiesenthal Center, on the other hand, lies to raise money, lots of it, more than Simon Wiesenthal ever dreamed of, and its political agenda is a lot darker than Wiesenthal's. It includes public hate-mongering of Muslims, regular appeals to a neo-fascist form of Zionism, and relentless provocations to religious war in Israel/Palestine.

In the late spring of 2006, Douglas Kelly, editor of the *National Post*, a Canadian newspaper, became aware of an item in a column by Iranian exile Amir Taheri indicating that the Iranian Parliament might require Jews to wear yellow stars. The editor assigned to investigate this story could have saved everybody a great deal of trouble by checking out the reputation of Mr. Taheri. Besides being associated with Benador Associates, a shadowy neo-conservative group set up after 9/11 and since disbanded, Taheri has been accused by many people of planting false stories in many different venues over the years. Just before the election of 2008, to cite a recent case, Taheri quoted Rev Jesse Jackson as telling an international conference that if elected, President Obama would implement unspecified "changes" in his policy toward Israel. It turned out that Jackson hadn't even attended that conference, much less said the things attributed to him by Taheri.

The Post editor then made his second and biggest mistake. For reasons unknown—but probably because he sincerely thought it a reputable organization—the editor called up the Simon Wiesenthal Center in Los Angeles and spoke to Rabbi Abraham Cooper. Rabbi Cooper then sent an e-mail to the *Post* saying that the story about Iranian Jews being forced to wear yellow stars was "absolutely true." A reporter from the *Post* then called Rabbi Marvin Hier, Dean of the SWC, who again confirmed the story and added, to drive the point home, that the Wiesenthal Center had sent a letter to UN Secretary-General Kofi Annan pleading with him to take action on the matter. Later on, Hier would admit that the Wiesenthal Center did not independently check out any part of the story—yet both Cooper and Hier insisted to the *Post* that the story was true, although they did nothing, by their own admittance, to find out if it actually *was* true. On May eighteenth, one day before the story appeared in the *Post*, the SWC sent the letter to UN Secretary-General Annan, with all the press releases and fan-fare the Wiesenthal Center is known for.

One can see why Hier and Cooper liked the story. It had institutional persecution of Jews in Iran, a country that was a sworn enemy of Israel; and it brought up the Holocaust, since it was reminiscent of the Nuremburg Laws that preceded and prefigured the Holocaust. For the *National Post*, it was a scoop. Having received a confirmation from the two top leaders of what they believed to be a reputable human rights organization, the *Post* went ahead with the story, and on May 19 it ran on Page One. The headline read IRAN EYES BADGES FOR JEWS, accompanied by a 1935 photo of two Jews wearing yellow badges in

Nazi Germany. It was a sensational story, and was picked up by daily journalism around the world, not to mention electronic media—Rush Limbaugh and others on AM Radio quickly made it their main story. For the *National Post*, in terms of pure impact, it was one of the most popular stories they had ever carried. Many of the newspaper that picked up the story also ran pictures of Jews wearing yellow stars in Nazi Germany. There was only one problem, which was that the story was a complete fabrication.

On May 19th, the day the story broke in the *Post*, Taylor Marsh, a political analyst located in Washington DC, called Aaron Breitbart, a senior researcher at the Simon Wiesenthal Center, to check out the story. She later reported him as "eager to confirm it," using words like "throwback to the Nazi era," "very true," and "very scary." In fact, Breitbart said that Rabbi Marvin Hier, Founder and Dean of the Simon Wiesenthal Center, had been on the phone four hours confirming the story. This was a bit confusing to Marsh, who wondered why it would take four hours to confirm such a frightening story. But despite Rabbi Heir's enthusiastic attempts to confirm it, it quickly became clear to all that the story was not going to fly.

On May 19th, the very day the story ran on page one of the *National Post*, a veritable host of Iran experts began stepping up to denounce the story as bogus. The trickle of denunciations turned into a storm. Practically everybody who knew anything about Iran pointed out that the story was a fabrication. On Wednesday, May 24th, Douglas Kelly, editor of the *National Post*, was obliged to carry a long and detailed apology to *Post* readers, which he carried on Page Two. In his apology he confirmed that the story about Iranians forcing Jews to wear yellow starts was untrue, and also referred directly to the *Post's* contact with both Cooper and Hier at the Wiesenthal Center, mentioning pointedly that they had both, on separate occasions, confirmed the story. The sense of having been betrayed by the Wiesenthal Center was palpable.

For Hier and Cooper, however, it was a considerable victory. They were able to get a well-known daily newspaper to carry a sensational story, which was quickly picked up and run on front pages throughout the world, including and especially US media, where it became the subject of morbid fascination in both print and digital media for weeks. As Hier and Cooper knew it would be, the story fascinated people because it played into the public's obsession with Hitler, Jews and Nazis, now magically resurrected in a new venue (allowing everybody to forget for the moment that it was Christians, not Shiite Muslims, who had originated the practice of making Jews wear identifying garments). The actual verisimilitude of the story momentarily became unimportant, becoming important again only after everyone had been given the chance to process—and write about—their morbid obsession with the yellow stars. Once the story had implanted itself in the public's mind, in other words, it developed a life of its own, despite the fact that it wasn't true.

Neither Hier nor Cooper ever acknowledged that they had deeply hurt a newspaper that had trusted them, nor did they apologize for doing so. As for the SWC letter to UN Secretary-General, Kofi Annan, his spokesperson at first replied cautiously that the "passage of such a [sumptuary] law has been called into question," adding that the UN was "looking into it." Later, Annan declared the report to be false, and the Simon Wiesenthal Center acknowledged that it was untrue—managing to do so in a way that implied that without their vigilance, it very well *might* have been true. But they never apologized, because they did not see themselves as doing anything wrong.

A similar brazenness regarding their motives could be discerned in the Wiesenthal Center's misrepresentations regarding a story about Venezuela's Hugo Chavez, who in 2006 made a speech in which he criticized the wealthy of his country. In this speech he lashed out at Venezuelan wealthy classes, saying at one point rather ungrammatically that the "world is for all of us, then, but it so happens that a minority, the descendants of the same ones that crucified Christ, the descendants of the same ones that kicked Bolivar out of here and also crucified him their own way over there in Santa Marta, in Colombia. A minority has taken possession of the wealth of the world..."[18]

The Wiesenthal Center then doctored the quote, taking out the reference to Bolivar. The Center then insisted that Chavez was making a reference to "Christ-killers," despite the fact that Chavez had said nothing even remotely like that. This astonishing bit of disinformation was quickly denounced by several established Jewish organizations—the American Jewish Committee, the American Jewish Congress, and the Confederation of Jewish Associations of Venezuela—all of whom pointed out the ridiculousness of the Wiesenthal Center's assertion. Since the Wiesenthal Center deliberately misquoted Chavez by removing his reference to Bolivar and then fabricated an anti-Semitic comment that he didn't make, this wasn't just an exaggeration, but a deliberate lie.

This propaganda gambit against Hugo Chavez came at a time of high tension between Venezuela and the US; it seems likely that the Wiesenthal Center did this to support the neo-conservative clamor for US intervention in that country. This interventionist attitude shouldn't surprise us too much—the Wiesenthal Center once presented Jeanne Kilpatrick, a US diplomatic defender of the murderous Pinochet regime in Chile, with its Humanitarian of the Year Award. (And also such noted humanitarians as Ronald Reagan, Margaret Thatcher and Robert Murdoch.)

5

"At the outset of a new decade the Simon Wiesenthal Center is well-positioned to combat the ever-escalating challenges and threats to our people..." This is the lead sentence in a January 2010, email communication from the Wiesenthal Center. The hyphenated phrase *ever-escalating* is typical—almost everything put out by the SWC is formatted to give the impression that Jews are in peril everywhere, and that the peril, whatever form it takes, is by its very nature destined to get worse. The possibility that the behavior of the government of Israel (or the propaganda-mongering of the Wiesenthal Center) could be making things worse for Jews is contemptuously dismissed as anti-Semitism.

This same email update from the Wiesenthal Center references ongoing discussions with the social networking entity 'Facebook,' specifically mentioning the pressing need "to better service Jewish students on the frontlines around the world," including "embattled" students in Europe. (Apparently any Jew involved in higher education is willy-nilly involved in an apocalyptic battle against "ever-escalating" anti-Jewish plots.) Just so the reader will understand the gravity of the threat, Holocaust-related events and literature is extensively covered in the remainder of the email quoted from above; in fact every SWC communication, email or press release rarely goes for more than a paragraph without mentioning the Holocaust. This reminds us that the Wiesenthal Center, besides seeing itself as the world's premiere advocacy organization for Jews, also presents itself as a Holocaust education institution. The way their advocacy regarding the "ever-escalating" threat of anti-Semitism complements their Holocaust education could be boiled down to this formula: a second Holocaust is imminent; therefore anything that the Simon Wiesenthal Center does cannot be questioned or opposed.

Even the Anti-Defamation League (ADL) has noticed the Center's tendency to play fast and loose with the truth regarding the dangers of anti-Semitism, specifically as part of their fund-raising efforts. In 1984 the late Justin Finger, an attorney and ADL official, circulated an internal memo within the ADL complaining that a fund-raising letter on behalf of the Wiesenthal Center was filled with "factual misstatements and exaggerations" about anti-Semitism in Europe and the US. It's not surprising that Mr. Finger would have been sensitive to that—he was formerly an investigator for the famous New York Waterfront Commission of the 1950s, and therefore a gentleman of a more exacting investigatory school, before the fight against anti-Semitism was politicized by the neo-cons.

He was widely known for organizing an investigation into anti-Semitism in the Louis Vuitton luggage company; and when the allegations were proven incorrect, he treated the company heads to a testimonial dinner. Anti-Semitism, he said, "was a bad rap and can damage a person or an institution badly."[19] Sadly, these are not the kind of values pursued by the Simon Wiesenthal Center. (Of course, the ADL could have gone public with Mr. Finger's information about the Wiesenthal Center's use of disinformation, but chose not to.)

The ubiquitous former *New York Times* journalist and current Fox News diva Judith Miller got off a few clever quips at the expense of the Center's cheesy fund-raising techniques in her book *One, by One, by One: Facing the Holocaust*, in which she criticizes the vulgarity of making money off history's greatest crime. "I do not feel comfortable with the Holocaust being used as the vehicle for these huge fund-raising dinners for this [Simon Wiesenthal] center," she said in an interview after the book came out, referring to such public spectacles as "the 'celebratisation'" of the Holocaust." She added, "Using the Holocaust to raise money to sell Israel Bonds is not an appropriate way to contribute to those who died. I really don't want to see the

Holocaust become another fund-raising vehicle for any group. I'm not even comfortable with all these private, large donations to the US Holocaust Museum."

In the interview quoted above, and in other interviews, Miller also objected to public invocations of the Holocaust being used to generate political support for Israel. But in *Facing the Holocaust*, she focuses specifically on the uncanny ability of the Wiesenthal Center to commercialize the Holocaust: "The enormous success of the Simon Wiesenthal Center has given new meaning to what was once a macabre in-house joke… 'There's no business like *Shoah* business.'"

Norman Finkelstein is on record as calling the Simon Wiesenthal Center part of an "extortion racket" aimed at using emotional blackmail by playing on Holocaust guilt, anxiety and trauma. (He also characterizes the SWC as "a gang of heartless and immoral crooks, whose hallmark is that they will do anything for a dollar.") The Wiesenthal Center tried to stop publication of Finkelstein's book *The Holocaust Industry* in France, maintaining that the book was filled with "Holocaust revisionism" and incitements to anti-Semitism. (In reality, Finkelstein's parents are Holocaust survivors, and his findings regarding exploitation of the Holocaust have been validated by no less than Raul Hilberg, dean of Holocaust scholars.) The Wiesenthal Center failed spectacularly in their efforts to censor Finkelstein's book, but the very fact that they tried to do so, something no legitimate human rights group would do, validates Finkelstein's point about their ruthlessness.

The use of the Holocaust by the Simon Wiesenthal Center—and their constant reiteration of the danger of another Holocaust—has been phenomenally effective in fund-raising. The center's high-rolling backers include Roland Arnall, Ivan Boesky, Gary Winnick, and Mortimer Zuckerman, publisher of the *Atlantic Monthly*. The Wiesenthal Center was where Arnold Schwarzenegger made his lugubrious appeal for public redemption from his father's Nazi party membership in Austria—and to close the deal, of course, he made a hefty donation to the Center. (He did not publicize the exact amount, but it was rumored to be more than a million.) In that single interaction, the morally-challenged Schwarzenegger revealed an astonishing truth about public life in an America obsessed by the Holocaust: the best way to redeem oneself of a Nazi past is to vigorously support the suffering and torment of Palestinians in the future, by giving money to rightwing Zionists—thus continuing into an indefinite future the suffering unleashed by Nazism.

One source of the original Nazi-hunter Simon Wiesenthal's appeal was that he created a kind of political spectacle that allowed many Europeans to come to terms with the Holocaust without looking too closely at their own culpability. Wiesenthal, the outspoken survivor, tracked down Nazis and brought them to justice, like a detective in a detective novel, rounding off his career by supposedly capturing the Nazi arch-villain Adolf Eichmann. Well, we now know that his claims were at best overblown, and quite often false—he did no tracking, he did research and public advocacy; and he was responsible for bringing only a few Nazis to justice, which he accomplished by making a commotion until various European governments found the political will to arrest them. The public persona created by Wiesenthal served another purpose, besides providing Wiesenthal himself with celebrity status and a comfortable living—it allowed Europe to ignore its own bad conscience about what had transpired only a few years before, through the simple expedient of catching a few egregious super-villains for everyone to excoriate publicly. "It wasn't *us* who looked away when our neighbors were taken away," Europeans were saying, "it wasn't *us* who were too frightened to speak up—it was those Nazis who were the bad guys, it was these Nazis that made us do it!"

The Simon Wiesenthal Center has attempted to extend the run

of this threadbare public theater piece into the twenty-first century with another annoying "Nazi-catcher," Dr. Efraim Zuroff, who is the director of the Simon Wiesenthal Center's office in Jerusalem. (Zuroff is also, to the great exasperation of the Yad Vashem Holocaust memorial, deeply involved in the controversy surrounding the Wiesenthal Center's so-called "Museum of Tolerance" in Jerusalem, about which more a bit later.) In the reverential Wikipedia entry under his name, Zuroff is credited with playing "an important role in the efforts to bring Nazi war criminals to justice during the past 28 years." The same entry states that he has thereby earned the sobriquet of "the last Nazi hunter," because he is "the coordinator of Nazi war crimes research worldwide for the Wiesenthal Center" and since 2001 the author of its annual Status Report "on the worldwide investigation and prosecution of Nazi war criminals."

This is eerily reminiscent of the original Nazi-hunter Simon Wiesenthal, since there is a lot more information in the Wikipedia entry about what Zuroff does to catch Nazis than any hard proof that he has ever caught any. Zuroff claimed in 2005 to have "located" Aribert Heim, who had been an SS doctor at Mauthausen-Gusen concentration camp, known to Mauthasen inmates as Dr. Death. But the entry goes on to explain that Heim probably died in 1992 in Cairo, Egypt. In other words, the heroic Efraim Zoroff, "the last Nazi-hunter," hadn't actually located the infamous Hiem, but had located the place where he *may* have died *back in 1992*. Zuroff isn't quite sure about that either, of course—nobody knows if Heim really died in Cairo, or when he died, or even if he's really dead. (Nor where his corpse is buried if he *is* dead.) But Zuroff believes that he "probably" died there in 1992 and on that basis claims to have "located" him.

Such is the fate of the last Nazi-hunter in a world without Nazis, who are mainly dead or dying out at an alarming rate. Precisely because of the dire possibility that they might soon be *entirely* dead, the Wiesenthal Center has launched "Operation

Last Chance," a campaign to track down Nazis "before they die of old age." But how many real Nazi war criminals are actually left, at this late date? And why should we care if they are, when it is so much more important to identify and deconstruct systemic evil being acted out in the present moment?

6

Although it promotes itself as a human rights organization, the Simon Wiesenthal Center has been very active in the promotion of religious bigotry. Their more overt activity in this area is relatively recent, and involves their promotion and showing of the violently anti-Muslim film *The Third Jihad,* which was a project of the Clarion Fund, a shadowy rightwing Zionist operation that produced *Obsession: Radical Islam's War with the West.* The fundamental premise of the Wiesenthal Center is that they, like Simon Wiesenthal himself, are engaged in tracking down evil-doers who would harm Jews; but as Nazis die out, a new agent of Pure Evil must be found. This new figure of Pure Evil is the Muslim Terrorist, who is a composite of Palestinian, Arab and Muslim, but mainly a stand-in for Palestinians in the territories occupied by Israel.

Since most Muslims around the world, as well as most Arabs, identify with Palestinians (Jerusalem is sacred to Islam, as well as to Judaism and Christianity), they are likely to be critical of the government of Israel—not to mention the foreign policy of the US, since the US uncritically supports Israel; thus the Simon Wiesenthal Center seeks to represent Muslims everywhere as terrorists, believing that they are helping Israel by doing so. In this way the SWC embraces the neo-conservative concept of permanent war in the Middle East by representing Muslims as being the new Nazis, whose defeat must be accompanied by an international religious war between the West and Muslims generally. (Needless to say, the Wiesenthal Center vigorously advocates war with Iran, and as we've seen likes to represent Iran as the Nazi menace dressed up in new clothes.)

But there is a domestic franchise connected to the neo-con dream of an apocalyptic world struggle between Islam and the West. That franchise is the dissemination of religious hatred against Muslims in the US, which the Simon Wiesenthal Center now manages. This was kicked off by their collaboration with Aish HaTorah, a group that Jeffrey Goldberg has referred to as "just about the most fundamentalist movement in Judaism today,"[20] and which has strong ties to the racist settlers in Israel's occupied territories. The nonprofit Clarion Fund became a loosely-constituted front group in America for Aish HaTorah in 2003, when its operatives produced a film alleging Palestinian incitement against Israel and Jews; and then, still in the heady post-9/11 atmosphere, the Clarion Fund went ahead to produce *Obsession*, and then *The Third Jihad*, both wildly inflammatory films that were supposedly about a minority of "radical" Muslims, but which made fantastic allegations about Muslims generally. Furthermore, the second film actually named specific Muslims organizations in the US (mainly the Council on American Islamic Relations, or CAIR) as being part of a hostile international plot to infiltrate and take over America.

The film *Obsession* was far from being the first attempt to use film to promote war, fanaticism and religious bigotry—cinema has been used many times for that purpose, most famously in Leni Riefenstahl's *Triumph of the Will*. Ironically, *Obsession* mimics many of the cinematic tropes of Riefenstahl's Nazi propaganda, depending heavily on continuous but cleverly edited footage of chanting, marching and demonstrating Muslims. *Obsession* and *The Third Jihad* try to suggest an aesthetic of violence in Islam similar to that of Hitler's Nazis; but ultimately the film reveals much more about the extent to which the film's makers are attracted to, and are prepared to use, fascist propaganda techniques. Most important, however, was that *Obsession* was the first film project by a religious group based in a foreign country that attempted to influence an American election. They did this by spending millions of dollars during the 2008 election campaign of Barack Obama and John McCain in a bizarre mass distribution scheme in so-called swing states, where voters tended to be somewhat conservative but could have voted for either man.

Just before the 2008 election, DVD copies of the film *Obsession,* which had been produced in 2005, were offered as a free insert to as many as 70 newspapers. (They also distributed 28 million DVDs by mail, again in those states generally referred to as swing states.) Newspapers carrying the free DVD as part of an advertising supplement included the *Charlotte Observer, Miami Herald, Raleigh News and Observer* and (interestingly) *The Chronicle of Higher Education*. To its everlasting shame, the overtly Zionist and Likud-supporting *New York Times* put 145,000 DVDs in the national editions of their newspapers to be sold in Denver, Miami, Tampa, Orlando, Detroit, Kansas City, St. Louis, Philadelphia and Milwaukee. Other newspapers flatly refused to carry the supplements containing *Obsession* DVDs, among them *St. Louis Post-Dispatch,* the *Detroit Free Press,* and Cleveland's *Plain Dealer*. In North Carolina, the *Greensboro News and Record* similarly refused, its publisher Robin Saul giving this reason: "We were told its purpose was education. We didn't see it as educational at all. It was fear-mongering and divisive."

Since the DVDs were targeted for swing states, and a pro-McCain ad was seen on a Clarion Fund Website, the Council on American-Islamic Relations asked the Federal Election Commission to investigate whether the Fund was trying to influence the outcome of an election. Nothing came of this complaint, but all indications were that the distribution of the film was intended to do just that, although nothing could be proven. (Otherwise, why were the DVDs distributed only in the swing states?) Furthermore, the connection to Israel was not hard to find for anybody willing to do a little digging—Raphael Shore, one of the principal producers of *Obsession,* is also the director of the Hasbara Fellowships, which aims to bring young people to Israel and expose them to Aish HaTorah's patented racist, pro-Likudnik propaganda. Furthermore, most of the translations in *Obsession* were done by MEMRI, the Middle East Media Research Institute, whose pro-Israel distortions are well-known. And finally, according to reporter Pam Martens, it was close associates of Charles Koch, of the super-rich Koch brothers, who gave millions to the Clarion Fund, which distributed the DVDs. The controversy had little effect, however, since people in the swing states were beginning to feel the effects of the credit-market recession. When you are losing your home, it's hard to become excited about endless footage of people marching in the streets of Tehran.

In the spring of 2009, after Obama had been inaugurated as President, the Clarion Fund released *The Third Jihad,* which turned out to be even weirder—in fact a lot weirder—than *Obsession.* In Los Angeles, it was the Simon Wiesenthal Center that agreed to feature this inflammatory film, a film overtly biased against American Muslims and also clearly designed to stir up negative feelings toward them; in fact the Wiesenthal Center opted to sponsor its West Coast premiere on May seventeenth, 2009, thereby making it a major event in their spring calendar. It was co-sponsored by the American Freedom Alliance, an unsavory far-right group that is unabashedly Islamophobic, anti-environmental, pro-torture and authoritarian (books by John Yoo and Marc Thiessen are on sale at their website). Their main link to the SWC seems to an obsessive hatred of Islam, and an uncritical support for extreme rightwing Zionism based on the likelihood that it might involve killing, torturing or otherwise hurting Muslims.

The Washington D.C. opening of *The Third Jihad,* which also occurred at the same time as the SWC event in Los Angeles, was co-sponsored by the International Free Press Society, another unsavory rightwing group, this one authentically neo-fascist. Two months before the Washington Premiere, the IFPS had been involved in publicizing and promoting Geert Wilders, a notorious Dutch neo-fascist with links to several far-right parties in Europe. Wilders, who has campaigned to ban the Qu'ran from The Netherlands and believes that "moderate Islam does not exist," is associated with Vlaams Belang (VB), a Flemish neo-fascist party. Wilders is so far to the right that he has even been criticized by the Anti-Defamation League for being "inflammatory, divisive and antithetical to American democratic ideas." (Vlaams Belang is on record as demanding amnesty for Dutch Nazi collaborators, and at least one person associated with it is doing jail time for Holocaust denial.)

As the date for the May seventeenth premiere of *The Third Jihad* approached, several groups in Los Angeles pleaded with the Wiesenthal Center to cancel their premiere. CAIR, which had unsuccessfully opposed the distribution of the free DVDs of *Obsession*, sent a letter to Rabbi Marvin Hier on May fourteenth, 2009, pleading with him and others at the Wiesenthal Center to cancel the film's West Coast premiere. "It is unfortunate that, per your institution's stated mission, it apparently continues to believe it is benefiting the state of Israel by promoting anti-Muslim prejudices and propaganda," the letter, written by Hussam Ayloush, said. "I urge you to cancel the film screening and join the American Muslim community and many other Americans in finding ways to bring about peace and harmony among all people."

Rabbi Hier and the Wiesenthal Center were not about to reconsider its plan to show *The Third Jihad,* partly because they wished to escalate their campaign against CAIR and other organizations in the organized Muslim community in the US. It was also an opportunity for Aish HaTorah, the fundamentalist Jewish group, to get even for CAIR's complaint to the Federal Election Commission's concerning its alleged attempt to influence the 2008 election. Furthermore, they were quite annoyed that it had been necessary to remove some particularly libelous footage concerning CAIR from the film shortly after its release. Hussam Ayloush referred to this in his letter to Hier:

"Following the release of *The Third Jihad* last year, the producers were forced to remove demonstrably false information. The film's narrator, Zuhdi Jasser, also makes the false claim that CAIR avoided participating in a Muslim rally against terrorism he sponsored in Arizona 2004. In fact, representatives of both CAIR's Arizona and national offices asked to join in the effort, but Jasser refused."

The Wiesenthal Center, perhaps receiving more bad press than they had anticipated, took the position that they were honoring, not attacking, the "moderate" Muslims of the world, represented by Dr. Zuhdi Jasser, the narrator and the obligatory "good" Muslim in the film. But what exactly made him "good," and other Muslims "bad?" Jasser, a former activist in CAIR, at some point had a falling-out with that organization, and left to form his own organization in Arizona, the American Islamic Forum for Democracy. Jasser's single issue (his obsession, one might say) is opposition to what he called "political Islam," or "Islamism," which he never gets around to defining, at least in an American context. Sometimes he says political Islam is opposition to "separation of mosque and state," but there are no Muslims agitating to make Islam part of any American government, whether federal, state, municipal or county.

Other times Jasser seems to believe political Islam means Muslims who take strong political positions—but his own website is full of strong and usually extreme political opinions, ranging from innocuous to absurd. (As an example of the latter, Jasser recently assailed some remarks by John Brennan, the Assistant to the President and a Deputy National Security Adviser, by suggesting that Brennan and the Obama Administration "may as well register as publicists and promotional agents for the Muslim Brotherhood and their ideology.")

So if political Islam equals terrorism, what exactly is the political identify of Dr. Jasser? Jasser is a rightwing Republican who supported George Bush and later Rudy Giuliani, and is a member of the Committee for the Present Danger. He speaks at the Hudson Institute, writes for the *National Review*, and was a guest of Glenn Beck on the Fox network. Jasser is, in short, a Muslim neo-conservative, joining a short and not particularly savory list of people from the Middle East including Nonie Darwish, Brigette Gabriel, Wafa Sultan, Amir Taheri, and the fraud Walid Shoebat who are regularly presented as "experts" on terrorism and Islam by the neo-con foundations, the Israel Lobby and some of the extreme Hillel groups. Although a sworn enemy of "political Islam," Zuhdi Jasser is a veritable fount of political opinion and invective, insisting that Rep. Keith Ellison "promotes Islamist causes," criticizing Hilary Clinton for giving Tariq Ramadan a visa to get into the US, and viciously attacking one of the few Muslims to run for office in Arizona because of her "anti-Israel activism." He personifies, in other words, the complete neo-con fantasy of the "good" Muslim, who is appropriately grateful to live in American, gratifyingly humble to his primarily Christian audience on TV, and who never, ever criticizes American foreign policy or the state of Israel, for to do so would be "Islamism," and thus terrorism.

The movie *The Third Jihad* opened at the Simon Wiesenthal Center to a slightly jittery audience that was nonetheless elated to have Dr. Zuhdi Jasser present, and were only too ready to make nice to him because of all the bad press the film—and the Center—had been receiving. The film itself was an astonishing exercise in conspiracy-mongering, and one that had a creepy resonance with Jewish history, but a resonance that not everybody in attendance wanted to dwell on. There was a predictable disclaimer at the beginning of the film by Dr. Jasser specifying that it was not about most Muslims, who are "good" Muslims, but only about the minority of "bad" ones. (The fact that Dr. Jasser has extreme rightwing views almost no Muslim in America would agree with was left unsaid.)

The story told by *The Third Jihad* is this: There have been three big military pushes by Islam to take over the world, and this is the third. (To demonstrate, huge swatch of green marked with a star and crescent are periodically shown moving around the map, making the viewer wonder how they could possibly represent only a tiny minority of Muslims.) This third jihad aims to take over America. Since Muslims are a small religious group within America, and lack both the capital and the political clout of Christians and Jews, it might seem that they are not in a position to take over even a small village, much less one of the largest countries in the world. An organized, nation-wide revolutionary plot to subvert all branches of government seems a bit much.

But the film's narrator Jasser, presenting himself as the film's protagonist, announces that he has discovered that in 2003 the Federal Bureau of Investigation miraculously uncovered a subversive document—a "Grand Jihad Manifesto"—outlining a Muslim plot to take over America. The plot is already underway and even now threatening America's security. (Why the FBI isn't making arrests, if the plot violates the laws, is left unanswered for the moment.) One would like to see the actual document in question, simply to see where the makers of this fantasy are able to take it. But no, the document cannot be released to the general public, perhaps because the effects of reading it would demoralize the nation. (Or perhaps, on the other hand, it really doesn't exist) But the producers of *The Third Jihad* insist that it does exist, and that it outlines a *cultural* strategy. "The 15-page document outlines goals and strategies for the infiltration and domination of America from within," they say. "Among the strategies discussed is the establishment of 'moderate' groups, mosques and Islamic centers across North America in an effort to strategically position Islam so that it might weaken western culture and promote the implementation of Sharia Law."

This is spectacularly wrong on several counts. A manifesto is by its nature a public document, one that attempts to appeal to the widest number of people, not a secret communication spelling out a secret strategy. Secondly, there is no reason to believe such a document exists if it cannot be produced; or that such a document, if one exists, could be of any importance if it was not widely disseminated. Third, why would American Muslims, who are universally seen as well-integrated into American society, want to conspire against American democracy, especially since so many of them came to America to get away from authoritarian regimes? Fourth, how exactly is western culture "weakened" by exposure to a minority religion, especially in America, where religious liberty is a core value? Finally, how could Muslims impose Sharia law on a nation in which there are a hundred million evangelical Christians, at least that many confirmed secularists, not to mention the powerful neo-cons? It's a rightwing fantasy from beginning to end, with no basis whatsoever in reality.

Propaganda efforts like *The Third Jihad* have had relatively little success, but if the neo-cons can get American into a war with Iran, or involved in a religious war with the Islamic world, it will be much easier to promote domestic discrimination against Muslims. The well-known "paranoid style" of American politics has already started to re-assert itself, in the campaign to ban "Sharia Law"; and the neo-con operatives and foundations are already arguing for internment of Muslims or political outlawing of Muslim organizations, which has always been one of their main domestic political goals. *The Third Jihad* appeals to religious bigotry, but that can probably be turned into *institutional* discrimination against Muslims only if we're at war.

Finally, of course, there was the uncanny resonance of *The Third Jihad's* claim to have discovered a secret document detailing the conspiracy of a religious minority to take over the world. The similarities to "The Protocols of the Elders of Zion" were immediately noted by progressive Jews, who realized that it was now clear that well-heeled Jewish backers of the settlers' movement in the West Bank (such as the Koch brothers) had no hesitation in playing the "Protocol" card in the efforts to demonize Muslims. The search for secret documents that would "prove" Islam's intent to dominate the West had been the focus of a number of writers, principally Gisele Littman, whose texts are a favorite of European Islamophobes. But this was arguably the first time American neo-cons had tried to promote their version of The Protocols of the Elders of Mecca, and it should not surprise us that they chose to do so through the Simon Wiesenthal Center. For better or for worse, the Simon Wiesenthal Center has become the main institutional promoter of hard-right neo-conservative ideas—and of religious bigotry against Muslims—among conservative Jews in Los Angeles.

7

This dissemination of religious hatred by the Simon Wiesenthal Center was soon to be overshadowed by an even more hateful operation, which was clearly aimed at igniting religious conflict on the ground in the Middle East. In June 2005, the Simon Wiesenthal Center began construction in Jerusalem on a new facility, variously referred to by Rabbi Hier as the "Center for Human Dignity," the "Center for Human Dignity—Jerusalem" and most pretentiously, the "Center for Human Dignity—Museum of Tolerance." (Ground-breaking had occurred in 2004, giving Arnold Schwarzenegger the opportunity to fly to Israel for yet another photo op with Rabbi Heir.) This sprawling structure was built on a parking lot that was supposedly adjacent to a historic Muslim ceremony; but which turned out to be on top of a part of it.

The cemetery, called the Mamilla Cemetery (*Ma'Man Allah* in Arabic), was an extremely old Muslim burial ground that was once the most important in Palestine, and in the Middle East. The Center for Constitutional Rights in New York, in a petition to the UN and other international organizations to stop construction of the Wiesenthal Museum, wrote as follows: "The Mamilla Cemetery is an ancient Muslim burial ground and holy site believed to date back to the 7th century, when companions of the Prophet Muhammad were reputedly buried there. Numerous saints of the Sufi faith and thousands of other officials, scholar, notables and Jerusalemite families have been buried in the cemetery over the last 1000 years. The Muslim Supreme Council declared the cemetery a historical site in 1927, and the British Mandate authorities pronounced in an antiquities site in 1944. It was an active burial ground until 1948."

"After the new State of Israel seized the western part of Jerusalem in 1948, the cemetery fell under Israeli control, and like other Islamic endowment properties, or waqf, Mamilla Cemetery was taken over by the Custodian for Absentee Property. Since then, Muslim authorities have not been allowed to maintain the cemetery." At that time, in 1948, the Israeli Religious Affairs Ministry itself acknowledged Mamilla "to be one of the most prominent Muslim cemeteries, where seventy thousand Muslim warriors of [Saladin's] armies are interred along with many Muslim scholars." It added: "Israel will always know to protect and respect this site."

But that is not what happened.

In the early 1980s, Muslims became aware that bodies were being disinterred, and that the cemetery was being encroached on, and protested to the United Nations Education, Scientific and Cultural Organization (UNESCO). In 1984 Israel responded to that protest by stating flatly "no project exists for the de-consecration of the site and that on the contrary the site and its tombs are to be safeguarded." In fact even as Israel said this, however, it was engaged in parceling off pieces of the cemetery for various kinds of private developments, even as they assured UNESCO that they were protecting it.

Sadly, Palestinians had no legal instrument by which they could stop this. Although Mamilla cemetery is on a list of "Special Antiquities Sites," it is not protected as a *religious* site. All of the cemeteries in Israel that are protected as religious sites are Jewish. (The Israeli government designates 137 holy sites that receive such protection, but *all are Jewish*, a fact that the US State Department's International Religious Freedom Report of 2009 protested against.) Furthermore successive governments have sought to obliterate reminders of Palestinian culture in Jerusalem; successive governments parceled out sections of Mamilla for buildings, then the parking lot mentioned above—and in 1992, the site was transferred to the Jerusalem municipality. At one point the government built a park over a part of the cemetery, which they named Independence Park, a reference to the founding of Israel in 1948 (and a clear attempt to provoke and humiliate Palestinians).

This is completely unlike the treatment meted out to Jewish cemeteries. On the Mount of the Olives, for example, the Jewish cemetery has been lavishly refurbished and even expanded, and finally transformed into a "heritage site." On the other hand, Israel's Muslim cemeteries have been allowed to fade into disuse, and are even destroyed when the government thinks it can get away with it. The 900-year-old Hittin mosque built by Saladin in the Galilee region has been deliberately fenced off and allowed to go to ruin. According to Bethlehem-based journalist Jonathan Cook, some mosques are used by rural Jewish communities as animal sheds. "And yet more," he writes, "have been converted into discos, bars or nightclubs, including the Dahir al-Umar mosque—now the Dona Rosa restaurant—in the former Palestinian village of Ayn Hawd."

Meron Benvenisti, a former Deputy Mayor of Jerusalem who wrote *Sacred Landscape: Buried History of the Holy Land Since 1948*, has been vocal in pointing out that Muslim groups, contrary to what the Simon Wiesenthal camp is saying, pleaded over the years to be allowed to officially refurbish and keep up their sacred sites and cemeteries, but were never allowed to do so. Many important Islamic sites, he has written, have been "turned into dumps, parking lots, roads and construction sites."

Of a tour of East Jerusalem in late summer 2010 Phillip Weiss wrote on his website *Mondoweiss*:

> *Maybe the most pitiable sight I saw yesterday, inside the West Bank but close to the north Jerusalem colonies of Ramot and Ramat Shlomo, the hilltop tomb of the prophet Samuel, which is worshiped by Jews and Muslims. The tomb is both a mosque with a minaret and a Jewish place of worship. Well when we visited, busloads of Jewish schoolchildren were arriving and Israeli soldiers were in the tomb davening and Hasidic boys were descending, too.*

But next door it's a different story:

> *And meantime the Islamic portion of the tomb is dead. The door is chained; pigeons fly into the outer rooms, the Palestinian who runs a store there told us that the authorities had shut down the minaret. There are no Palestinian worshipers.*

Weiss points out that this is an Israeli National Park in the West Bank, which is supposedly Palestinians land and supposedly—if there were actually ever to be a two-state solution—the future site of a Palestinian state. But being under the authority of the Israeli state, the Jewish site is protected as a *religious* site, whereas the Muslim worship facility next to the tomb of the prophet Samuel has been closed down. It is hard not to conclude that closing down or deliberate degradation of Muslim religious sites has become a general policy of the Israeli government as part of its slow ethnic cleansing aimed at Palestinian Muslims. The message seems to be, "If you don't like what we're doing to Muslim holy sites, why don't you leave?"

The Simon Wiesenthal Center similarly claims that Mamilla deserves no protection as a *religious* site, citing the fact that in 1964 the government set up a Muslim trust and that the head of that council "deconsecrated" Mamilla—he supposedly declared it no longer sacred ground and opening it up to development. But this person was a government toady introduced by the state of Israel to give political cover to those interested in making money by developing the cemetery. (The 1964 proclamation was aggressively overturned—or ruled "void"—by the Shari'a Court of Appeals in Israel, which found the sanctity of cemeteries "eternal" in Islam.) Certainly this single state factotum trotted out by the Israelis in 1964 cannot speak for Palestinian families today who have ancestors buried at Mamilla. Although some tombstones appeared to have been replaced in recent years, individual attempts at upkeep haven't been as successful as organized efforts would be.

In *Death in Jerusalem,* Noga Tarnopolsky writes of a friend named Sari Nusseibeh, a Muslim philosopher and university president, who located the tomb of two illustrious ancestors in the Mamilla cemetery. "Nusseibeh then contacted a friend working at the Ministry for Religious Affairs and requested permission to place a plaque on the crypt. 'I thought it was important to commemorate this, and to tell people that in the case of a family like mine, we are not claiming roots here in the abstract or national sense, but in the familial sense, which is a much closer thing,' he said. Nusseibeh secured permission and affixed a stone plaque explaining that the tomb belonged to Islam's Kabrkabiyyan period and contained the remains of one Prince Iddaghji and a certain Judge Nusseibeh. The next day it was removed by municipal workers, who claimed sole jurisdiction over the entire park." This was despite the permission he had supposedly gotten from the Ministry for Religious Affairs.

This could stand as a paradigm interaction between the Israeli state and Palestinians. You can jump through all the hoops, do all the paperwork required of the state; but if you are Palestinian you can be stopped at any moment simply because you have, from the government's point of view, the wrong religion and the wrong ethnicity. And your attorney will be able to do nothing for you, because in Israel the legal system is completely skewed against Palestinians.

Thus the location for the Simon Wiesenthal Center's "Museum of Tolerance" had already been contested ground for some time, which Rabbi Hier knew very well; and in the opinion of most Palestinians it serves today as a prime example of Israel's rampant intolerance. Even the design for the new structure—by the internationally-known architect Frank Gehry—seems to have pleased nobody. (Gehry claims that it represents a bowl of fruit, a strange idea that got little traction in Jerusalem.) Meron Benvenisti complained of its "geometric forms [that] can't be any more dissonant to the environment in which it is planned to put this alien object." Noga Tarnopolsky characterized its design as "the image of a supernatural edifice resembling nothing so much as a crab in the process of hatching a sapphire spider with huge, glassy eyes. It is neither beautiful nor ugly; it is striking and odd." The management of the Vad Yashem Holocaust memorial were unhappy about the competition in Holocaust tourism (there's a good comic novel in there somewhere; Philip Roth, where are you?), and the people of Jerusalem, perhaps wary of busloads of ecstatic Wiesenthal-inspired tourists from Southern California, were generally mystified by Heir's grandiose ideas.

The "Museum of Tolerance" is being built on a parking lot that was supposed to be *adjacent* to Mamilla cemetery. In reality it was built *over* part of it. This fact became painfully clear to the Wiesenthal Center as workers began to encounter human remains. (Laying electrical cables and sewer lines had apparently required digging deeper than had been required for building the parking lot.) At first the presence of human remains was kept secret by the SWC, but it couldn't have surprised many people in Jerusalem, since they knew that the government had been parceling off the cemetery for some time. What they didn't know was how resentful of this Palestinians had become over the years, especially those families with ancestors buried in Mamilla.

Reports vary, but the Wiesenthal Center workers apparently encountered remains of about two hundred people; and a decision was made—according to Wiesenthal spokespersons—to take the remains to another Muslim cemetery and re-inter them there. (Exactly what really happened hasn't been confirmed.) The centuries-old remains have been the main sticking point for Hier and the SWC, the seriousness of which can be inferred from Hier's insistence that they "respectfully" re-interred the bones. If the Wiesenthal Center is simply building something on a parking lot, why were they digging up human remains? And if claims by local Muslims are invalid, why was the Wiesenthal Center re-interring the remains they uncovered in another Muslim cemetery?

In fact, Hier and the Wiesenthal Center had known for a very long time that they were building on top of a Muslim cemetery. During the building of the original parking lot back in the 1960s, hundreds of graves were disinterred, which caused anguished protests by Muslims, and also in 1984, when they appealed to UNESCO. Furthermore, as early as 1993 the municipal authorities offered the Wiesenthal Center the parking lot for the building of the project. Both Teddy Kollek and Ehud Olmert had encouraged Rabbi Hier to build the current or similar projects at precisely this site, and they above all were in a position to know that the parking lot had been built over part of the Mamilla Cemetery. Therefore Kollek, Ehud Olmert and Rabbi Hier knew exactly what lay under the parking lot. In fact, the case can be made that Hier *wanted* to build on a Muslim cemetery, given his apocalyptic ideas about the inevitability of war between Muslims and Jews. What could be better for fund-raising than a nice little religious war, with Rabbi Hier leading his faithful troops into the fray?

In 2005, Gideon Suleimani, a Palestinian archeologist, personally warned representatives of the SWC that the area was an antiquities site; at Suleimani's request, the Israeli Antiquities Authority (IAA) allowed test trenches to be dug, and it was revealed that hundreds of graves—as many as four layers of graves—were located under the parking lot. One has the sense that Suleimani thought that he could get the Wiesenthal Center to back off if only he could appeal to their common humanity. If so, he didn't know the group he was dealing with—the SWC continued in spite of being so advised; and when reports surfaced of their digging up remains and carrying them away surreptitiously in boxes, several Palestinian families in the area decided to act.

The Israeli Antiquities Authority (IAA) then moved to investigate further. Suleimani, who was appointed Chief Excavator, found that there were "at least 2000 graves," on at least four levels, with exhumed remains dating back to the twelfth century, and the lowest level dating back to the eleventh century. But, as Suleimani later testified in an Affidavit,[21] people from the Simon Wiesenthal Center began to put pressure on the IAA, as did interested politicians who were invested in getting the construction done. For their part the IAA, according to Suleimani, tried to get him to stop his excavating and to alter his report. Suleimani also said that "representatives of the SWC started coming by on a daily basis, pressing for the excavation to progress quickly, to prevent the Muslims from stopping the project," not to mention entrepreneurs whose connection to the site was unclear, but who were now threatening to sue the Israeli Antiquities Authority.

In 2006 a lawsuit was filed that resulted in a court order that temporarily stopped construction. But the pressures were growing on the government. The Israeli Antiquities Authority decided, while defending against the lawsuit, *to suppress the evidence their Chief Excavator Gideon Suleimani had uncovered.* The High Court of Israel never found out that there were around 2,000 graves under the parking lot, going down four levels, the lowest level of graves dating back to the eleventh century. They did not find out about it because the IAA suppressed the evidence that it had asked Suleimani to collect. In another astoundingly cynical move, the IAA apparently lied (according to affidavits by Suleimani) about his finding that only about ten percent of the excavations had been done, instead claiming that ninety percent was done.

What caused these criminal misrepresentations to the High Court, the first of which was suppression of evidence, and the second of which was perjury? The Simon Wiesenthal Center had arranged to pay the workers doing the excavation, perhaps a violation of the law, but one that gave the SWC greater leverage over facts on the ground. And there is some circumstantial evidence that the "Museum of Tolerance" was part of a larger deal, which may not have been open to public scrutiny (since it may have involved secret deals or patronage from politicians). If not, why did the IAA falsify the report they had initiated, and what did they receive in return from the Simon Wiesenthal Center? The truth about this could probably be established only by a special commission of inquiry, but the corrupt Likud government would never permit that.

The deck was stacked against Palestinians seeking justice at every level of government in Israel, including the judiciary. And despite Israel's promises in 1948, there has been an ongoing process of destruction and marginalization of historical Islamic religious sites, a tragedy engendered by greed and prejudice, justified in some cases by the idea that any historical sites associated with the Palestinian community might arouse Palestinian nationalism. On the contrary, the *destruction* of those sites seems far more likely to arouse Palestinian nationalism, and the rest of the world is likely to agree with that perception.

The High Court allowed construction to continue in October 2008. Efforts were made to appeal this, since the Israel Antiquities Authority had repressed the only evidence that really counted in this case, which was testimony (and evidence) of the Chief Excavator assigned by the IAA itself, Gideon Suleimani. Despite the suppression of everything he had to say and all the evidence he had obtained, the court refused to open the case again, and insisted that construction must proceed. Exhumation of human remains resumed, and there was nothing that could be done about it. This constituted the exhaustion of appeals within the Israeli system of justice, and made the later appeal to the United Nations inevitable.

The disinterring of human remains by the SWC workers would be considerable, because contrary to what the IAA had told the High Court, ninety percent of the area still had to be dug up. The Israeli Antiquities Authority claimed that the disinterring of remains occurring after October 2008 involved manual removal after documentation so that they could be re-interred; but both the Simon Wiesenthal Center and the IAA have engaged in extreme secrecy, and it is impossible to say exactly what they did with the remains. (Needless to say, they refused to consult with appropriate Muslim authorities.) It was reported by the Palestinian News Network that during one week in 2009, some 300 Muslim graves were opened up, and the remains dumped into a mass grave. It is impossible to confirm this, but one can imagine how such reports affect the Palestinians that read them. The apparent collusion of the IAA and the Simon Wiesenthal group, and the extreme secrecy with which they operate—not to mention the violent rhetorical attacks on any who oppose their projects as terrorists, anti-Semites, and "Islamists"—have for the time being removed hope for resolution using any of the instruments of Israeli civil society.

Therefore on 10 February 2010, in New York, Jerusalem, Geneva and Los Angeles, a petition was filed with several United Nations agencies to stop desecration of Mamilla Cemetery by Israeli authorities and the Simon Wiesenthal Center. (Press conferences were held in Geneva, Jerusalem and Los Angeles.) The UN agencies to whom this was appealed were the UN Special Rapporteurs on Freedom of Religion and Belief and on Contemporary Forms of Racism; the Independent Expert on Culture; the High Commissioner for Human Rights; and the Director General of UNESCO, the agency that was involved in investigations of previous desecrations of Mamilla Cemetery in 1984. The Petition was filed on behalf of some 60 Palestinians from 15 Jerusalem families whose ancestors, going back to the twelfth century, are buried in the cemetery. The filing was done by the Center for Constitutional Rights located in New York, which has made information about the campaign to save Mamilla available at www.mamillacampaign.org.

The press release accompanying the filing said as follows: "This will be the first known time Palestinian individuals have taken collective action against Israel to bring such an issue before a UN forum and comes after all remedies in Israel were exhausted. The families, NGOs, and attorneys argue the desecration of the cemetery violates international conventions protecting cultural heritage, the manifestation of religious beliefs, and the right to family." Maria LaHood, a Senior Attorney as CCR, added: "Left with no recourse in Israel, families of people buried in Mamilla cemetery have come together to petition the United Nations to safeguard their international human rights to be free from discrimination, to manifest religious beliefs, and to have their cultural heritage protected. We call on the international community to denounce this shameful desecration of a historic Muslim cemetery in Jerusalem."

In the international arena, the CCR sees itself as "dedicated to advancing and protecting the rights guaranteed by the United States Constitution and the Universal Declaration of Human Rights." Predictably, the Simon Wiesenthal Center sees the Petition filed by the Center for Constitutional Rights as a scheme to overthrown the authority of the Jewish state, rather in the same way as the Goldstone Report—or any other attempt to document Israeli violations of international law—is seen by the SWC as the use of international law to destroy Israel.

In the New York *Sun* and certain elements of the Jewish press, the Simon Wiesenthal Center has recently presented evidence, in the form of a story from the Palestine *Post* of 1945, that the Supreme Muslim Council of Jerusalem was planning a business center on the site of the Mamilla Cemetery in 1945. In the Wiesenthal Center's view, that means that they can do anything they want with Mamilla Cemetery. But the Palestine *Post* (precursor to the Jerusalem *Post*) was violently Labor-Zionist in its politics, and in 1945 it was not the best source for news originating within the Palestinian community, nor the best advocate for its interests. Furthermore, the nominal head of the Muslim Council at that time was the notorious Mohammad Amin al-Husayni, who although out of the country in 1945 was still the Grand Mufti of Jerusalem; and who, besides being one of the worst anti-Semites of the twentieth century, was also an enthusiastic propagandist for Hitler and the Nazis. (Besides making propaganda broadcasts for Hitler, al-Husayni tried to recruit Bosnian Muslims to the Waffen SS.) Furthermore, the entire Muslim Council in Jerusalem at that time was rife with cronyism, corruption, and the infighting of various Jerusalem families.

It could be said that Al-Husayni and Jerusalem's Muslim Council in 1945 represented a snapshot of exactly what a great many secular Arab nationalists (not to mention the later Islamic Revival throughout Muslim-majority countries) aimed to get rid of—not merely cronyism, greed and class oppression but also, in the case of Al-Husayni, European-style fascism and anti-Semitism. The fact that neither Arab nationalism nor the Islamic Revival was entirely successful in doing so does not change the fact that Al-Husayni and the Muslim Council of 1945 engaged in behavior that the best Arab thinkers were irreconcilably opposed to. It was for precisely this reason that the Palestinian Liberation Organization was careful to sideline al-Husayni and to downplay his influence in the years before his death in 1974.

In any case, neither al-Husayni nor the Muslim Council of 1945 are guides to important cultural and political decisions in Israel/Palestine of 2010, for the Palestinian community today is entirely different than it was in 1945. Sadly, that is difficult for Rabbi Hier and the Simon Wiesenthal Center to accept. For them, there are only "the Palestinians," much as Christians once referred to a mysterious entity known as "the Jews," who were supposedly the enemy of Christendom.

But Hier's rhetoric is the self-delusion of the bully, who projects his own bad conscience onto his weaker victim. In reality, there is no *they* in those organizations and individuals who seek to defend Mamilla Cemetery, but Palestinians, Christians and Jews in many countries and of many different temperaments and affiliations, whose guiding interest is in preserving one of the most important religious sites of the Middle East. But Mamilla Cemetery is also a dispute in which a dominant group of people have the power to hurt and humiliate another, weaker group of people whose religious sites receive no protection from the government; and as we all know, such total power over an entire people, and the impunity to use that power to hurt those people, is the most dangerous thing in the world—to nations, to religions, and to individual human beings.

8

The Simon Wiesenthal Center is an extreme rightwing Jewish organization, tinged by neo-fascism and with many of the characteristics of a hate organization. It is based almost completely on a vulgarized, pervasive form of religious nationalism. Its vision for Israel is consistent with the neo-fascist Jabotinsky tendency within Zionism that was modeled on Italian fascism, and it also promotes the Likudnik doctrine that Judaism itself has no practical or demographic existence separate from Israel. The SWC supports the neo-con belief in permanent war in the Middle East, and it engages in the vigorous dissemination of religious bigotry against Muslims in the US. It portrays anti-Semitism as worse than it is, partly for fund-raising purposes and partly to establish victim status as the highest good. It similarly uses the Holocaust both to discourage criticism of Israel and to justify Israel's own violence, teaching that every criticism of Israel is aimed at destroying the Jewish people. The Simon Wiesenthal Center supports the complete nationalism of Judaism by the apartheid state of Israel, which would mean a moral collapse at the heart of both religious and cultural Judaism. Above all, the SWC is a dangerous political and cultural force that seeks religious war as the standard for religious authenticity.

What kind of people make up the "400,000 member-families" claimed by the SWC as supporters in southern California and the US? If the SWC does indeed have that many families that contribute annually, it is a mass organization, which means that it must be taken seriously. One has the sense that Hier's followers are primarily lower (and middle) middle-class, perhaps small businesspersons and conservative professionals whose level of cultural literacy is not particularly high, and who reject traditional Jewish concerns for social justice. The frenetic and frequently duplicitous advocacy emanating from the Simon

Wiesenthal Center has a pronounced middlebrow flavor—that is, it is pretentious, self-congratulatory and sometimes unintentionally funny. (Last year an e-mailed Passover invitation to SWC members billed Rabbis Marvin Hier and Abraham Cooper as "featured Scholars-in-Residence at the Arizona Biltmore Hotel and Spa.")

Rabbi Hier's followers probably share a common characteristic of many religious constituencies, of interpreting their leaders' lies as a form of religious enthusiasm. They are also likely to be people who lack sufficient historical insight to understand why Hier and Cooper's half-truths and lies are dangerous, and why they might be capable of igniting religious war. Above all, they have been indoctrinated with the idea that the state of Israel, the Simon Wiesenthal Center and the people that support them are never wrong, and never at fault, because criticisms directed against them are really the work of anti-Semites aimed at destroying the Jewish people. It is especially easy, then, for them to believe, like the followers of many Messianic movements, that they are serving a higher morality that cannot be questioned.

Rabbi Hier and the SWC know very well about the bodies buried under the parking lot at Mamilla Cemetery. They have reportedly contemplated buying the site since at least 1993; they have been repeatedly warned that the site was built over a historic cemetery; and they have repeatedly refused suggestions to build somewhere else. The Simon Wiesenthal Center cannot say that it did not know the potential for conflict in their choice. At its core the conflict over the Mamilla Cemetery is one more attempt by rightwing Zionists to redefine Judaism as a religion that will redeem the Holocaust by hurting and humiliating Palestinians and attacking Islam. Words like "Tolerance" and "Dignity" from the liberal and social-democratic past of European Jewry are gleefully flaunted by the SWC, but are used in the same way that Stalinists used words such as "democratic" or "liberation," to disguise the real nature of Stalinism.

There is nothing "ironic" about the use of such words, because it is a conscious ploy for political purposes; it also serves the function of Orwellian language, which is to communicate contempt for logic, and to distract with its absurdity. Finally, it is an expression of raw illegitimate power, saying in effect to the Palestinians: "We control everything, even language. If we say that black is white, we will force you to accept it, because we have the power to humiliate and kill you." And as often happens in extremist movements and institutions, people in the leadership of the Wiesenthal Center will lie and misrepresent things anytime they think they can get away with it.

The Mamilla Cemetery site was chosen for a reason. The Simon Wiesenthal Center's real objective in building the "Center for Human Dignity—Museum of Tolerance" in Jerusalem was almost surely to ignite religious conflict. It is this pathological aggression that makes the Simon Wiesenthal Center dangerous. This is a dispute in which Rabbi Hier, the very incarnation of the charismatic but morally corrupt religious fanatic, seeks to invent a new Judaism that, like medieval Christianity, defines itself by its ability to wound and torment the underdog. As the neo-conservatives made clear in their famous letter to Netanyahu in 1996, the American empire they seek depends on a state of permanent war in the Middle East; and that is also what Hier, Cooper and their Likudnik patrons want. What Hier seeks, what he has always sought, is religious war; for what could be more apocalyptic, what could be better for fund-raising, than a violent religious war in which he could portray a new Holocaust as being ever more imminent?

9

Why the extraordinary aggression of the Simon Wiesenthal Center, its need to lie and provoke conflict? It begins with the Wiesenthal Center's belief that the Nazi Holocaust is the pivotal event in human history—not *a* pivotal event but *the* pivotal event. It comes also from the Wiesenthal Center's dangerous idea that the Holocaust must be personally internalized as a central component of Jewish identity. Just as the Holocaust is the pivotal event in history, it should become pivotal to Jewish identity, so that one's personality and social identity as a Jew can be built around it. These two aspects of the Simon Wiesenthal Center's message are constantly reiterated in one form or another. To live in the same world in which the Holocaust occurred, the Wiesenthal Center is saying, you must accept it both as history's biggest crime and the most important determinant of Jewish identity. But that is a mistaken strategy, because it gives too much power to the Holocaust. You cannot base *identity* on the Holocaust without internalizing its *aggression,* because you cannot take in one without the other. The result is an unconscious identification with the power-worship at the heart of Nazi violence, which goes a long way toward explaining the Wiesenthal Center's striking lack of morality and common sense. Looking into the abyss, they become the abyss.

The second reason for the astonishing amorality of the SWC derives from the uncanny ability of the Nazi Holocaust to corrupt all those that would use it for personal and organizational gain. That is the great danger of manipulating trauma to manipulate people—sooner or later it results in identification with the trauma itself. Using the Holocaust to make money and promote disinformation has thoroughly corrupted the Simon Wiesenthal Center; but it could be argued that this is merely a continuation of a process that began earlier, with the foundation of Israel. After the Second World War, the Zionist movement used the Holocaust for their own rhetorical purposes, presenting the state of Israel as the *only* realistic deterrent to further violence against Jews. The defeat of Hitler suggests that the opposite was true—that people of all faiths and nationalities worked together to defeat the Nazis, and could therefore work together to defeat anti-Semitism in the West. (A concrete example of this was the Catholic Church's jettisoning claims of collective Jewish guilt for Jesus' crucifixion.)

But Zionists' used the trauma of the Holocaust to browbeat surviving European Jews, some of whom were still struggling with the after-effects of their trauma. This political misuse of the Holocaust—using guilt and emotional blackmail to impose bad policy—has had massive, toxic effects on the West, especially in America. The Wiesenthal Center simply continued this toxic use of the Holocaust, although in a typically vulgar and buffoonish way, using it to intimidate critics, guilt-monger the rich and the politicians, and make money for its founders and board of directors. But for just that reason, the Wiesenthal Center isn't likely to end its constant references to the Holocaust anytime soon, or its tactic of proclaiming that a new Holocaust might be on the way. The Center's funding and its power—political and cultural—depend upon stirring up unresolved negative emotions originally put in play by the Holocaust. The result is a continuation of Holocaust trauma in a new venue.

10

The main interior of the Simon Wiesenthal Center's Museum of Tolerance in Los Angeles—that is, most of the total space—is dedicated to memorializing the Nazi Holocaust. The Wiesenthal Center's project was one of three such museums in the US built in the 1990s, the other two being the United States Holocaust Memorial Museum in Washington, and the New York "Museum of Jewish Heritage—a Living Memorial to the Holocaust." Are such memorials a good thing? The entire experience of the Simon Wiesenthal Center suggests that such museums are extraordinarily vulnerable to misuse by charlatans. That doesn't have to be invariably the case, however—the memorial in New York includes artifacts typical of Jewish life before and after the Holocaust, which strikes a more positive note than the Wiesenthal museum. But the tendency to use the Holocaust for political purposes—and for fund-raising—is definitely there.

The very name of the New York museum suggests the depth of the problem: there really can't be a "living" memorial to the Nazi Holocaust, because genocide is about death. A better response to the Nazi Holocaust would be to build a museum dedicated to the people who *opposed* the Holocaust—that would at least give us an idea of how some people tried to defeat systemic evil. But don't hold your breath—such a strategy takes us toward a resolution of the problem of evil, and if there's one thing the Wiesenthal Center doesn't want it is to deconstruct the trauma of the Holocaust; that would rob them of the fear-mongering they need to raise money. Besides, a museum about those who fought the Nazis would inevitably cause people to wonder how they would act in a similar situation, and that could make them uncomfortable—perhaps so uncomfortable they might not want to shell out good money for it. On the other hand, simply focusing on the Nazi death machine has a dark voyeuristic pleasure to it; and it completely disengages the moral imagination, since the Nazis are so evil nobody has to wonder what they would do in their place.

Another problem with Holocaust museums as that their ability to teach causal factors is highly limited. Viewing computerized dioramas in a darkened hallway is not going to tell you much about militarism in German society, the traumatic humiliation of Germany by Versailles, the popularity of pseudo-Nietzschean ideas, nor even the inability of the German Left to unite. Had not Stalin taken over the Communist movement and turned it against the Social Democrats, could they have formed an electoral front that might have staved off Nazism? The Wiesenthal Center cannot help us answer that, because it doesn't ask that question in the first place. Nor does it attempt to communicate the immensely creative but dangerous spiritual malaise of Germany in the 1920s, its weird mixture of cruelty and bohemianism, and the fundamental hostility to democratic sensibilities that underlay everything.

To understand the Holocaust, you must read about it—you can no more understand the Nazi Holocaust from a museum than you could learn tax law from a graphic novel. One should start with the first and best account of the Holocaust, Raul Hilberg's three-volume *The Destruction of the European Jews,* published in 1961. But to appreciate fully this first and best historical account of the Nazi Holocaust, one must remember that no commercial publisher or university press was willing to publish it when Hilberg first finished writing it. Publishers did not want to publish a history of the Nazi holocaust because people did not want to know about it. This subject, which is now such an obsession with Jews and non-Jews alike, was once a taboo subject, something that people didn't want to know about.

For one thing (as Norman Finkelstein has pointed out) it was considered rude to West Germany, because it was America's new Cold War ally against Communism. Hilberg's monumental study was such a non-starter that it only became publishable when a wealthy Czech-American put up $15,000 to have it published. In other words, one of the most important works of history ever written had to be self-published, because no established commercial and academic publishing house would touch it. Why? For one thing, by documenting that the worst genocide in history occurred in the supposedly civilized West, Hilberg's book was an indictment of Christian Europe. (And why *did* all those German Christians follow Hitler? Could there be something fundamentally *wrong* with Christianity?) It also seemed to reveal that evil really does exist, something that progressive, right-thinking people no longer believed—and that systemic evil in a highly-industrialized country was worse than anyone could ever have imagined. Hilberg was one of this century's great prophetic intellectuals, who lived to do one thing: to write a book that nobody wanted to publish because it contained information about humankind that nobody wanted to know.

The press at Princeton University considered Hilberg's book for two weeks, but Hannah Arendt—who was reading the book in manuscript for Princeton—told Princeton not to publish it. Consciously or unconsciously, however, during this reading she took some of Hilberg's best ideas, and later used them and claimed them as her own. Arendt was a calculating—and sometimes scheming—veteran of international academic politics, and does not come out of this encounter looking very good. (Just as today her most famous ideas often do not, for one reason or another, convince.) No matter. Rightly or wrongly, Arendt and Hilberg have to be considered together, because they represent two necessary stages in understanding of the Holocaust. Hilberg tells the story of the Holocaust, and Arendt tries to interpret how it all arose from, and at the same time affected, the personalities of individual people involved. And she did so in terms of *the universality of human good and evil,* in that she saw cupidity and cowardice in Jews as well as aggression by Nazis, without losing sight of the fact that the Nazis were the proximate cause of the catastrophe that befell Europe and the Jews.

Hilberg, like Arendt, frequently outraged powerful Jewish interests. His most independent-minded decision was to support the research of Norman Finkelstein over others such as Daniel Goldhagen, who became a rock star of the neo-cons. Hilberg acted as he did because he thought Finkelstein was a better political scientist; but Finkelstein was also an outspoken defender of the Palestinians, which was one reason the Likudniks in Israel and the US neo-cons typically promoted Goldhagen. There were also objections from the Israelis that Hilberg was insufficiently respectful to the Zionist worldview. In a stunningly petty—but telling—act of political censorship, Yad Vashem, the home of the Israel's Holocaust Memorial, refused to let Raul Hilberg use its archives, because he wrote that certain attitudes of Eastern European Jews made them especially vulnerable to the tricks of the Nazis. So deeply was Yad Vashem awash in idealized Jewish victim-hood—so deeply, in other words, was Yad Vashem immersed in Zionist national mythology—that it denied its archives to the world's most reputable Holocaust scholar, Raul Hilberg, because he dared to suggest that Eastern European Jews were neither idealized victims nor Zionist *uebermenschen,* but imperfect human beings with recognizable human traits.

In retrospect, it is clear that the most troubling aspect of Hilberg's story was that it documented a depth of human evil that no one really wanted to see. The reaction of American intellectuals to this was interesting. Many Jewish intellectuals grasped what Hilberg's book implied about human nature, but few understood what this meant in a secular world in which religious precepts of evil are fading; fewer still grasped that the eclipse of God might cause traumatized Jews to worship the state of Israel. Christians took the position that Christian anti-Semitism was a big mistake, but couldn't explain why it somehow persisted generation after generation for 1600 years. Instead they allowed themselves to be guilt-tripped into supporting the crimes of Israel against the Palestinians, writing one more chapter in the long history of the wretched Christian addiction to redemptive violence. Other intellectuals viewed the evil uncovered by Hilberg's work as specific to European anti-Semitism, which made it seem less universal, and therefore less threatening. And as Hilberg quickly learned, Zionists sought to idealize Holocaust victims, the better to use them for propaganda purposes in the war of ideas in the Middle East, rather than acknowledging their humanity.

"It has taken me some time," the rebellious Hilberg wrote late in life, "to absorb what I should always have known, that in my whole approach to the study of the destruction of the Jews I was pitting myself against the main current of Jewish thought."[22] Put another way, his research did not always lend itself to the uses of the institutional leaders of American Jewry, when they used the Holocaust to score political points for the state of Israel. Hilberg, on the other hand, was primarily concerned with getting the history of the Holocaust right; and it is there that interested parties should begin. The significance for the Simon Wiesenthal Center and other Holocaust museums is this: it is impossible to get from two hours at a museum the information one can only get from a few days or weeks reading a first-rate written history.

Perhaps the most publicized Holocaust scholar is Daniel Goldhagen, whose book *Hitler's Willing Executioners* has been widely criticized for its many historical mistakes, but which many neo-cons and Zionists loved for its propaganda value. (Raul Hilberg wrote that Goldhagen was "totally wrong about everything,"[23] a strong criticism even by Hilberg's curmudgeonly standards.) Goldhagen saw the systemic evil of the Holocaust as unique to Germany, which neatly took care of the problem of good and evil. Neo-cons and Jewish leaders in the US tended to accept this idea, also embracing the idea that the Holocaust itself was unique, and therefore could not be compared to other historical events. But the evil itself was in no way unique. The Germans did what Christians had been doing to Jews for centuries, and simply used better technology and organization, and depended on the willingness of the world *at that time* to look the other way while Jews were gassed.

What is missing from Goldhagen and his supporters was the melancholy awareness that the capacity for evil, the desire to torture, humiliate and murder and then lie about it, is present in Jews as well as non-Jews. (And can be triggered very quickly by particular circumstances, as the Milgram 'Obedience Study' chillingly demonstrated.) The best critique of Goldhagen's thesis regarding German uniqueness is simply to look at what is happening in Israel/Palestine. Hitler and Stalin killed more people in modern times, but that fact does not mean that they invented murder, or that there will not be much more mass murder in the future. The fact that Hitler and Stalin engaged in more systemic evil than their rivals likewise does not mean they invented evil; they simply had the organization and the technology to do more of it—and they were aided by the indifference of the world to human rights. Like it or not, evil is universal—what happened in Germany could also happen in the US, and also in Israel. Jews, Germans and everybody else is capable of it. It is precisely for that reason that human rights must be universal.

11

Films, publishing and media can't seem to get enough Holocaust-themed material; the death camp has become the modern archetype of hell on earth, the black-and-white striped prisoner uniforms instantly recognizable to any film or TV viewer, leading to a kind of fascination with Nazi sadism that is very nearly pornographic—or at least voyeuristic. (Why pornographic? Because Nazis did it, so I can watch it without feeling complicit.) There are so many books published about the Hitler and the Nazis, or alluding to them, that one could easily fill a bookstore with just those published since 1985. It is an astonishing and somewhat demoralizing thing, but publishing insiders claim that the two most written-about historical figures are Jesus Christ and Adolph Hitler. What those two figures represent in the popular imagination is clear: salvation and pure evil. But the world is never that easy, since the Nuremburg Trials demonstrated rather conclusively that there were many degrees of complicity in Nazism's systemic evil.

But all the books, films, TV shows, conversation and information generally about the Nazi Holocaust has not improved our understanding of it very much—indeed, a kind of moral and emotional uncertainty principle has set in. Partly it is a problem of the human imagination, but partly also a problem of unconscious identification and comparison that sets it when people try to talk, write or think about the Nazi Holocaust. The underlying difficulty really lies not in the area of historical accuracy, but of human ownership of evil—a difficulty that is greatly complicated by the fact that modern secular society generally does not recognize the existence of evil.

We know that something *like* evil exists, something quite frightening and very dangerous—like the psychopathic serial killer who preys on single women, for example, or the sexual predator that organizes his life around the stalking of innocent children—but many are loath to call it evil, because people are not entirely convinced that evil isn't a religious concept. But evil *is* real; all kinds of people do evil things, and evil happens to all kinds of people, the irreligious as well as the religious. We just haven't yet gotten a clear idea of how to describe it as a psychological or perhaps naturalistic phenomenon, much less begun to find a way to stop it.

But this problem begins to disappear when we acknowledge that the capacity for evil exists in ourselves—and that in fact the capacity for evil is actually a part of our own personalities, and even part of the way the Self defines itself. This candid ownership of evil may be one of the few ways we can comprehend evil in secular, naturalistic terms, because it can be reduced to a narrative that we can tell in the story of our own lives, both the evil we have done and the evil done to us. Without question such a narrative is the best way to explore evil for most of us, because once we take ownership of the capacity for evil we are talking about the evil that interests us the most. Unfortunately, few people are willing to comprehend evil in their own personalities, greatly preferring to see it only in their perceived religious, political or geo-political opponents.

In fact, the closer our own aggression gets to our conscious minds, the more we feel compelled to see it in other people. That is one way we have for hiding evil, for pushing it back into the subconscious mind, by quickly accusing others of the same aggression we sense in ourselves. No credible moral philosophy, ethical system or moral code can be relevant in the twenty-first century that does not begin with an acknowledgement of one's own capacity for evil. That is—that *must* be—the starting point for a new moral psychology. Translated into political terms, when we look for evil we must look first in *our* country, *our* tribe, *our* race and class, *our* political interest group. Above all, we must see it in ourselves, although we do not have to speak about it publicly. But we do have to learn how to denounce evil publicly when we see it in our own tribe or country.

But simply to *know* about systemic evil is never enough—we must respond to it appropriately, which means we must learn to oppose it. When we see it in ourselves, we must work to weaken its power—that is no more than a natural function of the survival instinct. But such a moral compass is also necessary to organize the cautionary tale we are telling about our lives, about how we affect other people, because that must have a beginning, middle and end. Yet we do not yet know the end, whether we are personally able to avoid complicity in evil, or not. All we can say is that it is a process in the service of which we must exert our maximum effort, because it is linked to our feeling of authenticity as persons; and once we connect our identities to our moral psychology, we are ready to learn how to deconstruct it. It begins by learning how one recognizes evil to keep from being influenced by it, which invariably takes us back to out own capacity for evil. That's really a rather simple transaction: *To the extent that we recognize evil in our personalities, to just that extent can we try not to act on it.*

But how does one put this kind of personal ownership of evil in a Holocaust museum?

It might help if the people who set the thing up acknowledged their own capacity for evil, but the Simon Wiesenthal Center is unlikely to do that—the entire premise of their existence is that they are right, and everybody else is wrong. Furthermore, such personal ownership of evil would no doubt remind people that the SWC supports Israeli apartheid, and it might also remind them of the Wiesenthal Center's extensive record of over-the-top lying. Setting this embarrassing set of facts aside for a moment, how *would* one convince the garage mechanic, the beautician, and the kindergarten teacher that they are capable of the worst kinds of evil, if they got into the wrong situation? There isn't a lot of cultural support for the idea of the omnipresence of evil, except among evangelical Christians; but they feel no need to advocate against evil, whether in themselves or in the world, because it can all be redeemed retroactively by Jesus. In short, you cannot get personal ownership of evil in most museums, for the same reason that you can't get ownership of evil anywhere else.

Again, the best way to learn from the Nazi Holocaust is to learn about the people who *opposed* the Holocaust—people who hid Jews, Jews that fought back, people that organized escapes of Jews, resistance figures that arranged to be smuggled into and out of death camps, and so forth. In order to understand the moral dimension of the Holocaust you must, in other words, study the motives and personalities of people who are not completely different from oneself, but who yet *fought* the Holocaust. If you are Jewish, you must be prepared to study the motives of non-Jews that tried to overthrow Hitler, and vice versa. And if you study the motives of the perpetrators, you must be prepared to see that part of yourself that would be tempted to go along with the evil—you must see, for example, the immature, cranky idealist that might respond to the grandiose screaming of a Hitler. Everybody has a Nazi and an anti-Nazi in them. They're both in there. One must own both, if one wishes to act on the anti-Nazi rather than the Nazi.

12

Understanding the Holocaust is a dialectical process in which the universal nature of evil is always acknowledged, but the universal possibility of good is likewise possible. You must understand the necessity of making a moral choice, while refusing to minimize the difficulty of that choice—and you must learn from the motivations and emotions of those who made the right choices. Otherwise a Holocaust museum is simply studying the repetition of organized violence, which is just as likely to result in a fascination with evil as a determination to oppose it. But studying the courageous, often difficult individuals that risked their lives resisting the Nazis, anti-Semitism and the Holocaust, is an intrinsically fascinating project, since the love of justice is both emotionally and intellectually engaging. The motives and backgrounds of such people are remarkably varied, and have the added quality of being highly inspirational.

But the Simon Wiesenthal Center will almost surely never build a museum celebrating those who fought Hitler, or those who tried to stop Nazi genocide. For one thing, such people would probably include more non-Jews than Jews, since in World War Two most Jews were in hiding or on the run. That would never do, since the main purpose of the Wiesenthal Center is to stimulate religious nationalism and promote uncritical support for Israel. Furthermore, the Wiesenthal Center has a marked preference for portraying Jews as victims, or potential victims, rather than protagonists.

In Israel, non-Jews that actively opposed the Holocaust are safely ghettoized as "righteous Gentiles," an interesting phrase that prevents us from seeing Jews and non-Jews as people cooperating together to combat anti-Semitism. (It's also a phrase that manages to suggest that Gentiles are less likely to be righteous than Jews.) Nor is the SWC likely to talk much about the many other people that perished with the Jews in the gas chambers, because they were Roma, intellectuals, Serbs, socialists and communists, the developmentally delayed and the mentally ill.[24] This exclusive focus on Jewish deaths out of the many millions that reportedly perished in the gas chambers, or that were murdered by the Nazis in other ways, handily plays into the right-wing Zionist hard-sell of anti-Semitism as a uniquely virulent evil that can only by deterred by an armed Jewish state that has nuclear weapons and brutalizes Palestinians.

Nor is the Wiesenthal Center likely to build a museum to memorialize the history of *all* genocides. That would place the Holocaust in a continuum of radical evil proceeding and following Hitler, thereby minimizing the distinctive and allegedly unique nature of the Nazi Holocaust. It would show how the Armenian genocide prefigured the Nazi Holocaust, and how it gave Hitler encouragement to proceed with the Final Solution. ("Who remembers the Armenians?" Hitler reportedly said before launching his *Endloesung*.) Likewise it would feature the genocides in Cambodia, Bosnia, Bangladesh and Rwanda, and the people who opposed them and worked to arouse world opinion against them—but again, that would take the focus away from Jewish suffering.

That puts off the day when people start to examine seriously the precursors of genocide, because they will find them strikingly similar—mass trauma, a national mythology of persecution and victim status, a craving for extreme or apocalyptic solutions, and steadily escalating waves of organized public hate and violence.

The study of genocide as a universal rather than singular phenomenon is something that must happen, not least because many of the most telling characteristics of systemic evil begin before the genocide begins. Those signs began to appear early in the revival of Serbian nationalism before the Bosnia genocide, for example, and they also appeared decades before the genocide in Rwanda; and they are now starting to appear in Israel. Perhaps that is one reason for the genocide denial maintained for years by the Israeli government and its proxies regarding the Turkish genocide of the Armenians. (Now that Israel and Turkey has fallen out, the Israelis are only too happy to acknowledge that Turkey committed genocide against the Armenians.)

Israel's position for decades was that the Armenian genocide wasn't really genocide, but a "tragedy" that somehow didn't deserve the "genocide" label. The reason usually given at one time was that Israel didn't want to offend Turkey, until recently its only ally in the Muslim-majority countries; but another huge reason, as most Israeli progressives freely acknowledged, was that it detracted from the Israeli conception of the Nazi genocide as being the most important because it had the most victims. Therefore everybody else's genocide had to be belittled, because it didn't have enough victims. If someone you loved perished in a genocide, whether in Turkey, Africa, Cambodia, Bangladesh or Europe, the final body count probably makes little difference to you—it's that precious family member that died, and the circumstances under which they died, that is probably important to you, and rightfully so. But in the patriarchal world of Israeli genocide denial, size matters.

In fact, it's the *only* thing that matters, since the object is all too often not to understand or stop evil, but rather to get something out of it: fund-raising, political advantage and uncritical support of whatever political party has gotten itself into power in Israel. A far better goal would be to empower people confronted by evil, by helping them identify with people who have found the strength to oppose it. What would a museum look and feel like that invokes an *opposition* to evil, rather than invoking the evil itself?

13

On a June day in Berlin in June 1990, I stood in the courtyard of the Bendlerblock, which is now a museum to the *Widerstand*, the German resistance to Hitler. A few feet away from where I was standing, four anti-Nazi army officers had been shot dead by a hastily-assembled firing squad in the early morning of July twenty-first, 1944. They had just tried to kill Hitler and overthrow his Nazi government—in fact the conspirators had planned their anti-Nazi coup in this very same building, working in telephone communication with a few thousand others across Europe. Today the Bendlerblock is a museum to honor the *Widerstand,* not just the officers of the July 20 attempt to overthrown Hitler, but a memorial to all the German men and women that resisted and tried to defeat Hitler, many of whom gave their lives. The memorial certainly isn't lacking in gritty historical detail; as I stood near the spot where the leader of the coup attempt, Claus von Stauffenberg, had been shot with three other anti-Nazi officers, I noticed a faint stain of what looked like blood on the wall.

Yet the overwhelming sense of the place was not of defeat but of an intense celebration of the moral imagination. The entire museum is devoted to telling the stories of people who knew evil when they saw it, and refused to become willing victims or Hitler's willing executioners either; and in most cases made good their insight by acting against the evil they saw. Many of them died at the hands of the Nazis, but in reading their words and seeing their faces it is impossible not to feel a sense of overwhelming victory.

As I stood there that day in June, I found myself wondering, "How is this possible? How is it possible that those who tried and failed to overthrow Hitler still manage to impart such intense hope and victory?" Because they show us, in their words and deeds, that it is always possible to fight the good fight against tyranny and sadism no matter how hopeless the situation may seem. They show us that even in hell, evil cannot replicate itself in the lives of those that have found a way to deconstruct its power.

Outside the Bendlerblock, on what is now called Stauffenbergstrasse, busloads of students of all ages, from children to young adults, arrived to be taken through the museum. Inside there were many rooms divided up into the various kinds of resistance to Hitler: the Left resistance, the Jewish resistance, the intellectuals' resistance, the student movement against Hitler, the labor resistance, and so forth. There was a noticeable feeling of exhilaration in the air—you can't read and talk about such lives without feeling uplifted—and the feeling was contagious. One read story after story of people who saw an overwhelming challenge, and somehow met that challenge.

As I continued to walk through the exhibits, I felt there was something about the presentations that inspired a profound exhilaration, not unmixed with melancholy, perhaps, but still unmistakably a kind of joy. Here one was in direct communication with the best that was in humankind—and that, I freely admit, was a feeling I never would have associated with a museum. The exhibits gathered here weren't only about the aristocratic Stauffenberg and his followers, who came rather late to the German resistance and who had their own reasons for wanting to kill Hitler. There were hundreds of even more interesting people who, each in their own way, fought the Nazi madness; and in so doing, demonstrated for all time that even under totalitarian conditions it is possible to know evil and call it out.

For me the most interesting figures of all have always been Hans and Sophie Scholl and their comrades of the White Rose in Munich—incredibly brave young people, most of them, many driven by Catholic idealism, but others simply appalled at the brutality of Hitler and the criminality of the war that he was waging. The White Rose had received reports of the campaign to destroy European Jewry, as well as reliable accounts of the atrocities against the Poles and Russians. They tried to rally the German people against these inhuman acts with leaflets of a surpassing beauty, which even today are taught in the classroom as stunning examples of discursive writing. It is no wonder that allied planes dropped hundreds of thousands of these leaflets on Germany as the war wound down. The passionate words they wrote, which continued to touch hearts and change lives long after the White Rose activists had been murdered by the Gestapo, were better than any propaganda could ever be, because they were an argument not for politics but for decency. After all these years, the leaflets of the White Rose still speak directly to the heart.

Even the aristocratic Stauffenberg himself is compelling—he rebelled knowing that he probably wouldn't succeed in overthrowing Hitler, but acted anyway so that in the future young Germans would have someone to look up to. That's hard for many Americans to understand ("How can he be a hero if he didn't succeed?"); but Stauffenberg knew well that the young that came after him would need concrete examples of Germans that stood against Nazi totalitarianism—indeed, the dashing Stauffenberg is a perennial favorite of those that study the *Widerstand*, and not just in Germany.

What made the exhibits in this museum special, in addition to the intelligent use of text and photos, was that the museum was located in the very heart of what had once been a Nazi bureaucracy—and the exhibits celebrated the lives of people that had conspired in this same building to bring that Nazi bureaucracy down. The layers of irony were breathtaking and almost a bit too much—one was dizzy, being so close to the rooms and halls where so much murderous Nazi drama was acted out; not to mention the halls in which the doomed attempt to overthrow Hitler was acted out; and yet in reading the texts and viewing the photos that are now situated inside it, one came to feel the desperate hope of the conspirators as they met in the very belly of the Nazi horror.

I spent a long day taking in the exhibits, the school-children around me chattering like birds, docents and teachers explaining and answering questions, people conversing quietly among themselves, all the time under the pictures of people who had faced evil and succeeded in defeating it, at least in their hearts. You could see the power of it in the way in which the people some forty-five years later looked up at their faces and read their words; you could see it in the way they nodded, the way they smiled and talked softly to each other.

Why should one honor Stauffenberg or the White Rose, when they did not succeed in overthrowing Hitler? Why honor failure, however honorable its intent? To paraphrase Brecht, the people who ask this question have not yet heard the terrible news. They do not yet understand the depth of the moral crisis we are in, and perhaps choose not to. Hitler's system was totalitarianism based on unremitting aggression, and the fact that there were Germans who could break the bonds of the sheer trauma that Hitler was imposing on Germany, Europe and the world—that they could deconstruct it while living at the belly of it—means there is hope for humanity, that it is not necessary for humankind to destroy itself. (Whether humanity will do so anyway is a separate issue.) And that is where we must begin, in that still, small space of the heart, where we learn to resist the weight of organized evil used by governments to bond us to further evil.

That the German *Widerstand* existed at all tells us that there is no government edict, no national consensus and no trauma powerful enough to take away *your* conscience or *my* conscience completely, even as it reduces millions of others to moral autism. The fact that some ordinary people in the Third Reich could see through Hitler and the trauma he created, and still had the will and courage to act against him, creates the possibility—indeed, the likelihood—that you and I might see evil when we encounter it. That is the hope they bequeath us. (How we deconstruct that evil, and act out our own appropriate defiance of it, is a separate issue, one that we will address in a later book.)

Interestingly, teaching about those who *resisted* evil is also the best strategy for teaching Americans—especially American schoolchildren—about slavery. If the Nazi holocaust is the nightmare of Germans and Jews, so slavery is America's Original Sin; and so likewise are Americans still haunted by it, to the extent that many Americans (both white and African-American) still cannot fully deconstruct the effects of racial segregation in their personalities, especially in the South. Slavery must be taught in the schools if Americans are to understand who we are, who we were, and who we want to become. But mind-numbing recitals of the tormenting of slaves by sadistic slave-owners can engender trauma, guilt and anger, especially among children; and to put on them the freight of that trauma is unfair, and could demoralize and bond them to new forms of systemic evil. We must be careful how we teach about American slavery—just as we must be thoughtful about the way we teach the Holocaust.

If you do not think the past evil of slavery and racial segregation cannot bond people to present evil, consider the case of William Faulkner. When he was a child, he was taken to a Negro graveyard by his father. "Once we *owned* these people," his father said, pointing to the graves. The traumatizing effect of this knowledge, and the deliberately abrasive way it was intruded upon his consciousness by a trusted parent, can hardly be overstated. If you once *owned* the dead, and you are made aware of that by a parent, you are being bonded—however little the parent may understand what he is doing—to a system of racial, class and regional oppression. One could say that Faulkner was forever imprisoned by the past; but the bond that pulled him backwards into that half-remembered, half-hallucinated past was the sense of an evil that was stronger than life *or* death; and the traumatizing weight of that perception was placed upon him by the powerful example and rhetoric of similarly-burdened adults in the Old South.

It is not surprising, then, that he ended up identifying with that powerful evil called racial segregation, because it was the most powerful thing in his world; and even as he struggled to escape from it, even as he knew its essential vulgarity, that social system became the standard for the strongest thoughts and feelings and rhetorical devices that defined him as a writer.

Even very young students *can* and *will* understand slavery and racial segregation, if the teaching of it concentrates on the exciting lives of those who *resisted* it. In fact, it all becomes clear to children when they study the lives of people who decided *against* slavery. That is, in fact, one primary goal of public education, to educate free people in the shared rights and responsibilities of democracy by teaching them alternatives to social injustice—and the best way to do that is to learn about Americans that have already chosen such alternatives. Otherwise sensitive children studying slavery can easily be left with the hopeless feeling that the world's evil is too strong to oppose. The excessive identification with the victim can be as bad as identifying with the perpetrator, because it often amounts to the same thing. When one identifies too much with a victim, one is also internalizing the power of the system that brought him down—which is why it is important to promote identification *with people who refuse to be either victims or executioners.* Such people insist on being protagonists in the story of their lives. It is something we want young people to learn.

These things I thought as I walked through the Bendlerblock on that June day of 1990.

I went out in the courtyard of the museum and immediately fell in with a group of young people, mainly Germans and a couple of British students, who were talking with great emotion about what they had seen in the museum. I have forgotten who brought it up, but at some point we found ourselves deep in a discussion about the White Rose. The Germans were delighted, and mildly surprised that an American would know about such German culture heroes, and I answered them in English and my *gebrochenes* Deutsch. The daylight was starting to fade, and still we talked. Our conversation turned inevitably from the history of resistance to Hitler by the *Widerstand* to the miracle that was happening down the road a mile or two from where we stood: students were tearing, tearing, tearing down ever-larger chunks of concrete from the Berlin Wall, as the last great imperial tyranny in Europe came crashing down, down, down.

A punk-rock singer had sung a concert a week before while standing on top of the Wall (my memory wants to believe that it was Nina Hagen, but it might have been someone else), shaking her backside at the *Stasis* and wearing a garter belt that would have made Dietrich blush. You could already sneak across the Wall if you were careful, and I had been doing it every night for a week—if you saw any *Volkspolizei* a bribe would usually suffice to head them off. Each night families would risk their lives sneaking over to the West in the subways, wading through the dirty water with goofy smiles on their faces, carrying their belongings in plastic bags. The night before, in East Berlin, I had gone with a group of East German civilians through a hole in the Wall to a watchtower abandoned by the *Volkspolizei*, and watched as they wordlessly, methodically, and with great attention to their task dismantled every gun emplacement in the watchtower.

Now I stood in the courtyard of the Bendlerblock, a few feet away from where Stauffenberg had shouted his last contested words of defiance before being shot by a Nazi firing squad. There was a rock band playing by the Berlin Wall, not far from Checkpoint Charley; and the small group of us standing there could hear each roar of the crowd as another slab of the wall came crashing down. We could see the Brandenburg Gate clearly on our right, like some monumental hallucination from the past—and we heard, as if in ethereal counterpoint, the shouts of young people no more than a mile away tearing down the remnants of Soviet totalitarianism. It will seem incredible to one who has not felt such a wild and intoxicating hope, but at that moment it felt as though the incandescent spirit of the White Rose had once more arisen, and again ignited the hearts of Europe, pulling it and the world forward in an unseen but unstoppable current, relentlessly sweeping its yearning people by the millions into democracy and social justice, and the freedom of the coming century.

It was sweet to be alive.

14

Building a museum to the *experience* of the Holocaust, rather than to those that opposed it, is unconscionable, particularly when there are people who seek to profit from it. One might as well build a museum to serial rapists. A similarly negative function is served by Claude Lanzmann's nine-hour 1985 film, *Shoah*. But wait—what about all those intellectuals that say that *Shoah* is a breakthrough of the moral imagination, not to mention human consciousness itself? Claude Lanzmann is a darling of the French Left, partly because of his participation in the Resistance during World War Two, and partly his association with Jean-Paul Sartre and other French intellectuals. But his film is hardly a breakthrough documentary, since it is strategically and dishonestly composed to misrepresent what really happened during the Holocaust. To make a particular political point Lanzmann distorts some important facts, including the testimony of his main informant.

Lanzmann interviews people who were alive during the Holocaust, and divides up those he interviews about the Holocaust into three archetypes: Perpetrators, Bystanders and Survivors. This trilogy was first presented by Raul Hilberg, who was trying to demonstrate how the Holocaust happened—and indeed, most people fell into those three categories. But there was more to the story, as there always is. In every moral disaster, there are always some that resist, even if they do not succeed in stopping evil; and in order to prevent the next moral disaster, we must study the motivation of that minority in order to identify what motivates them. Neither Hilberg nor Lanzmann recognized this to any significant degree, and in Lanzmann's film—since it is narrative art—it gradually becomes a glaring omission that robs his marathon film of passion and moral imagination.

That was unfortunate, because Lanzmann knew better. One of

the key people Lanzmann interviewed in the film was a man named Jan Karski, who knew more about the day-to-day operations of Auschwitz than almost any living person at the time that Lanzmann made his film. But Karski had not been a perpetrator, bystander or a survivor—Jan Karski repeatedly risked his life in an effort to stop the Holocaust, and he was in a position to make a difference. But these facts didn't fit well with Lanzmann's need to present the Holocaust in a particular way; so he simply cut all evidence of Karski's resistance activities out of the film—after promising Karski he'd leave it in.

In 1940, Karski, an important member of the underground Polish resistance, organized a courier service between the resistance and the Polish Government in Exile. He was captured and tortured by the Gestapo, but survived. In 1942 he was twice smuggled into the Warsaw Ghetto, and then sent to Britain to testify to the mass extermination of Jews by the Nazis. He first reported to Polish Prime Minister-in-Exile Wladyslaw Sikorski, and then to officials of the British and American governments, providing all with extensive microfilm evidence of what was happening to the Jews. The Polish Foreign Minister of the Government-in-Exile then circulated a letter to allied governments called *The mass extermination of Jews in German occupied Poland*, published in pamphlet form in English, perhaps the first full report of Hitler's genocide against the Jews. Karski gave a detailed report to Prime Minister Anthony Eden, and personally reported on Hitler's extermination of Jews twice to US President Roosevelt. In the US he spoke with Cornell Hull, Stephen Wise and Felix Frankfurter, the latter of whom refused to believe what Karski was telling him about the gas chambers. Karski angrily denounced the film *Shoah*, but the true story of Jan Karski and his extensive efforts to alert the world to the *Shoah* can be read in *Karski: How One Man Tried to Stop the Holocaust*, by Thomas Wood and Stanlislaw M. Jankowski.

The world turned its back on the Jews, but not the whole

world. In every moral catastrophe, I repeat, there are always heroes. So who are we going to study, the heroes or those that did nothing? Lanzmann neatly evades that question out of consideration by simply ignoring—that is, suppressing—evidence of resistance to Hitler's Final Solution. Thus his version of the Holocaust is a tedious, self-congratulatory over-simplification dressed up as *avant-garde* profundity, at the center of which there is no moral conflict because the behavior of everybody represented is completely predictable. But it fits well into the rightwing Zionist narrative, because if nobody did anything to resist the Holocaust the only way to stop it the next time is through an armed Jewish state with nuclear weapons.

And it is in that way that the film is being used today. Pauline Kael was close to the truth when she said, "the heart of [Lanzmann's] obsession appears to be to show you that the Gentiles will do it again to the Jews if they get the chance."[25] Indeed, one could see how and why she might think that, even if that wasn't Lanzmann's intention at first, because his telling of the story plays up the world's indifference to what the Nazis were doing, while he systematically suppresses the fact that some people resisted the Nazis. And that's how it's being used by neo-cons and rightwing Zionists today, to suggest the inevitability of the Holocaust by ignoring evidence of those that opposed it. There was a fair amount of hoopla about the re-release of *Shoah* from cultural forces associated with the neo-cons and the Israel Lobby, but sooner or later the truth about Lanzmann's distortions of Karski's testimony will see the light of day. Given the overwhelming nature of Nazi evil, isn't it important to know about those that resisted it? But the uncritical supporters of Israel are not interested in considering that point.

And what are we to make of Hannah Arendt's supposedly earth-shaking study of Nazi evil in *Eichmann in Jerusalem: a Report on the Banality of Evil*? One admires Hannah Arendt for her willingness to stand up to conservative elements in the US Jewish establishment, in the process creating some space for independent discussion of systemic evil in the Holocaust. But Arendt's ideas were never particularly persuasive as an explanation of evil. Her "banality of evil" theory worked perfectly to explain the motives and rationalizations of opportunists, but did little to explain why so many Nazis risked life and fortune—as Eichmann himself did toward the end, especially in Hungary—to act out the insanity of genocide. In fact, Arendt's archetypical flunky who is just following orders would not have pursued a defense so self-exculpatory when caught, as Eichmann did in Jerusalem, if he didn't realize how evil his work had been. (A good soldier-bureaucrat who was "just following orders" wouldn't have bothered to present a defense, but would have given up his life without a murmur, secure in his ultimate loyalty to the Fuehrer.)

In the end, banality just doesn't play as either a description or an explanation of evil. What about all the evidence that Eichmann hated Jews, at least partly because he was called "the little Jew" as a child? (Eichmann looked stereotypically Jewish both as a child and a balding old man.) And what about the statements made by Eichmann about his loathing of Jews? Arendt presents herself as a fount of paradox and profundity, and to be sure her theory is original, but finally most of her ideas are simply too lightweight to fly—and those that do, sadly, seem mainly lifted (perhaps consciously, perhaps unconsciously) from her surreptitious first reading in manuscript of Raul Hilberg's monumental work on the Holocaust.

Typical of Arendt's naiveté is the way she makes a big deal about the findings of the six Israeli psychiatrists that talked to Eichmann that he was "normal." But of *course* he acted and talked normal when the shrinks talked to him—he had no reason *not* to act normal. Arendt also marvels at what a considerate, thoughtful and altogether wonderful father and husband Eichmann was. But Eichmann was not alone in that—in fact the literature of Nazi death camp operators, officers and officials is full of stories about what great parents and spouses they were. But of *course* they were all wonderful family members, because they discharged all their aggression at work. Killing thousands in their day jobs, they had no need or energy left to beat up their wives and children—to moonlight, one might say—after a hard day's work.

After a long day killing Jews, Roma, leftists, the insane and the developmentally delayed, they could come home and treat the vexations of wife and *kinder* with all the serenity of Little Flower. These were criminals, but their specialty was a strict and extremely self-disciplined emotional division of labor, for which their participation in Nazi military organizations had been excellent training. Their working lives gave them a perfect opportunity to act out the enormous aggression they felt, leaving them kind, thoughtful and thoroughly pleasant people afterwards. Their military orientation gave them the ability to act out their sadism at work, with little or no leftover or underlying aggression afterwards.

15

So why is the Holocaust so difficult to comprehend, and why can't we even begin to agree on what it means? Because the Holocaust is not history, it is still happening—it drives thought and behavior in the present moment. As Faulkner said of the weight of racial segregation, "The past is never dead. It isn't even past." Evil enters the world through specific institutions and crimes, then it takes on an emotional life separate from history, because it isn't finished with us, and won't be until we figure out how we can deconstruct its negative effects on us. Until then, it changes us by engaging us on an emotional level. Don't fool yourself, reader, as you read about the Holocaust, don't think that you are not being affected by the information being discussed—evil sometimes has the power to impose emotional orientations on your psyche when you least expect it. Evil does not have a *physical* existence separate from human emotion and behavior; but since we still do not understand it completely, it seems oddly transcendent and somehow separate from us, as though it is attacking us from beyond ourselves.

But this does not make the Holocaust something inexplicable, nor is a retreat into mysticism justifiable. As Yehuda Bauer has observed, if the Holocaust was carried out by human beings, human beings can figure out why it happened. (The present writer would add: *we can also figure out how to abolish its malignant influence in the present moment.*) But the Holocaust has a tremendous ability to corrupt people, and especially it has the ability to corrupt people who want to use it to make money, or use its trauma to get political power—and that in turn corrupts many more, because they dare not see, talk or think about what is happening.

Norman Finkelstein's *The Holocaust Industry* caused a storm of outrage precisely because he demonstrated how the Holocaust had corrupted Jews who discovered that they could make enormous amounts of money from it—in some case billions of dollars, which quickly went into their personal projects, often Zionist projects in Israel and America, and also into their own overblown salaries and outrageous legal fees. Other ambitious men discovered that the Holocaust could be used to get political power. Also corrupted were those who went along for the ride, who threw away their agency as free human beings capable of choosing between good and evil, and in the process threw away a prime Jewish value—and one of the most precious possessions of humankind—freedom of moral choice. That's how the spiritual contagion was spread, that's how the evil of the Holocaust replicated itself in this situation.

And the money made by the crooks mentioned in *The Holocaust Industry*—money actually made *from* the Holocaust by manipulation of Jewish suffering for private gain—that money was often used to commit further crimes against the Palestinian people, once Holocaust guilt and trauma was cashed in and reinvested in Israeli apartheid. The reason why humanity must deconstruct the systemic evil of the twentieth century is not just to understand the Holocaust, but to free us from its power over our lives. Auschwitz was liberated in 1945, but we have not yet been liberated from Auschwitz.

16

Of course, clichés abound, not least because of a certain queasy fascination with Hitler and the Nazis, which has become for many an ongoing guilty pleasure. Trivializing a terrible thing, it turns out, is probably an instinctive defense against psychological damage by it. (Of course humor is a better defense, the classic example being the movie version of *The Producers*, but few have the comic genius of a Mel Brooks.) If a fascination with Nazism is a kind of pornography, as many have suggested, one could credibly question whether people obsessed by Nazis are internalizing Nazi sadism, or compensating themselves for previously internalized aggression. (The difference would probably revolve around the extent to which the aggression is connected to national myths that people are likely to act on.)

An interesting outgrowth of this fascination is "Godwin's Law," a mock-serious invention of online icon Mike Godwin, also known as Godwin's Rule of Nazi Analogies: "As an online discussion grows longer, the probability of a comparison involving Nazis or Hitler approaches 1."[26] The moral collapse that occurred in Germany under Hitler contains too much useful information about how people can be manipulated by lies and violence for people not to use it as a metaphor—but for just that reason, Godwin and others might point out, it is important to reject invalid comparisons to Hitler and to Nazi Germany.

But where do the invalid comparisons to Hitler and the Nazis come from? They come from the fact that people can't stop talking and thinking about Nazis. People find Nazis fascinating—but refuse to look at, or think about, the Nazi inside their own personalities; and as a result end up feeling vaguely guilty about it without knowing why. The classic essay about this guilty pleasure is Susan Sontag's *Fascinating Fascism*, which makes the point that liberal intellectuals are just as obsessed with

Nazism as conservatives. (The liberal fascination arises not from death-worship, as Sontag surmises, but because liberals are fascinated by the explicit nature of Nazi aggression.) The public mania for Nazis is also well-known to television's History Channel, which at one time ran so much footage involving the Third Reich that it was known to many as the "Hitler Channel." The rightwing Tea Party movement in the US compared their political foes to Nazis so often that comedian Jon Stewart suggested a "million moderate march" in which political moderates would hold signs that say, "I don't agree with you, but I'm pretty sure you're not Hitler."

In Germany, on the other hand, people go out of their way *not* to bring up the *Hitlerzeit* unless absolutely necessary. The definitive comment on this version of the Nazi hysteria came, appropriately enough, from a comedian. It was advanced by the satirical genius Harald Schmidt, who sometimes appears on his TV show in Germany costumed as Adolph Hitler. When the German film *Der Untergang* (Downfall) came out, with Bruno Ganz playing Hitler, Schmidt did a skit in which he portrayed Hitler bitterly castigating Ganz for his bad acting. There was an immediate public uproar directed against Schmidt's alleged bad taste; Schmidt promptly upped the ante on the air by promoting a mock device called the Nazometer, a highly sensitive screening apparatus that would monitor polite conversation and everyday German speech.

This interesting device would give off a warning alarm at seemingly innocuous words such as "Autobahn" or "Eva," because such words might trigger certain associations with the Third Reich. Once such associations were made, whether conscious or unconscious, they might release every kind of negative or threatening emotion, setting loose torrents of conflicted feelings and threatening social chaos.[27]

17

Avraham Burg, a former speaker of the Israeli Knesset, addresses the weight of the Holocaust on Israeli sensibilities in his book, *The Holocaust is Over, We Must Rise from its Ashes,* a harrowing and unusually honest examination of Israel's national obsession. For much of the time he was working on his book, Burg's working title was *Hitler Won,* the premise being that Israeli and American Jews have so completely internalized everything having to do with the Holocaust—with almost daily public references to it in Israel—that they have given Hitler the ultimate victory.

In the "Introduction" to the English-language edition of his book, Burg tells of being accosted by an older man in Israel. It was a few days after the book appeared, and Burg was on the street, and the following exchange occurred:

"Burg, I'm very angry with you!"

"Why?" I asked.

"Because of what you wrote."

"And what did I write?"

"You wrote against the Holocaust!"

"And you?" I wondered aloud, "would you write in support of the Holocaust?"[28]

The exchange ended in silence: the old man walked away. His observation that Burg wrote "against" the Holocaust is indicative of the extent to which he identified with the Holocaust—not a very positive thing to identify with, one would think, but that is exactly the problem. It is also interesting that he had no reply to Burg's rejoinder, and that he declined to continue the conversation. One senses that he had caught a glimpse of something in himself that he did not wish to think about.

Avraham Burg's father was from Germany, and both he and Burg's mother (a survivor of the Hebron massacre of 1929) worked hard not to let trauma burden their children. "The secret language between them was Heine's German," Burg writes rather mysteriously, "not the Holocaust German of the survivors." (But what exactly is *Holocaust* German? Did his parents create a romanticized, a-historical and perhaps lost world of nineteenth-century High German culture to block out the brutality of the twentieth-century world?) Burg wonders at certain points in his narrative if his parents were somehow able to use family life to "erase" their own traumata—stressful for the parents, one would imagine, but a more responsible expedient, one must say, than passing it on to the children.

"The Shoah industry that would develop in Israel in later years would be foreign to me," Burg writes, adding that as a child he "was never exposed, emotionally or practically, to 'Shoahization,' though this cultural movement has become second nature to us Israelis." (Burg usually uses the Hebrew word Shoah for the Nazi Holocaust.) This lack of conscious or unconscious Shoah-indoctrination was important: "To many, the Shoah was and will forever be an incurable wound. To others, the Shoah is the nucleus of their identity." And for many others, one must say, the wound and the identity are the same thing.

Burg sees a troubling but irreducible connection between Germany and Israel. Much of that came from his father, who idealized the intellectual penetration and creativity of the German-Jewish ethos. "My father was warm, his love was inexhaustible, but something of the German tradition was at the foundation of all our lives, and since then we have been yearning for the extraordinary culture that was destroyed forever. Germany committed suicide—killing herself and us—and significant parts of our Jewish identity perished in smoke, together with the cultural models to which we could and should subscribe."[29]

Burg's idea that Germany committed suicide is correct—without its Jews, German *kultur* is living on its capital, as philosopher Walter Kaufman long ago pointed out. But Burg understands other troubling connections: many of the ideas of Zionism are to some extent derived from German nationalism, and German imperialism—that is, from the worst rather than the best parts of the German ethos. And it was the rise of Hitler that kicked off the momentum for the creation of Israel in the generation of survivors in Europe after 1945. Most disturbing of all, Burg also believes that Israel is starting to resemble Weimer Germany, with the same extremes, the same worship of victim status, and the same corruption and weird attraction to aggression and violent rhetoric.

"The Shoah and the atrocities that the Nazis committed against us are an inseparable part of the active Israeli present," Burg asserts, adding a page later: "Since those [Nazi] days in Germany, we have been holding on painfully to the little that we have, not letting go. We hold the memories and the traumas and they do not leave us. We cling to the tragedy and the tragedy becomes our justification for everything."[30]

Why does a trauma that occurred sixty years ago actually *grow* in its power to affect behavior after sixty years? Partly because the further it is removed from the events that caused it, the less we understand about it—the more outrageous it becomes, the more of an affront to our cognition, the more it overwhelms us with its increasingly inexplicable horror. (And the more removed we are from it, the less we can see the Nazi in ourselves.) At the same time we look to it to give up some secret about the nature of things, which is a big mistake—only thoughtful human beings can give meaning to their trauma, invariably in retrospect, by unraveling the worst aspects of trauma's after-effects. Trauma by itself does not have the ability to guide or to enlighten, but can only overwhelm. Trauma cannot, in other words, deconstruct itself. Only the traumatized themselves can do that.

In Israel trans-generational (or multi-generational) trauma is endemic—but that is to a very large extent because it is encouraged by the government and the political class. "One day my daughter came home from her high school in Jerusalem," Burg writes. 'Today,' she said, "we had a lesson to prepare us for the trip to Poland. Over our family dinner, I asked her about the lesson. 'The school principal said we are all Shoah survivors,' she replied. Eventually she and her friends, in what has become the custom for many Israeli teenagers, traveled to Poland and returned as changed Israelis. Only my youngest son, Noam, did not join the trend. He, like me, does not want to base his Israeli, Jewish, and universal identity on the worst trauma in human experience."[31]

But the rightwing leaders of Israel wants to make sure that young people *do* base their identity on "the worst trauma in human experience," because they want to *use* that trauma—that is why donors pay millions to support these trips to Auschwitz, and why they are encouraged so intensively in Israel's schools. Adolescents hardly able to comprehend their own bodies, much less the rise of fascism in Europe, are the subjects of this indoctrination; and because they are so young, they are easy prey, which includes being traumatized by the Holocaust when they are brought to where it originally happened and subjected to the speeches of rightwing Zionists inside the walls of the death camps. Thus the state can use their disorientation (and their trauma) to indoctrinate them. There is plenty of state *apparatchiks* present on these little jaunts to Auschwitz, to tell the teenagers what to feel and what to think. And what they tell them is that Auschwitz could very well happen again, if they aren't willing to join the army and do what the state tells them to do. The only way to live in a world with Auschwitz is to become a good citizen-soldier—a loyal, unquestioning servant of the Israeli state.

No, these rightwing teachers and security specialists, anxious to indoctrinate with the Zionist ethos, will not encourage their students to love and respect universal human rights. Instead they will reiterate the trauma of the Holocaust to insist, repeatedly and insistently, that the world hates them because they are Jews, that Jews can trust nobody, and that anyone that criticizes Israel is an anti-Semite. To survive, they must defeat Arabs in general and Palestinians in particular, whom the Liked government portrays as simple continuations of the Nazi menace without any kind of self-interest or intentionality whatsoever—they are simply evil *golem* that arose solely to hate Jews. (Pity the poor Palestinians that must go through check-points manned by teenage soldiers indoctrinated at Auschwitz on these little expeditions to the heart of darkness.)

Burg's Israel has a cult-like fixation on trauma and aggression: "In Israel I live in one language, that of tensions and traumas, conflict and confrontation. Outside of Israel I use a different language, of building bridges, understanding, forgiveness, and of concession. In Israel I live according to the Talmudic self-defense rule, 'Rise early to kill that which rises to kill you.' It means, 'Either I defeat you and you die or I die.' When I was abroad, I learned the 'win-win' concept: 'I want to win, but not at your expense.' It is possible for two parties to benefit from the same outcome."

"As the years pass, the schism between the two languages I use deepens and tears me apart. I am increasingly convinced that the language of my land—not the spoken Hebrew but what is practiced—is based on a false premise. Israel accentuates and perpetuates the confrontational philosophy that is summed up in the phrase, 'The entire world is against us.' I often have the uneasy feeling that Israel will not know how to live without conflict. An Israel of peace and tranquility, free of sudden outbreaks of ecstasy, melancholy, and hysteria will simply not be. In the arena of war, the Shoah is the main generator that feeds the mentalities of confrontation and catastrophic Zionism." And the accompanying paranoia arguably causes Israel (or at least the political class of Israel) to do things that actually contribute to anti-Semitism: "We must admit that present-day Israel and its ways contribute to the rise in hatred of Jews."[32]

It should be pointed out at this juncture that Burg is no outsider in Israel, but comes from the very heart of the Israeli political class. His father was a conservative leader who was a minister in Ben-Gurion's cabinet. Burg himself is on the left politically, and was a leader in the Peace Now movement. (He was injured in a grenade attack by fanatical rightwing Jews while participating in a Peace Now demonstrated.) He was an advisor to PM Shimon Peres, and was elected to the Knesset in 1988. In 1995, he was appointed Chairman of the Jewish Agency and the World Zionist Organization.

In 1999, Burg was again elected to the Knesset, and was soon elected Speaker of the Knesset, where he remained until 2003. He won again in 2003, but stunned Israelis when he published an article in *The Guardian*, a well-known British newspaper, called "The End of Zionism." That same year he also published an article that included the following candid sentence: "Israel, having ceased to care about the children of the Palestinians, should not be surprised when they come washed in hatred and blow themselves up in the centers of Israeli escapism."

In *The Holocaust is Over, We Must Rise From its Shadows*, Burg's great complaint is that the Nazi Holocaust has expanded to take the place of God, the Devil and everything else, including everyday reality. And he is quite aware that the Israeli government encourages this. "The crisis is already here. When I study the components of my identity and the cause of my identity crisis, I recognize only one common thread that connects us all: the thick shadow, the unbearable heaviness of the Shoah and its horrors. It is the source of all, and it absorbs all. So much so that sometimes I want to rewrite the Bible to begin: "'In the beginning there was the Shoah and the land had become chaos.'"

"The Shoah is more present in our lives than God. The *Musaf* prayer says of God that 'his glory fills the world'—here is no place in the world without the presence of God. Listening to the Israeli, Jewish, and even [the] wider world's discourse today reveals that the Shoah is the founding experience not just of our national consciousness, but that of the western world as a whole. Army generals discuss Israeli security doctrine as 'Shoah-proof.' Politicians use it as a central argument for their ethical manipulations. People on the street experience daily the return of the horrors, and newspaper are filled with an endless supply of stories, articles, references, and statements that emanate from the Shoah and reflect it back into our lives. The Shoah is so pervasive that a study conducted a few years ago in a Tel Aviv teaching school found that more than ninety percent of those questioned view the Shoah as the most important experience of Jewish history. This makes the Shoah more important than the creation of the world, the exodus from Egypt, the delivering of the Torah, the ruin of both the Holy Temples, the exile, Messianism, the stunning cultural achievements, the birth of Zionism, the founding of the state, or the Six-Day War."

"I have no doubt that memory is essential to any nation's mental health. The Shoah must therefore have an important place in the nation's memorial mosaic. But the ways things are done today—the absolute monopoly and the dominance of the Shoah on every aspect of our lives—transforms this holy memory into a ridiculous sacrilege and converts piercing pain into hollowness and kitsch. As time passes, the deeper we are stuck in our Auschwitz past, the most difficult it becomes to be free of it. We retreat from independence to the inner depths of exile, its memories, and horrors. Israel today is much less independent that it was at her founding, more Holocaustic than it was three years after the gates of the Nazi death factories opened."[33]

Yad Vashem is the place where every important visitor must first come—the stranger, especially, is required to go to the site before doing anything else, so that no one can doubt his fealty to the national obsession with the Shoah. (Yad Vashem is, of course, Israel's memorial to Jews that died in the holocaust.) Few, if any, have openly remarked on the implicit emotional blackmail in this protocol ("You will agree with us on security matters, or you will be on the side of the Nazis"). The pathology of this ritual arises not just from the fact that state visitors are required to go there, but that they are required to go there *first*, in that way affirming by their presence the primacy of death in the collective mind of Israel, and the maintenance of trauma as a primary goal.

"If you are an official guest," Avraham Burg writes, "you land at Ben-Gurion Airport, stop briefly in your hotel to refresh yourself, then you don a black suit and tie, perhaps a large velvet skullcap like that of a rabbi or a cardinal, and you are whisked to Jerusalem, to Yad Vashem." How can one really mourn the dead when visiting their memorial is a required pre-requisite to diplomatic negotiations? But Yad Vashem is not really about mourning, but is a preliminary ritual in the ceremonial worship of power. "A solemn face, a bouquet of flowers in hand, head lowered. Then a cantor chants the awe-filled *God Full of Mercy* prayer for the dead. Three steps backward and everyone gets back in the limos, off to the real business of politics and diplomacy."

So what is Yad Vashem, to which everybody of importance arriving in Israel must pay homage? Yad Vashem is the "storefront and the gateway" to the Israeli experience. It seeks to commemorate something that happened in the past, but since no one can deconstruct its trauma (indeed, the state seeks daily to exacerbate that trauma), it dominates everything in the present moment—and its influence is not a life-giving or liberating one. "Unlike other events of the past, the Shoah does not recede but is coming closer to us all the time. It is a past that is present, maintained, monitored, heard, and represented."

"The list of Shoah manifestations in daily life is long. Listen to every word spoken and you find countless Shoah references. The

Shoah pervades the media and the public life, literature, music, art, education. These overt manifestations hide the Shoah's deepest influence. Israel's security policy, the fears and paranoia, feelings of guilt and belonging are products of the Shoah. Jewish-Arab, religious-secular, Sephardi-Ashkenazi relations are also within the realm of the Shoah. Sixty years after his suicide in Berlin, Hitler's hand still touches us."

By internalizing the enemy, the Israelis became like the enemy, Burg says. "In the end, we did what the rest of the world's bullies do: we turned an aberration into a doctrine, and we now understand only the language of force. It is true in relations between spouses and colleagues, and between the state and its citizens, and between politicians. A state that lives by the sword and worships its dead is bound to live in a constant state of emergency, because everyone is a Nazi, everyone is an Arab, everyone hates us, the entire world is against us."[34]

The Holocaust is invoked so often in Israel that it would have been a miracle if Israelis *hadn't* internalized the aggression of the Holocaust. The Israelis don't have to be convinced of the existence of evil, because they have internalized it. But having internalized it, they see no reason to use a different standard in their behavior toward the Palestinians than the Europeans used on them—they see no compelling reason to oppose the Nazi they have internalized. The world betrayed and brutalized the Jews, and they will return the favor. The behavior and policies of Israel and its proxies are therefore to some extent a *continuation of the Holocaust by other means.*

18

Why does the Holocaust's malignant ability to affect thought and behavior seem to be getting stronger with the passage of time? Can the constant reiteration of a past trauma enhance its effects on the human personality? The Holocaust is no more or less traumatic today than it was when the gas chambers were in use, or shortly after the camps were shut down; yet its influence on human thought and behavior is now much, much greater now than it was in 1945, when Auschwitz was liberated by the allies; or in 1955, when people still didn't care to talk about it. In fact it appears that *deliberate repetition* of information incidental to the Holocaust—almost invariably by the Israeli state and its US proxies such as the Simon Wiesenthal Center—has greatly increased the effect of the original trauma. Furthermore, this deliberate repetition is done intentionally by the Israeli government to keep the Holocaust alive and active in the minds of its citizens, and by its proxies who wish to keep the Holocaust alive in the minds of those it wishes to influence. It is used, in other words, as a form of state indoctrination, since these frequent references to the Holocaust are almost invariably accompanied by the observation that only the Israeli state can protect Jews from another Holocaust.

According to the work of psychiatrist Dr. Hans Keilson, a German Jew whose research was done in the Netherlands, there exists something known as "sequential traumatizing." If a traumatic experience is repeated—that is, if a traumatized person is victimized a second time in the same way—it creates a new trauma, but also enhances and exacerbates the original one. Could memory operate in a similar way? Could simply *hearing* about a past trauma enhance its negative effects in the present moment?

Jewish author Hajo G. Meyer believes that it can. He takes

Keilson's theory of "sequential traumatizing" and suggests that it might include repetition of trauma in memory: "An extension of Keilson's theory is called for....in order to account for the truly pathological preoccupation with the Holocaust and other disasters from the past, as well as for the paranoid feelings and fears that haunt so many Jews. According to my proposed extension of theory, so many previous sufferings of the Jewish people are time and again collectively remembered in ritual settings, that they serve the same role as the previous traumatic experiences."

"*Collective remembrance thus acts as fresh trauma.* Since the number of previous traumatic experiences that the Jewish people have suffered throughout history is so large, and as observing Jews have to remember many of them so often, the amplification of trauma is very great indeed."[35] (Emphasis added.) Meyer makes a similar point about multi-generational trauma: "Terror learned by hearsay may leave a deeper impression than that experienced directly, since many of the people who were actually imprisoned in the camps had time to get used to the horrible experiences, and experienced a sort of psychic numbness that helped them survive. More important, perhaps, is the fact that members of the second and third generation were brought up by deeply traumatized parents. This is in contrast to the parents themselves, who in general grew up under normal circumstances and have more or less normal childhood memories."[36]

Meyer suggests that trauma becomes harmful when "collectively remembered in ritual settings." But how much more harm does this process do, when it is promoted by a government as a form of indoctrination, customized to today's Jewish fears and anxieties as well as collective memories of victimization and suffering—especially when it is aimed at creating obedience to the state, and hostility to enemies chosen by the state?

19

Israelis aren't just haunted by the Holocaust. They are also mightily haunted by the Naqba. If you aren't familiar with the word 'Naqba,' don't worry—few people are, since it, and what it means, have mainly been suppressed both in Israel and in the West. (The Israeli Knesset passed a law in 2011 making it illegal to commemorate it publicly, which is a good indication of how important it is to the Israelis, even though the political class says it never happened.) The 'Naqba' was what the founders of Israel did to the Palestinians in 1947-49: it was the ethnic cleansing of 750,000 Palestinians by the founders of Israel, done in order to give Jews the numerical majority they believed necessary to the creation of a Jewish state. (Another quarter of a million Palestinians were dispossessed during the 1967 war.) During the period of 1947-49 the Zionist settlers conducted strategic massacres of civilians to terrify people into running away from their homes, then taking their land, farms and houses and very carefully preventing them from returning. Nobody knows exactly how many massacres occurred, but probably there were slightly more than twenty of them, in various locations throughout Mandate Palestine. The massacres came as a shock to the mainly unarmed Palestinians, enough to make 750,000 of them leave their homes and go to neighboring countries. But the real shock came when Palestinians prepared to come home and take up their lives again. They were not allowed to return to their towns, neighborhoods, farms and villages by the Israelis.

Palestinians call this "the Naqba," which in Arabic means "the Catastrophe." The Naqba wasn't anywhere near as bad as the Holocaust, as Zionists like to point out, but it was a lethal down-payment on what may someday be even worse, since the bitterness it generated doomed Israel to ten wars over the next sixty years; and it was the first in a sequence of events that is now becoming a worldwide showdown between Islam and the West. Worst of all, it changed the very nature of Judaism, which went from a religion based on universal values to one based to a large extent on defending a small but highly contested patch of real estate in the Middle East. It is common nowadays to say that the Palestinians paid the price for the crimes of the European anti-Semites, ending with the Nazis; and in emotional terms that is exactly what happened. But for just that reason, it is important to point out that the expulsion of Palestinians was not dictated by historical necessity, but happened because of certain fateful and brutal choices made by the Zionist founders of Israel, many of them planned well in advance. They wanted to create a country in which having the right religion and ethnicity was the thing that counted, not your character, your talents, or your intentions.

If Jews had simply come there to live, or had founded a secular state based on shared rights and responsibilities, there would have been no reason to dispossess 750,000 indigenous people, and Palestinian refugees would have come home after the 1948 war with no interference by the state. There would have been tensions between Jews and Palestinians afterwards, to be sure; but if rights and responsibilities were equally shared, expulsion would have been the last resort rather than the first, and it would have been punishment for individual crimes, not expulsion of a whole people. There were tensions between Palestinians and Jews in Mandate Palestine before 1948, but again, that was because the Zionist settlers came with the avowed purpose of founding a Jewish state and not a secular one—and most of their leaders had been talking about expelling Palestinians for as long as there had been a Zionist movement.

The Zionists never wanted to set up a secular state with shared rights and responsibilities. They always wanted a theocratic Jewish state, which according to Zionist dogma required a Jewish majority. Why a Jewish majority? So the Jewish state would have the political will to go to the rescue of Jews anywhere who were experiencing anti-Semitism. The Zionists couldn't *prove* that there'd be future attacks against Jews, but their world-view required them to *believe* that the world would always hate them—hadn't Jews always been hated in the past? In any case, by the late 1940s Palestinians were still in the majority in Palestine, so 750,000 Palestinians were ethnically cleansed to give the Zionists the demographic majority they wanted. The descendants of those refugee Palestinians are still in the Middle East today, and there are about seven million of them, some in territories occupied by Israel and some in refugee camps in the surrounding countries.

Although those Palestinians that stayed in Israel are citizens, they are victims of intense racism, their towns and neighborhoods don't receive the services that Jewish towns and villages do, they are prevented from buying any but the worst property, they are almost never given permits to non-violently picket or protest, and they are prohibited by law from telling the story of what happened to them. In other words, they are second-class citizens inside the green line—and in the Occupied Palestinian Territories, the territories Israel took over after 1967, they have no more rights than a colony of feral cats. Murder, torture and collective punishment are practiced on a mass basis, and the Israel Defense Forces almost never have investigations of these horrors although they claim to do so.

After the Naqba (which went on from 1947 until 1949, although 1948 is often used as a kind of shorthand for the entire three-year period of ethnic cleansing), Zionists made a second crucial and tragically mistaken decision, one that would decisively change world history and transform the nature of Judaism. They decided to lie to the world about what they'd done to the Palestinians. They discovered that because of Holocaust guilt and because of long-standing racism toward Arabs, the Christian West would believe anything the Israelis told them, no matter how unbelievable. So the Zionists spun the line that nothing very bad had ever happened to the Palestinians, and that the Palestinians that were claiming that they've been ethnically cleansed were liars who liked to say such things because they hated Jews.

This decision by Zionists—and their short-sighted proxies in the West—to lie about what had happened to the Palestinians had several toxic effects that have gotten worse with every year. For one thing, by lying about what had happened, uncritical supporters of Israel effectively took the idea of reparations—that is, compensation for the homes, farms, orchards and property taken from the Palestinians—off the table. (It is very hard to compensate people after you've spent years telling everybody that nothing bad ever happened to them.) Furthermore, the Zionists begin to see that Christian guilt about the Holocaust gave them a form of power. And by being unwilling even to listen to what the Palestinians had to say about what really happened in Israel/Palestine, the Christian West became complicit in the crimes committed against the Palestinians by the new leaders of the theocratic state of Israel. That was fine with most leaders of Christianity in the West—all they wanted was for people not to probe too deeply into why the Holocaust happened, and why it was done exclusively by Christians.

When the early Zionists lied about what they'd done to the Palestinians, and Jewish leaders around the world went along with it, the aggression that had been committed against the Palestinians was changed into something different, something harder to deconstruct. That is because aggression alone is not evil—it is aggression plus deceit that is evil, and when a state does the lying it becomes systemic evil. It is when the sociopath invents a narrative in which he is completely innocent (and sociopaths are particularly inclined to do that), it is then that his aggression really becomes a form of evil. If the sociopath didn't lie about his crimes, and took responsibility for them, they would still be acts of aggression worthy of punishment—but it wouldn't be evil. When Israeli leaders lied about what they'd done to the Palestinian people, their aggression became a form of evil; and since it was being promoted by a state and its proxies, it became a form of systemic evil.

People that lie about their crimes telegraph the fact that more crimes are on the way, because their evil is in the process of becoming systemic. When aggression is accepted by a political class—and that same class lies consistently about it, to conceal it from the world—systemic evil is created. A similar situation existed in the American south when African-Americans were oppressed through a system of indigenous racial terrorism involving law enforcement and millions of complicit whites who benefited emotionally and economically from the oppression of their African-American neighbors. Such a system of evil is always progressive, like an addiction is progressive—that is, it only can get worse unless people inside or outside the system intervene to stop it. When a state is given impunity for its violations of human rights, in the way that Israel is given impunity by the US and the West, it will always get worse until it ends with war, genocide or a completely corrupt and unlivable society. It may take some time, but that is always the destination toward which systemic evil heads.

To keep the crimes against the Palestinians secret, the early Zionists had to adopt the line that Palestinians (and by extension, Arabs and Muslims generally) only criticized Israel because they hated Jews. This resulted in Israel contributing to one of the world's most pernicious forms of racism and religious bigotry, because Israel—and its proxies in the West—now had an incentive to portray Arabs and Muslims as evil. It also required Zionists to accuse people who criticized Israel of being anti-Semites and self-hating Jews, in order to intimidate everyone into silence. (This habit of calling everyone anti-Semites who criticize Israel began early and is still going on; and since it usually isn't true, it corrupted and still corrupts the Jewish leaders and organizations in the West that use this gutter tactic.) Christians in the West didn't want to hear anything the Palestinians said, and in a way, this hurt the Palestinians—and all Arabs—perhaps most of all, because by denying something without investigating to see if it was true, the Christian West was saying that Arabs have no standing as human beings. In fact, the West *took pleasure* in their contempt toward Arabs, in the mistaken idea that somehow they were helping the Israelis by doing so. That is called racism, and is the most prevalent and toxic form of racism in the West.

Zionists argued that the only way Jews could be protected from another Holocaust was by an armed Jewish state—such a state would need a majority of Jews, and the only way to achieve that majority was expelling the Palestinians. This was one of the first glaring examples of the capacity of the Holocaust to corrupt people morally and politically. Palestinians who remained in Israel became second-class citizens; and although injustice to Palestinians was not the whole story concerning Israel, any more than injustice to African-Americans was all there was to the American South before the 1960s, it was prevalent enough to define and influence everything else.

Above all, it had a disastrous effect on Judaism in Israel, not to mention Jewish culture and religion in the Jewish Diaspora. Of course, at first almost all Jews, except for some on the Left or those that had studied the situation in Israel/Palestine, believed the fabrications that were retailed by their own community leaders. Those Jews that knew the truth about the ethnic cleansing of the Palestinians kept their mouths shut, because anybody who told the truth about it would typically be subjected to virtual excommunication from the Jewish community.

Interestingly, however, in the 1980s the Israel political class took a fateful decision: they decided to open the military archives for the first time. A group of Israeli historians, all of them Jews, rushed to take advantage of it. These Israeli historians—often called the New Historians—were specifically interested in finding out what really happened during the founding of the state of Israel, and they went out of their way to document what they found. They included Benny Morris, Ilan Pappe, Avi Shlaim, Tom Segev, Baruch Kimmerling, Hillel Cohen and Simha Flapan. The importance of this group of scholars can hardly be exaggerated in affecting the way the world views Israel, but what they bore witness to was not good news.[37] It was something that many—perhaps most—Israelis already knew about, but they weren't anxious to get it out in the open where the world could find out about it. (If this sounds sinister, that is because it *is* sinister—whenever any group of people lie in a systematic way to cover up an injustice, they are engaging in systemic evil.)

The New Historians discovered that almost everything that the Israeli government said about the displacement of the Palestinians was a lie. Just as the Arabs had been claiming all along, the Zionist settlers had, indeed, engineered a series of massacres across Palestine during 1947-1949 with the intent of driving a majority of the Palestinians out of the country; and they had then refused to let them return to their homes. (The largest of these massacres was engineered by the Menachim Begin at Deir Yassin, killing about 250 unarmed civilians, men, women and children.) About a thousand innocent civilians were killed in these massacres. A thousand is a paltry number when compared to the genocide of Muslims in Bosnia by the Serbian militias, let's say, but bad enough if you happened to be one of the Palestinians killed or had to watch as your family members were killed.

In Illan Pappe's book, *The Ethnic Cleansing of Palestine,* he was able to document the extent to which the ethnic cleansing was planned and discussed by top Zionists long before 1948. The New Historians also discovered that some Palestinian groups had sought an accommodation with the Zionists but were rejected. But the most devastating discovery was the extent to which so many people associated with the state of Israel, both in Israel and the US, were lying to others (and perhaps to themselves) about the expulsion of Palestinians in 1947-1949. The narrative presented by Jewish leaders in America was almost always a variation of the same lie. A great many Jews and non-Jews probably believed the lie, or tried to, but others simply repeated the party line because they were afraid to look for the truth on their own. People who tried to correct the lie were often shouted down, or retaliated against in some form. The extent to which religious leaders in the US cooperated with this ongoing deception was deeply disillusioning to many Jews.

One of these was Rich Siegel, a Jewish musician who lives in New Jersey. He started reading the New Historians rather innocently, hoping to find out more about Israeli history because he wanted to go there someday.

"I became appalled. I was raised with the notion that Israel could do absolutely no wrong and never did anything to harm anyone... I had believed that [w]e as Jews are privileged to be part of this group that the whole world hates for no reason—and by the way we're smarter than everyone. And by the way the Arabs also hated us for no reason, we just wanted to go there and be their neighbors...When I became aware that there were Jewish terrorists, and that Jews had sought to create an exclusivist territory, while still playing the victim card about the Holocaust—it's been a thoroughly appalling revelation. That led me to be active, just being so angry about being lied to. I was lied to all my life, by my synagogue, my family, by my Jewish community."[38]

In the "Introduction" to his book *Prophets Outcast*, Adam Shatz writes about Israel and growing up Jewish. "In the Sunday School I attended at a Reform Synagogue in Massachusetts, we read about the 'birth' of Israel, but not about the expulsion of Palestinians; Zion, after all, had been a barren country, waiting to be discovered by hardy Jewish pioneers, 'a land without people for a people without land.' We were told of the glories of Israeli democracy—but not of its peculiar limitations: for instance, the ways in which it denies equal rights to Palestinians (the 'Israeli Arabs'), in effect turning them into internal exiles. We were told of Arab terrorism, which was real enough, but never of what provoked it. We were told that not only the Arabs but the *goyim* could never be trusted, and that the only conceivable reason someone would have for faulting Israel was animosity toward the Jews. We were thought to think of ourselves as eternal victims, despite the obvious affluence of our suburban surroundings."

But in the late 1980s, during the first intifada, Shatz began to doubt the indoctrination he'd received, especially after reading Isaac Deutscher's *The Non-Jewish Jew*. So did his parents. "Around the time that I discovered Deutscher's book *The Non-Jewish Jew* in my father's library, my liberal parents were finding their sympathies for Israel sorely tested by the growth of settlements, the repression of the intifada, and by the rise of the radical religious parties in Israel, with their power to define who (and what) is and is not Jewish."

"A year into the first intifada, they stopped giving money to the local Jewish Federation, concerned that their money was going to support the creation of more settlements. The federation wouldn't let them off without a fight. First there were the calls to the home, and then there were visits from 'representatives.' Finally a man from the Federation showed up at my father's office, accompanied by an Israeli general on an American tour. They proceeded to tell my father he had no right to criticize Israel, no right to ask how his money was being used—and no right to stop giving. My father showed them the door."

"Who have you been talking to?" they asked him on their way out.

This inquiry—*who have you been talking to?*—is indicative of the cult-like atmosphere that had grown up around the subject of Israel in the organized Jewish community by the late 1980s. (One of the characteristics of cults is that members are warned not to talk to "outsiders," because mental and organizational discipline can't be maintained if questions and opinions from the outside are discussed and considered within the cult.) For many decades the Israelis took the line that Palestinians didn't exist, so therefore they were referred to with euphemisms until roughly the time of the Sadat peace initiative. (Usually they were called 'Arab Israelis' by Israelis.) But it went on much longer than that in the US, among people who had been to some extent indoctrinated with a pro-Zionist line. The extent of the unacknowledged guilt, fear and aggression around this issue can be gauged by the reaction of some Americans to the very *word* 'Palestinian.'

The present writer once worked at a newspaper in Massachusetts where I was accosted by a co-worker who once stopped me in the hallway clutching a copy of *From Time Immemorial,* by the Zionist propagandist Joan Peters. This co-worker refused to let me pass unless I admitted, as he put it, that 'there's no such thing as a Palestinian.'

It was the late 1980s, and I had never talked to him about Palestinians, or anything else—I knew that he had strong feelings about the Middle East, but he was a bit too intense, and I'd avoided getting to know him. I don't think he'd every come in contact with any real Palestinians, but somehow this paragon had found out that I was married to a Muslim woman; and that was the proximate cause, however weirdly, of his demand.

I told him that I didn't care why Palestinians were so important to him, nor did I know why he wanted me to say that Palestinians didn't exist.

I simply didn't know what he was talking about, I told him. I figured he was in a bad place, but I didn't want to go there with him.

Probably he just wanted to be a good Jew, and thought this was the right way to do it.

At last he stepped aside and let me pass. That's how charged the word 'Palestinian' was, as late as the 1980s—and in some ways, it still is. The entire interaction reminded me of the guilt and anger I'd observed among southern whites in New Orleans in the late 1950s, when they talked about Martin Luther King and the Civil Rights Movement. They, like the guy at the Massachusetts newspaper, were caught up in something that was a lot bigger than they were, and were on fire with anger, guilt and aggression.

20

Organized resistance by Palestinians in 1948 was close to nil, since the main fighters had been wiped out during the Arab Uprising of 1936-1939. The twenty or so massacres of Palestinians were relatively small—most of them less than fifty people—but the Jewish militias were very good at publicizing the gory details, making sure that Palestinians found out what had happened. In Jerusalem, an underground Zionist militia drove around in a truck full of Palestinian men, women and children for almost a full day, so that people in the Arab neighborhoods could see them. Then the Zionists killed the lot of them. In Haifa, crowds of Palestinians were forced into the sea by gun-wielding settlers, where a great many drowned, causing a mass exodus of Palestinians from the area.

The surviving Palestinians clearly left their homes with the idea that someday, after the fighting was over, they would come back to their villages, farms, vineyards and neighborhoods; but after most of the Palestinians had been driven out, the Israeli borders were closed. The Palestinians ended up in hastily-constructed refugee camps. In the next year or so, Jewish militias and armed forces kicked off an astounding campaign to destroy all physical traces of the 500 or so most important Palestinian villages. The Israelis laboriously plowed under between 500 and 600 Palestinian villages, destroying crops and homes, shooting animals and, in some cases, villagers who tried to hide in the ruins. (The US did something similar in Vietnam, moving villagers to so-called "strategic hamlets," but after the Americans were driven out the Vietnamese went back and rebuilt their original villages, because their ancestors were buried there.) The destruction of the villages was perhaps the most heart-breaking part of the ethnic cleansing of Palestinians.

The Zionist settlers plowed under the villages intending to

make sure that there was no visible remainder to show that a Palestinian village had ever been there, and took care to give whatever remained—a hill, rubble, cultivated earth, and orchards—Hebrew names.

The intent was to change the map of the area completely, an amazing and extensive and well-documented campaign considering that so many otherwise informed people in the world prefer not to know about it (or angrily insist that it never happened). Trees were often planted where the villages had been, sometimes paid for by idealistic liberal Jews in America giving donations to "make the desert bloom"—the Zionists even gave Hebrew names to places that had been known by Arabic names for many centuries. The Israelis did this part of the ethnic cleansing with enormous deliberation, because they were well aware of the extent to which Palestinians identified with their villages. The intent was to destroy the hearts and soul of Arabic-speaking people of that area, by smashing Palestinian culture; and they thought that the best way to do that was to wipe out Palestinian villages.

Westerners have often pointed out rather disparagingly that there was little national feeling among the Palestinians, and to a large extent they're right. The Palestinians didn't think of themselves as belonging to a country—their connection to the region went deeper than the imagined community of a nation. The Palestinians were village-centric, tribal people, and tended to think of themselves as belonging to a particular village; many came from extended families that had been identified with particular villages going back 700 or 800 years. The Palestinians especially had a connection to these villages because that's where their ancestors are buried. The Zionists knew that. They knew that the villages were the soul of the Arabic-speaking people of that region, and they determined to crush all hope of its resurrection.

When Palestinians speak of the Naqba, they are referring to

everything the Israelis did to them in 1947-1949; but they are most often referring especially to the Israeli destruction of their system of villages and neighborhoods that defined the word 'home' to Palestinians. When those villages were physically destroyed and plowed under, and it became impossible to go back to them physically, the trauma of the Palestinians was incalculable. It sent shock waves through the entire Middle East, where the concept of ethnic cleansing to ensure a religious majority was unknown. (At that time about ten percent of the population in the Arab countries was Christian.)

But there's always a price to pay. At the same time that the Jewish Zionists were destroying the culture and society of the Palestinians, they were already well-launched into the simultaneous destruction of the core values of European Judaism. The devastation of this loss would not be fully understood by Jews until later, when the extent of the emotional and spiritual destruction started to become more apparent. The expulsion of the Palestinians represented the defeat of social-democratic Jewish values, and the near-total defeat of universal social justice as a Jewish ideal, at least among Jewish leaders. Israelis did not see that at the time because, since most of them were Europeans, they often did not even think of Palestinians (or Arabs generally) as people. (Those that did rationalized it by saying that their own tragedy had been worse than anything they could do to the Palestinians.)

Astonishingly, what the Zionists did in founding the state of Israel was one of the stupidest and most self-destructive things an aspiring people has ever done to itself, or could possibly do—if you accept the claim that they were trying to create a refuge where Jews could be safe. Since the Zionists would neither let the Palestinians return to their homes nor give them compensation (because they claimed nothing bad had ever happened to them), they had in one fell swoop made endless wars inevitable. It is hard not to believe that this tendency toward extreme self-defeat was not there in Zionism from the beginning; and it is even harder to believe that so few people saw that self-destructive tendency at the beginning.

At the very same time that the Zionist leaders were proclaiming that they were setting up a safe haven for all Jews, they were doing things that would make conflict with their neighbors inevitable. That is undoubtedly because the true reason, one must suspect, for the founding of Israel—that is, the real if unconscious motivation—was never to create a refuge for Jews, but to start a war with Arabs that would allow Jews to prove themselves as warriors, in the process redeeming the shame of the Holocaust, and doing to the Arabs what the Christians had done to them. Because the underlying motivations of the Zionists were so different from their public proclamations, and the differences between their real motives and their idealistic proclamations claimed so many lives, Zionism is without question the most destructive False Messiah in a long history of False Messiahs that have plagued Judaism. Religious nationalism goes in only one direction, to the right, and ends at only one junction, at religious fascism, with multiple wars along the way—but that is the real motivation for the creation of a mono-cultural, theocratic state. The Zionists sought generalized destruction to punish a world in which the Holocaust could happen.

After the Holocaust, Christendom—which had traditionally believed that Jews were collectively guilty of Christ's death—could now be accused of something very close to collective guilt itself. This gave ambitious Jewish leaders an enormous political leverage; and it also gave the more aggressive of the Zionists ammunition for special pleading and emotional blackmail. Simply by talking about the indifference of Christian leaders during the Nazi Holocaust, Zionists could expose institutional Christianity for what it too often was—a corrupt money-making racket enmeshed in imperialism, exploitation and war.

Therefore the Christians would allow themselves to be bought off, not the first time they had made money off their own dishonesty. Nor were conservative Christian leaders unhappy to see the corruption of Judaism in the founding or Israel, and Zionism's descent into the kind of colonial system of aggression, lying and racism that institutional Christianity had often promoted. Fascism in Europe had failed in its goal of the physical destruction of all Jews, but the worst elements within Christendom could now take pleasure in knowing that they had contributed to the corruption of Judaism from within, by giving the state of Israel impunity to commit its crimes without being held accountable for them.

Thus did the most conservative Christians train Israelis in the arts of colonialism. Indeed, the US corporate upper class began almost immediately transforming the wealthier Jews into junior partners in empire, a profitable political tendency that the neo-conservative movement arose specifically to service. It was not the first time that rich Christians had put Jews in an impossible situation, or that opportunists had accepted such a position for short-term power or profit. But this time it corrupted both Christians and Jews much more quickly than before, because of the ability of the Nazi Holocaust to corrupt all who sought to use it without deconstructing its inherent evil. Again, the most egregious corruption was this—the Zionists presented Israel as a refuge for Jews; but by dispossessing the Palestinians, they ensured that Israel would be attacked for generations. By dispossessing the Palestinians, Zionists made Israel not a haven, but the most dangerous place on earth for Jews.

This ethical, practical and organizational disaster was not forced upon Jews by anti-Semites. It was a breathtaking miscalculation made entirely by traumatized Jews who adopted the corrupt and racist values of Zionism; it constituted probably the most egregious self-sabotage by an aspiring people in history. And the real reason why this was done had nothing to do with making things safe for Jews—it was always about aggression.

The Zionists claimed that they "had to" expel the Palestinians to have a Jewish majority; but why did they need a Jewish majority? They "had to" have such a majority because of their fears of a new Holocaust; but in what universe are you allowed to commit crimes based on what you fear in the future? And one must ask, why were Israelis so convinced that the world was against them? Probably in part because of their unacknowledged guilt about what they'd done to the Palestinians, mingled with an unconscious identification with the European aggression that had traumatized them. Whatever the reasons, Zionists made a right turn that would compromise and quickly began to destroy the culture and religion of European Judaism, at least in Israel.

Ethnic cleansing of an entire people can't be justified by someone's fears about what *might* happen in the future—it can't be justified by anything. The Jews that stole the farms and homes and orchards of the Palestinians had fully internalized the trauma of the Holocaust, but without deconstructing its evil. Therefore they had no reason to seek a better way than what they had learned in Europe, and instead began to do to the Palestinians what the Christians had done to them. And because they receive impunity for their crimes from the West, their discrimination, their torture of Palestinians, their theft of Palestinian land, their administrative detention of thousands for no reason, becomes more egregious with every year.

21

The expulsion of the Palestinians in 1948 and the disastrous decision to lie about it made an Israel Lobby in America necessary. Christians were willing participants in this destructive process from the beginning. The stated purpose of "interfaith dialogue" in the US after 1945 was for Jews and Christians to work together to oppose anti-Semitism on American soil—and there's no reason to suspect that that most participants weren't completely sincere about that. But Christians were also looking to Jews to help them manage their guilt and their bewilderment about the Holocaust. In some ways this was relatively easy to do, because US Christians did not have the same tradition of anti-Semitism as European Christians. But helping people manage their trauma is a tricky business, because those who do so can quickly learn to exploit it. Of course, Jews were more traumatized by the Holocaust than Christians, but they understood it better—it was simply a much larger and more terrifying version of what they had always gotten from Christians. On the other hand, the immensity of the Holocaust was too much for most American Christians to comprehend.

This was to some extent because Americans also have a kind of willed innocence where certain unpleasant realities are concerned—thinking and talking about the Holocaust upset certain middleclass sensibilities, although most decent American Christians probably would have agreed that it was important to try. The entire Holocaust seemed unbelievable—nobody could really explain why it had happened, or even *how* it happened. The world turned to Jews for an explanation, since they had been most directly impacted. And indeed it was Jews (Hilberg, Arendt, Milgram) who generally came up with the most informative writing about the Holocaust, with Stanley Milgram arriving at perhaps the most satisfying explanation of *how* it had occurred. But Jews concentrated on the psycho-social aspects of systemic evil in Nazism; as a result the religious—that is, the Christian—roots of anti-Semitism were often ignored by both Christians and Jews.

If American Christians really wanted to know what caused German Christians to murder millions, they might have looked closely at their own belief in the redemptive violence of Christ's crucifixion. Throughout the history of Christianity in Europe, it was usually when public displays of emotion around Christ's crucifixion were most visible—around the time of Easter week, for example—that anti-Semitic outbursts were likely to happen. If Christ's bloody death redeemed followers to eternal life, what about the Jews that voted to crucify Jesus, and continued to reject him in modern times? But it was precisely this troubling core dynamic of Christian thaumaturgy, and its historical association with anti-Semitism, that Christians didn't want to look at. Such an inquiry was likely to lead American Christians to a dark place where they weren't ready to go.

In addition to reading the writing of Jewish intellectuals, meeting with leaders of the organized Jewish community offered Christians some sense of meaningful response to the horror of Auschwitz. And both Jews and Christians could do this in the name of community-building in the US, without either side required to explain or explore their own beliefs. By simply showing up for "interfaith dialogue" with Jews, Christians were able to convince themselves that they were doing something important about ending anti-Semitism. That, in turn, helped them get a handle on the guilt and horror they were feeling, as it became clearer that the political anti-Semitism that led to the Holocaust had arisen directly from long centuries of Christian anti-Semitism. The power of the Israel Lobby was prefigured by the rich irony of American Jews absolving "good" American Christians of guilt-by-association with "bad" German Christians, which became an unspoken and often unconscious dynamic of interfaith dialogue between Christians and Jews.

But why *had* anti-Semitism been a part of Christianity for so long? The unwillingness of US Christians to look critically at their own theology turned out to be a missed opportunity, for the liberal Protestant establishment was soon overwhelmed by a rightwing evangelical movement that greatly outnumbered them. The ultra-conservative Christians of the Religious Right generally belonged to denominations or embraced theologies associated with anti-Semitism in the past, but were quickly adjusting to the loss of anti-Semitism (which had now become a supreme example of political incorrectness) by finding new objects of hatred in gays, Muslims and "secularist humanists."

By the late 1960s and 1970s Jewish leaders were, on the other hand, beginning to identify with the new Jewish state Israel, which they saw as a kind of living representation of Judaism in the world of *realpolitik*. For the more important Jewish leaders, supporting Israel suddenly gave them legitimacy—now they were associated not merely with a religion but with an important geo-political entity. And there was another reason, again mainly unspoken: it made Jews look good in the eyes of the *goyim*—they were a people with no land who had taken over a land with no people, as the Zionists liked to say, and they had made the desert bloom! No more would they been seen as cloth jobbers, money speculators and subversive intellectuals with coke-bottle glasses—now their excellence as soldiers, farmers and nation-builders would be crystal clear to the non-Jewish world.

There was apparently no downside to the dream of Zionism—Jews in search of a Jewish identity need look no more. One became a good Jew by uncritically supporting the Jewish state, whereas Christians could prove how free of anti-Semitism they were by uncritically supporting it. After sixteen hundred years, major reconciliation of Christians and Jews! This happy picture was not sullied by any mention of the Palestinians' tragedy, partly because information about it had been suppressed in the West, and partly because those who knew something kept their mouths shut rather than face a firestorm of denunciation by ecstatic Jews sincerely convinced that it was all a lie. The role of the Israel Lobby would be precisely to make sure nobody *ever* found out about what had happened to the Palestinians in 1947-49, and to keep those who *did* know something from talking about it. They would do this by keeping the Holocaust in the public eye as much as possible. If Jews were the century' biggest victims, how could the Palestinians be victims? Public opinion in the US tended to accommodate only one victimized group at a time.

Because of the confluence of these mainly unspoken needs, Christians and Jews adopted certain unconscious but highly charged roles that would govern "interfaith dialogue" between Christians and Jews for the rest of the twentieth century. The main rule was, *Don't say anything bad about Israel.* After a decent interval (or indecent, if you prefer) this was followed by its inevitable corollary: *Say anything bad about Israel, and you will be publicly denounced as an anti-Semite.* But these extreme conditions didn't faze most Christians—if uncritical support for Israel was required for overcoming anti-Semitism, Christians were willing to give it.

None of this was conducive to speaking frankly, of course—nor, one must add, did it encourage anything like trust or respect. It did create an elephant in the interfaith parlor, which only got larger and more fractious as the years went by. The name-change of the National Conference of Christians and Jews to the more mundane National Conference for Community and Justice may have occurred partly because of a claustrophobic sense of divisions that nobody was allowed—or could allow themselves—to talk about. To speak candidly about the origins of Israel in front of certain audiences, to mention the undeniable fact that ethnic cleansing had been used to dispossess Palestinians, and that torture and death squads were regularly used on

Palestinians inside and outside Israel, was to incite a riot. Even today, campus speakers on Israel/Palestine that criticize Israel regularly require police protection.

Christians also used interfaith connections for their own corrupt purposes. As Peter Novick convincingly demonstrates in *The Holocaust in American Life,* Catholic leaders used interfaith connections to try to suppress the American production of *The Deputy,* asking "their Jewish dialogue partners to put pressure on the Jewish producer and director to cancel the play, or at least to join them in denouncing it." *The Deputy* (a play that questioned Pope Pius' unwillingness to speak out against the Nazi Holocaust) had been produced at a time of "tense politicking at Vatican Council II in Rome over a declaration repudiating anti-Semitism and absolving Jews of culpability in the death of Jesus." According to Novick, the American Jewish Committee "did its best, albeit unsuccessfully, to prevent the play from going on—and made sure that church officials knew that it had tried." The national tour was canceled, probably as a direct result of combined Catholic/Jewish pressure to do away with it.[39]

Needless to say, a play should never be closed down because it criticizes organized religion, *any* religion, and using it as a poker chip in such backstage *tummeling* is another example of how the Nazi Holocaust corrupts everything. If American Catholics and Jews had to suppress a play about the Holocaust to get the Pope to stop blaming Jews for the death of Jesus, the entire project of reconciliation had, certainly for the people involved in the suppression, no meaning whatsoever. Similarly, the postponement of candid discussion about Israel was both stupid and tragic, because as time went on the elephant in the parlor got bigger and bigger; and in the total absence of tough love from American Jews, the political class in Israel kept moving to the right until it had completely embraced the neo-fascist Jabotinsky form of Zionism. There was still no talk about what had happened to the Palestinians, because few people knew about it, and most Americans didn't *want* to know about it.

But the few people who did know were often Jews such as Noam Chomsky, who insisted on telling the truth. Chomsky was condemned by major Jewish leaders and organizations as a monster, a crypto-Nazi and a betrayer of all Jews everywhere. As a young man involved in union politics, I was told by "progressives" that Noam Chomsky suffered from a form of mental illness that caused him to criticize the government of Israel because he could not come to terms with the fact that he was Jewish. He was, in other words, a self-hating Jew. It was not until later that I discovered that he was simply a man who sought to tell the truth, and that the sobriquet of "self-hating Jew" was regularly used by the Israel Lobby.

It is important to remember, however, that the unspoken decision of Christians not to discuss their doubts about Israel with their "interfaith dialogue partners" was to a large extent the creature of institutional Christianity, both Protestant and Catholic. Why? Christians overlooked the evil of Zionism because they were overwhelmed by the evil of Hitler. Christianity, the single social instrument in the West that could both explain and expiate evil, had been itself complicit in the greatest example of evil the world had ever seen. If the only way Christians could reconcile to Jews was to support Israel uncritically, they felt they had to do it. Remember that there was no theory of evil, either secular or religious, that could even begin to explain why German Christians had behaved as they did. Nor was there any immediate explanation for the next potential genocide that was now looming on the horizon in the threat of nuclear war.

Indeed, it was because nobody could explain the sudden emergence of so much evil in the twentieth century that evangelicalism arose in Christianity, and extreme religious nationalism in Judaism. Both evangelicalism and religious nationalism actually fed the evil that they set out to oppose; but both, in the late 1960s, 1970s and 1980s, seemed to serve the need for apocalyptic solutions to apocalyptic problems. Most Jews had never had enough organizational power to engage in systemic evil, either in Europe or the US; but in Israel, for the first time, Jews had some power. With that power, they were to learn the addictive nature of sadism and aggression, which are not things that most people are anxious to discuss. And since nobody dared to talk about it, the political class of Israel, once they got a taste of it, naturally wanted more. How nice not to be the victim for once, and to try one's hand at a little oppression of the natives!

This was formulated memorably by the German Jewish journalist Henryk Broder:

> "Israel is presently more perpetrator than victim. But that is good and it is right. After all, for nearly two thousand years the Jews were in the role of the perennial victims, and their experiences in this role were bad indeed. Perpetrators mostly have a longer life expectancy than victims, and it is much more fun to be a perpetrator."[40]

This disgusting endorsement of brutality was made by Broder in the German forward to *A Case for Israel* by Alan Dershowitz.

What Zionists now wanted, in other words, was what Christianity had always had, which was redemption through violence—but the Zionist settlers of Israel had no idea how habit-forming it was, and especially they had no idea how dangerous it was to the future of the Jewish people. Nor did they realize how fast the world was changing, and to what extent people outside Israel were internalizing the idea of universal human rights. Meanwhile Israelis were still stuck in 1948, in a time when—according to Zionists—human rights for Jews could only be guaranteed by taking away the rights of Palestinians.

22

Before Hitler, European Jews were true believers in democratic values and not merely in the narrow sense of electoral democracy—it was social democracy, the rule of law, and political and religious pluralism that excited them. They overwhelmingly tended to support progressive, center-left and Left political parties. The Zionists, on the other hand, took positions that placed them well to the right of the liberal democracy that almost all Jews believed in, which is why most Jews rejected Zionism prior to the 1940s. The Zionists were basically religious nationalists, and like most nationalists they were rather arrogant, taking the position that *their* ideology was the only future that Jewry could contemplate if they wanted to be *real* Jews—not only did they insist that building a new Jewish nation in the Middle East was the only way that Jews could be safe, they also regularly implied that there was something more manly, more authentic, even more sexual, about being a pioneer in the desert, than being an intellectual in Europe. There was, in other words, a fair amount of patriarchy and aggression in Zionism, along with the idea that Jews had to be as militaristic as the Europeans if they ever wanted anyone to take them seriously.

Publicly, the Zionists put a lot of emphasis on building a new nation to keep Jews safe. That's what the Zionists said publicly—but that was not what was really driving them. What most wanted was what all nationalists want, which is to create conditions that could maximize the growth of a patriarchal warrior class. They believed that Jewish participation in a violent struggle to establish a homeland could redeem and authenticate Jews as a people. Why did they believe this? For the same reasons that European Christians believed in the redemptive violence of imperialist wars. At the same time that they were telling Jews that Zionism was the only way to keep them safe, Zionists were already making plans to ethnically cleanse the Palestinians, which would guarantee endless conflict with the Arabs. Did they not on some level understand the contradiction in what they were saying? I think some did, but they didn't care, because the resulting violence was what they were obsessed with all along. This dangerous tendency toward self-sabotage through deception and self-deception was present in Zionism from the beginning, but they may have picked this up from the Europeans, especially the Germans, since the so many Zionist leaders were German Jews.

David Ben-Gurion, who is generally touted in the West as a hero, once made the following statement, or words to this effect: "If I could save all the German Jewish children by transferring them to England, or save only half of them by taking them to Palestine, I would save only half of them, the half that I could bring to Palestine, because our [Zionist] concern is not only the children's lives but the historic interest of the Jewish people." I suggest that anybody who would sacrifice hundreds of thousands of children for an ideology based on some sense of "historic interest" of this or that group is both a fanatic and a criminal, and utterly despicable.

Zionism arose out of a certain kind of the nationalism typical of that time and place; and it was precisely that kind of extremism—and the obsession with race and religious identity—that put Zionists far to the right of most European Jews. It was only after the deluge, after the rise of Hitler and the Holocaust and after the old social, political and economic moorings of European Jewry were irreplaceably swept away, that Zionism finally triumphed. Ironically, the triumph of Zionism was irreducibly linked to the sowing of death and destruction in Europe by Adolph Hitler. It should not surprise us, then, that most forms of Zionism were not really an alternative to that death and destruction, but an internalization of the horrors the Jewish survivors had escaped. This meant that the Zionism that ended up defining daily life in Israel was actually a *continuation* of those forms of nationalism based on race and religion, which had given rise to that pan-Germanic nationalism of which Hitler was the last and most virulent spokesperson.

23

Christians were desperate to expiate their guilt for the Holocaust, and Zionists were more than willing to take advantage of that desperation. It was also for this reason that those postwar Christians and Jews in America that engaged in "interfaith dialogue" were really engaging in a kind of hypocritical game that neither could control. Certainly they never arrived at anything like real dialogue—or at least not the kind of dialogue one has with people if one happens to care about them. When Christians sat down to have dialogue with Jews, they really cared more about expiating their own guilt than they did about the Jews with whom they were supposedly in dialogue. One reason for this desperation was no doubt a growing (and usually unconscious) lack of confidence in the ability of Christianity to expiate sin. Christians were ready to let anti-Semitism go, but they did not really want to know why it had been there so long, nor did they want to know what was likely to take its place.

The evangelical movement in America quickly filled the vacuum with Islamophobia, the strident projection of guilt, anger and fear onto Muslims, and a world mission of defeating Islam and converting Muslims to Christianity in the "10-40 window," those 28 or so Muslim-majority countries located in the forty degrees north of the equator. Many rightwing evangelicals, including Franklin Graham, supported both the Gulf and Iraq wars because they saw it as a chance to proselytize Muslims; and almost all the evangelical churches that had missions began to concentrate on the "10-40" window. As always, there was little introspection about whether that mission might actually be simply another example of cultural imperialism from the Americans, and whether evangelicals could really help people in those countries, and if so how.

For Jewish leaders in the US, the rise of the ecstatic rightwing evangelicals was not such a bad deal as one might imagine. In fact, the growing political power of the Religious Right in the US produced a new kind of inclusive nomenclature, proving that American meritocracy extended to entire religions as well as to individuals—as long as the Jewish leaders involved did not look to closely at, or protest too strenuously about, the grandiose specifics of evangelical Christian world mission.

Jews were now to be upgraded to something known as "Judeo-Christianity," a bogus expression used by rightwing evangelicals to promote Christian nationalism and advocate in the public square for certain evangelical values without being called anti-Semitic. Jews were now to be allowed into that part of the conservative establishment that was encouraging coalition with the evangelicals of the Religious Right; and the expression "Judeo-Christian values" was rolled out to pre-empt any question of anti-Semitism. Jews were perceived as a difficult group that had a baffling tendency to vote Democratic, but whose institutional leadership was practically a domestic extension of the rightwing parties of Israel; it could therefore be used to whip the intelligentsia into line when American corporate interests were threatened in the Middle East. The expression "Judeo-Christian civilization" was used to reassure Jews that if and when the evangelicals succeeded in making their scabrous brand of Christianity into a state religion, Jews would have nothing to fear.

The entire issue of whether Christian evangelicals in America would continue to proselytize Jews was finessed in an interesting but dishonest way: the Religious Right would give uncritical support to the government of Israel; in return, institutional Jewish leaders would say nothing regarding the evangelical teaching that Jews would go to hell unless they converted to Christianity. Later the issue of proselytizing Jews would be even more subtly finessed by a little-known provision in the dispensationalist playbook—namely, that during the End Time (the

Christian evangelical term for the Second Coming of Christ), Jews would for reasons unknown suddenly convert to Christianity as the New Jerusalem arrived. The recalcitrant ones, those Jews who for some reason refused Jesus' kind offer of conversion to Christianity, would be mass-murdered by God, who would thereby neatly finish in the End of Days what Hitler had started back at the Wannsee Conference in 1942. As long as Jews kept quiet about the essentially anti-Semitic nature of this juvenile and astonishingly bigoted theology, evangelicals would give uncritical support to whatever government had gotten itself into power in Israel. In concert with this cultural development, the Protestant old-boy network that still controlled most of the capital in the American corporate upper class would let some of "them" into the conservative establishment.

The turning point was the emergence of Henry Kissinger as a modern Mandarin of American imperialism. Some report a moment in the early 1980s when Kissinger derisively referred to a roomful of people at the Council on Foreign Relations as "You Episcopalians—" Many of the Christians present were not Episcopalians (the days when Anglicanism dominated the boardrooms of America had passed some time before) but they all knew what Henry meant. There were going to have to open their ranks to let in some new blood. And the new ones would have to have power, not just vague and—to them—meaningless trappings of prestige.

This set the state for the empowerment of the neo-conservative movement. Neo-cons in those days were—and many still are—essentially upper-mobile, rightwing Zionists afflicted by an extreme case of ambition, aggression and power worship. They understood that if America continued uncritical support of the Likudniks in government in Israel, *no concessions to the Palestinians or the Arab states would ever be necessary*. Of course, the result would be permanent war, sometimes covert and sometimes hot, but *their* sons would never have to fight in it; and it would enable—and even encourage—the corporate upper class to set up a new neo-colonial apparatus in the Middle East. In return, Israel would become the mafia enforcers of American "interests" in Arabic-speaking lands, becoming in the process a super-militarized, highly armed camp of Arab-hating soldiers and fighter pilots, bristling with the will and the psychological need to kill Arabs on a regular basis. Most Jewish leaders in the US were seen—correctly—as uncritically supporting this process, by destroying or de-legitimizing every person or organization that questioned it. But the neo-conservatives went beyond the goals of most Jewish leaders, whom they wished to manipulate but not emulate. If the US could intervene in the affair of the Middle East, why couldn't it intervene everywhere in the developing world, openly and unapologetically?

The neo-conservatives hit upon the idea that America would be in a much better shape to intervene on Israel's behalf if overt or covert intervention were central to American policy everywhere in the world. Neo-conservatism was the Jabotinsky school of Zionism writ large, applied not just to Palestinians but to everybody in the developing world; and since this translated into a new and particularly lethal version of early twentieth-century gunboat diplomacy, a great many old-time conservatives were attracted to it, including people who cared nothing about Israel or the Middle East. People in the Third World who did what American policy-makers demanded of them would be rewarded; those who didn't would be imprisoned or killed. Realism, the reasonable pursuit of limited national interests, and a shared goal of a stable world would be set aside. Behind the policy-makers would be the US corporate upper class and its phalanxes of hired intellectuals, because only those leaders created by the marketplace could really be trusted.

The neo-cons were very savvy about public relations and influence generally, since they, like other Zionists, tended to see the defense of Israel as mainly a public relations problem. They invented extremely effective new methods (neo-con foundations, for example) to provide political cover for their activities and goals, also providing money to buy off their political opponents and marginalize the rest. Under the tutelage of neo-cons, the "Judeo-Christian" label was more about promoting American "interests" (that is, empire) throughout the developing world, in which effort the Israelis were to be the errand boys and arms suppliers.

But this idea existed and was promoted on pretty much the same wave-length as the rightwing evangelicals of the Religious Right during their rise in the 1980s and 1990s. Call it "Judeo-Christianity," or simply the neo-con's unapologetic appeal to American domination—it boiled down to the same thing: some lucky Jews were to be allowed to sit at the table of empire if they did as they were told, kept the Arabs in line, and agreed not to say anything bad about the ancient Protestants that still controlled the corporate upper class, particularly that part of it interested in keeping energy based on fossil fuels (the same part that would later swing the entire Republican party behind climate denial). The old-boy network of Episcopalians and other Protestants that had mainly controlled the corporate upper class before the 1980s would now do their part by increasingly including Israel, and certain of its rich American proxies, into their imperial calculations.

The Zionist part of this Faustian bargain was to help the Likudnik political class in Israel get what it wanted, which became critical after the collapse of final status talks in 2000. What the Likudniks now wanted was ethnic cleansing of the remaining Palestinians, either slowly (by making life unbearably difficult), in installments, or all at once. By building settlements that control almost half of the West Bank, the Israelis have made the two-state solution nearly impossible. Under current conditions, on the other hand, they would be able to do whatever they wanted to the Palestinians; and without question they will—*if there is no external or internal pressure that can stop them*—kill, ethnically cleanse or restrict the Palestinians to bantustans, perhaps moving quickly under cover of a military crisis with Iran. That would finish the job of ethnic cleansing begun in 1947-1949.

Zionism, and then neo-conservatism, were the outgrowth of western-style imperialism, and were only incidentally religious phenomena at first; but this desperate and mistaken collaboration between Zionists and the Religious Right has gradually become one in which religious nationalism is by far the most dynamic, unpredictable and dangerous factor within the conservative foreign policy coalition. It is all the more volatile because of the guilt, fear and anger arising from the Holocaust and the Nazi nightmare, a free-floating trauma that nobody has been able to explain or deconstruct. For that reason, ghosts from the past still drive decisions made about the present and the future. Christian evangelical leaders have recently striven to adopt a more mainstream image, and embraced centrist and even progressive concerns; but the evangelical voting bloc within the Republican Party will be a reliable source of support for imperial aggression for some time, not to mention torture, Muslim-baiting and obscurantism generally—as well as uncritical support for the Israeli state.

But the most problematic reality afflicting this coalition is that both rightwing evangelicals and Zionists are still quite prepared to give religious labels to their worst organizational fantasies. Tens of millions of US evangelicals believe that a war in the Middle East could usher in the Second Coming of Christ. And both Zionists and evangelicals believe in war as transformative and redemptive; both believe in a patriarchal warrior ethic. Therefore both are dangerously likely to support and promote the idea of a worldwide religious war against Islam, whether covert or overt. This all-encompassing and almost instinctual desire to engage in a religious war against Islam is by far the most dangerous outcome of the Zionist collaboration with the Religious Right, a problem of which most American liberals are still mainly unaware.

Of course, by virtue of its very extremism, the rightwing government of Israel has begun seriously to discredit itself, to an extent that even the Israel Lobby in the US cannot entirely paper over. By the time Israel has moved far enough to the right to discredit itself completely in the US, the new democracies of the Arab Spring may rise up against continuing apartheid in Israel/Palestine, or a new round of ethnic cleansing against the Palestinians. War in the Middle East might become inevitable. But by that time, Israel will have built so many settlements that a two-state solution in Israel/Palestine may be impossible. This is, and to a great extent always has been, the basic neo-con strategy.

24

Judaism, one of the world's oldest religions, was completely transformed in six short years. In 1942 began the Nazi extermination of European Jewry; in 1948 came the state of Israel. Surviving Jews who came to Israel, then, were battered by two related but equally incomprehensible traumas. On the one hand was the Holocaust, which the Israeli political class never stopped talking about; then there was the Palestinian Naqba, which nobody was supposed to *ever* talk about, or even *know* about. How could anyone make sense out of such dueling traumata? To put it simply, the Holocaust made it very difficult for Jews in Israel to feel or even comprehend the suffering they were inflicting on the Palestinians. Later on, they would understand that they were causing suffering to the indigenous people of Palestine, but they had already committed themselves to a Jewish rather than secular state—and they had no idea until they were in the thick of it how addictive tribal sadism could be, because they had never had the power to oppress anybody before.

The Holocaust and the Naqba are irreducibly connected, because the Holocaust convinced Jews that a Jewish state was necessary. But the sequential traumas tended to overlap. To begin with, the Holocaust overwhelmed everybody who had anything to do with it, because it forced people to see for the first time in the twentieth century the depth of human evil. Yet the Holocaust was also irreducibly connected to the founding of Israel, because it convinced Jews to accept the claims of Zionism, and the religious nationalism upon which Zionism is based; and secondly, the two things cannot help but be conflated in the mind and emotions because they happened so close together in time. They became further conflated because one (the Holocaust) was forever being used to justify the second (the Naqba). Paradoxically, however, although they became inseparable emotionally, they became separately inexplicable: that is, you cannot understand the Holocaust by studying the Naqba, nor can you really understand what the Naqba meant to Palestinians by studying the Holocaust.

The trauma of the Holocaust was exponentially complicated by the expulsion of the Palestinians. By surviving the Holocaust, Jews had become victims of recorded history's greatest crime. But they also expelled the Palestinian and destroyed their villages; that is to say, they became aggressors (or rather, victim-aggressors) barely four years after the liberation of Auschwitz. That is exactly how evil will always replicate itself, if no strenuous efforts are made to deconstruct the original trauma—people that are traumatized by human aggression tend, if the process is not interrupted, to seek out new victims against whom they will act out their internalized aggression. But it was next to impossible for Jews to see what was happening to them at that time; since they'd always been victims they'd never had the power to act out their internalized aggression on other people. But it was still a shock.

But Israelis quickly adjusted to their new ascendant status, as people always do. The transition from victim status to victim-aggressor became the fundamental process for socialization in the state of Israel: the victim-aggressor is Israel's emblematic and basic social type. But that does not mean that Jews were entirely aware of what was happening, because in 1948 that was not something Jews could handle cognitively, in the sense that they were not able to comprehend what was happening to them. Some psychological mechanism had to be developed that could be used to repress all consciousness of what the Israelis had done to the Palestinians, and to deflect any criticism from the outside world. Jews dealt with—or accommodated—the dueling but partly conflated traumas of Holocaust and Naqba by *psychologically retreating into total victim status*. This was enhanced by constant reiteration of the Holocaust by the Israeli state, soon picked up and mimicked by its US proxies and perfected by organizations like the Simon Wiesenthal Center.

In the beginning, this constant reiteration of Holocaust trauma was used mainly to repress and deflect criticism for displacement of the Palestinians. Only later did it become clear how important this reiteration was for the conditioning of victim-aggressors in a militarized Israel. In the West, reiteration of the horrors of the Holocaust was used to repress all consideration of Palestinians suffering and banish it from the polite conversation of middle-class society. The Zionists enforced this, insisting that anybody who spoke of Palestinian suffering were necessarily anti-Semites.

And in Israel, the assumption of total victim status soon led to an even more comprehensive denial. What the Israelis had done to the Palestinians was soon denied in its entirety, not just in Israel but in the US and by proxies in Europe. The horror of the Holocaust, the uncritical supporters of Israel insisted, could only be redeemed by accepting anything the survivors of the Holocaust did, not because of merit but because of their victim status. This insistence on victim status relied on a state of mind experienced by Jews who had completely internalized victim status. Above all, when indulged to the full, it completely banished all thought of Palestinians suffering, to the extent that if any memory of the Palestinian remained at all its moral significance was not only submerged but denied in its entirety. In comparison to the victim-hood of the European Jews, how could Palestinians dare compete? Thus did Israel administer to itself—and to Jewry in general—the narcissistic wound that would ultimately threaten to kill the best in Jewish culture and religion.

But Jews did not see this at first, because the advantages of victim status were too powerful. The deliberate inculcation of victim status by the Israeli state and its proxies in other countries could be used to bludgeon people into accepting virtually any crime committed by Israel. Furthermore, Jewish leaders could convince themselves that if anybody *did* dare to disagree with them, it must be because they hated Jews. This often led not just to the apotheosis of victim status among Jewish leaders, but also to a kind of juvenile Philo-Semitism on the part of liberals and the Left. If Nazis were bad, were not the victims of Nazis good? Therefore Jews, as the world's premiere victims, had to be good. Of course, the worst executioners are precisely those people who have been victimized, or imagine that they are victimized when they are not; but in the 1950s people still could not talk about the Holocaust. And even those who could talk about it couldn't see its connection to anything in the Middle East. Furthermore, as good modernists most people did not believe in the existence of evil, nor did they understand how it could affect the human personality.

Of course, making victim status into the central identity of Judaism and Jewish culture goes against the main thrust of universal human rights, which is about being *neither* a victim *nor* an executioner. It also contradicts one of the main selling points of Zionism, which was supposedly that a Jewish state would stop victimization of Jews. How could the Israeli state stop victimization of Jews while simultaneously embracing victim status? By becoming a victim-aggressor, of course. The retreat into victim status seemed the only way to handle the emotional demands of dealing with two traumas at the same time, the Holocaust and the Naqba. If someone questioned Israelis about the Palestinians, they could simply posture themselves as the ultimate victim: "I survived the Holocaust. How could you possibly suggest that I would harm anybody else? You must be an anti-Semite for even thinking that."

In fact, the most enthusiastic destroyers of Palestinian villages were precisely those Jews that had been persecuted most by the Nazis. But the world did not want to see that, any more than it wanted to admit that the social institutions in the world were to a large extent influenced by systemic evil. Therefore the world had then, and still has, a built-in incentive to sentimentalize the psychic realities surrounding systemic evil, and of good and evil in general. That makes popular opinion deeply vulnerable to the idea that victims should be idealized, and that they can't possibly oppress new victims because "they know how oppression feels." Of course, some victims—a minority—see though the cycle of violence in which they and others are caught, and refuse to act out the aggression they have themselves experienced. Such people become the teachers of humanity, and are extremely important to deconstructing the cycle of violence. But let us be clear: many victims of human aggression—perhaps most—tend to victimize others. That is the way aggression replicates itself. Abused children grow up to be abusers, or seek out relationships in which they will be abused.

We see traces of this retreat into victim status in the Israel Lobby. Powerful Jewish leaders in the US posture themselves as pitiful victims of religious bigotry; Jewish students in Berkeley are told by an Israeli Consulate to say that they "feel unsafe" every time the subject of Israeli apartheid comes up; and Israelis soldiers who break the legs of unarmed Palestinian boys insist tearfully on network TV that they are really victims of anti-Semitic hatred because the world criticizes them. Victim status is in, and moral responsibility is out, especially in Israel and among its uncritical supporters; and as long as it is, any honest examination of Zionism will have to be put indefinitely on hold.

That is why uncritical supporters of Israel cling so tightly to the Holocaust, and strive to keep its brutal memory alive in the present moment, even though most people on the planet weren't even alive when it happened. The Holocaust must be endlessly kept alive in the current moment to just the extent that Israeli aggression against the Palestinians must be concealed and repressed emotionally; especially now that Israel is setting up an apartheid system in the occupied territories, and a strong fascist movement is making headway inside Israel. These things must be concealed; and especially must Israelis and their proxies in the

Diaspora conceal *from themselves* what Israel does to the Palestinians.

Indeed, that is why there is so much anger at those who threaten to tell the truth about Israel—those who shout them into silence are very often trying to repress doubts about Israel in themselves. And the only way that can control those doubts from rising to the surface, is to punish and to scream at other people who threaten to express them.

A powerful sense of victim-hood is at the root of almost every kind of political extremism, and is especially at the root of nationalism and fascism. The trauma of Versailles was constantly invoked by Hitler, not to deconstruct the shame and fury associated with it, but to use it to justify his regime's state terrorism. Stalin presented himself as the savior of workers from victimization by the bourgeoisie; and on that basis justified show trials, mass murder, and the destruction of Russian society by the gulag. Victim status is the most profound motive for aggression of which human beings are capable. But that is not the only reason why Israel and its proxies adopted victim status, because it is more than a defensive strategy. The victim eventually becomes a victim-aggressor, and the Israeli state encourages this by glorifying war and militarism. Thus Israel promotes victim status as one element of a psychological system that both justifies aggression and generates more of it. *The logical culmination of victimology as a psychological continuum is a transformation of the victim into a victim-aggressor.* It is finally because of the extremely aggressive nature of this system that Zionist proxies like the Simon Wiesenthal Center want victim status to be at the center of Jewish identity.

25

Victim status is insanely attractive to a great many people, at least partly because it is a convenient escape from the pressures of freedom. Most particularly it allows one to avoid—that is, to refuse—the responsibility of moral choice. If one is a victim, one does not have to make choices, because the victim is always right. Assuming total victim status is a kind of freedom from the world's rules, laws and perceived moral codes. The advantages of this for the Israeli political class should be obvious.

Avraham Burg tells the following story, which indicates how deep this obsession runs in Israel:

> *Mr. D. is an outstandingly successful businessman, a native of Israel in his early fifties. Some time ago we tried to set up a meeting but it was cancelled again and again. He told me that he had to go on a business trip to Poland and I expected the meeting to take place a few weeks later. But a few days later, his secretary called and said that he was available.*
>
> *We met that same day, and I asked him what happened in Poland that cut his visit short.*
>
> *'I couldn't bear it any more,' he replied. 'Everything came back to me. I landed in Warsaw and it was cold and snowy. The same day we traveled into the Polish hinterland to check on a few opportunities that I was being offered. The snowy plains blinded me. It was cold to the bone and all we saw were birch forests and shrubbery. We spent the night there and then continued on a night train. The train traveled for many hours. The wheels and the cars shook and the ticket conductor was aggressive. Then a sudden ticket control. I just couldn't bear it anymore. Polish trains are too much for me. Everything came back to me. The following day, I hopped on a plane and came back.'*
>
> *I called him in the evening at home. 'Tell me,' I asked, 'where are*

your parents from?'

'From Iraq,' he answered.

How could it be that everything 'came back' to him, I wondered, if he or his parents had never been there? Did Hitler win over him, too?[41]

26

Victimology is a psychological continuum that arises when people build their emotional and communal lives around victim status. It is the dominant psychological system in Israel and is likewise promoted by US proxies, and is reinforced by the Israeli state through constant reiteration of the Holocaust, as well as not-so-subtle hints that a new Holocaust might happen. People under its influence talk like true believers, but their motivation is emotional rather than ideological. Victimology usually begins as a method for handling trauma, but evolves into a highly dysfunctional system in both the human personality and the culture of a nation; as a national phenomenon it is likely to lead to endless, reckless military and diplomatic adventures and ultimately national and personal implosion. People driven by victimology provoke or invent conflict, not to win the conflict but rather to lose it, thereby proving to the world their enduring victim status. Being defeated does not stop such people, since they define success as remaining a victim *while creating as much violence and aggression as possible*. Losing a conflict simply renews that person's connection to victim status as they wait for the next opportunity to generate conflict.

In county mental health systems in the US, there are always a certain number of clients who embrace victim status as their core identity. They tend to hang out together, very often in order to engage in various kinds of conflicts, and also in order to reiterate repeatedly their victim status. They are often people who were severely abused in childhood, but continue to identify with their early victimization into late adulthood, swapping horrifying abuse narratives and often competing with other clients using various forms of self-harm, including dramatic suicide gestures and attempts. As a mental health professional, this writer explained to such clients that simply being a victim is not a good thing. First one is a *victim,* then one is a *survivor,* and finally one is a *protagonist,* which means a person who can make decisions and engage in behavior that is no longer dominated—or critically influenced—by past trauma.

Sadly, many of these mental health clients identify so strongly with the victimization in their past that they cannot break free of it. Such people often make a remarkable adjustment to mental illness, which in the short term is a good thing; but in the long term their adjustment can be so good that they sometimes see no reason to get better. For one thing, they would lose all their friends, with whom they have a kind of tribal connection based on their powerful communal identification with victim status.

Because they do not really aim at winning, people driven by victimology engage in reckless strategies, and as a result often win impressive early victories in conflicted situations. But they almost always overreach, winning battles but losing the war. The most obvious purpose of victimology is to create a losing situation in which a person or nation cannot win; and the second underlying purpose of victimology is to maximize the aggression in every situation. It is this unstated but dangerous component that makes it socially and personally pathological, and quite often a central component of evil. (Because victimology trends almost invariably into a form of concealed aggression as the victim becomes a victim-aggressor.) It is particularly reckless because people under its influence unconsciously seek disaster. It is incapable of incremental strategies, often demanding apocalyptic, all-or-nothing approaches to conflict in order to maximize the aggression implicit in every situation.

The *central dynamic* of victimology in society is to excuse aggression while at the same time generating it. The *short-term purpose* of the system is to conceal aggression. The *long-term purpose* of the system is to generate more aggression in the form of personal attacks or military dictatorship or what have you. The *cultural outcome* of the system is the promotion of a patriarchal-warrior ethos. The *overall consequence* of the system is progressively escalating social conflict leading to war, government repression, torture, genocide and ultimately social implosion. Since victimology is an emotional orientation or system that automatically tends to conceal aggression—and aggression becomes evil when it is concealed by the aggressor—it is a widely-shared emotional state in nations in which *systemic evil* is acted out or encouraged by the state.

The goal, purpose and central psychological dynamic of victimology in Israeli society converge in the ultimate transformation of the victim into a victim-aggressor. The pain generated from feeling like a victim can then be acted out against a new victim. The value of this to a highly militarized state is obvious: it absolves the citizen-soldier from guilt and frees him of the moral consequences of his behavior. A soldier under the influence of victimology *acts* like an aggressor while *feeling* like a victim. The most thoroughly indoctrinated Israeli victim-aggressor is likely to feel like a victim at the exact moment that he is torturing or killing a Palestinian civilian. Victimology is seductive, dangerous, and addictive, and when permanent victim status is institutionalized in a society it creates victim-aggressors that are both supremely confident, and completely amoral. That is exactly the kind of citizen-soldier most desired by the Israeli state in the building of the apartheid system that Israel is currently creating.

The value of perpetual victim status to the Israeli state is clearly demonstrated in the following two stories. One is of Golda Meir, former Prime Minister of Israel. She was fond of saying as follows: "There is only one thing for which we will never forgive the Arabs, which is to make us hate them." This ridiculously self-congratulatory statement was widely quoted in the West as an example of moral sensitivity, but it is a particularly transparent example of victimology. The Zionists expelled the Palestinians, not the other way around—so how does Meir deal with that? She deals with it by posturing herself as a victim; and in her position of supreme executive power, that made her a victim-aggressor. The West loved it, perhaps recognizing in Meir the kind of duplicity that could be used in the future to sell American imperialism.

In the following exchange between Shimon Peres and Ariel Sharon, a more murderous form of victimology emerges. Sharon was the pugnacious Israeli general who was involved in the mass murder of 800 Palestinian civilians at Sabra and Shatila, whereas Peres was a center-left politician. Sharon was planning some horrific new collective punishment of the Palestinians, and Peres was trying to dissuade him, using reason and national self-interest.

"If we do this, the world will hate us," Peres said reasonably.

"The world will hate us anyway."

"Well," replied Peres, "maybe we should leave the world."[42]

I agree with Peres in this exchange, if by leaving the world he means to imagine a better one. But what is important here is Sharon, who reveals with great clarity the thinking of the victim-aggressor driven by a total internalization of victim status. Imagining that the world will always hate the Jews, he can do whatever he pleases—victim status justifies even the most heinous crime. The similarity of this kind of thinking to the self-exculpation of the sociopath is unmistakable. The difference, of course, is that the Americans give Israelis impunity for their crimes, whereas if arrested for theirs most sociopaths are likely to be punished.

27

When we talk about victimology we are also to some extent dealing with a malignant but extremely powerful psychological interaction called *trauma bonding*. Trauma bonding is the way that aggression and systemic evil replicate themselves in the world; therefore we'll take a detailed look at that in the next book of this trilogy, in order to understand what evil is and the circumstances that create it. The trauma bond is a psychological process by which a victim becomes imbued with the aggression of their attacker—it is what causes a victim of trauma to become a victim-aggressor. Victimology operates as a mainly unconscious emotional and cultural orientation that facilitates the trauma bonding process. The trauma bond occurs when people struggle with trauma as a result of human violence or exploitation, and end up resolving the resulting tension by internalizing the aggression of the aggressor. Victimology occurs before, during and after that transaction, and is particularly likely to be present in societies where victim status has become a fetish.

People do not simply wake up some morning and say, "I think I'll posture myself as a victim today, because I'm tired of making moral choices. If I'm a victim, I won't have to be accountable for what I do, which will allow me to attack and exploit other people with impunity." It's a more subtle process than that, and is likely to occur in response to powerful forms of aggression; almost all of the process is completely unconscious, and can be tracked only through concomitant changes in behavior. On the other hand, it rarely occurs on a mass basis if not encouraged by powerful social, military and ideological forces. Encouragement of victimology on a mass basis, by the state or some other power center, is one way that mass trauma bonding is facilitated.

Israel is the prime example of that in 2012, because Israelis still haven't come to terms with the horror and aggression of the

Holocaust. At the same time, the political class continues to bring it up, because the politicians realize how powerful multi-generational trauma still is; so ambitious men use it as a way to score political points. The worst part of it is that nobody has yet developed a theory of evil that can explain why it happened—nor can anyone explain why it continues to have such a disorienting effect on people. It is essentially incomprehensible, and therefore constitutes a maddening question mark hanging over the twentieth century that nobody has yet successfully confronted. So Jews that have heard or thought a great deal about the Holocaust often end up simply internalizing the aggression involved, precisely because it is incomprehensible. That is an example of trauma bonding.

But such trauma bonding would not likely occur on such a mass basis were it not for the Israeli state and its proxies, which use all their resources to convince Israeli and American Jews that the world is completely anti-Semitic, and that everybody is against them because they are Jews; and that therefore, victim status should be the central component of Judaism and Jewish culture. Thus they should no longer bother to make moral choices, because the world will hate them anyway. Their best bet is simply to do everything they can to uncritically support the policies of the Israeli state.

Victimology is, in too many cases, simply what happens when victims of emotional trauma get stuck. And if they're encouraged by their government to do so, that makes it even worse. The victim of aggression in such a situation *can't stop going back to the original trauma.* Most people and nations act out the violence they've internalized, but in so doing they usually manage to discharge it; and some are sensitive and smart enough to deconstruct the internalized aggression without acting it out. Victimology happens when the traumatized person or nation makes a spectacular fetish out of their original victimization, either because the state uses it for indoctrination, or because people get stuck psychologically as individuals. (In Israel, it tends to be both of the above, but with indoctrination by the state being the most powerful factor.) If they have completed the transaction to victim-aggressor, people experience themselves as victims even as they commit aggressions against new victims. They can't stop acting out the aggression they internalized; but because of the excited and increasingly cult-like nature of Israeli society they are never quite able to discharge or deconstruct the aggressive emotional orientations burning inside them. They're stuck with a painful addiction—even as they believe, as the Israeli state and its proxies want them to believe, that victim status is the highest good.

28

Avraham Burg writes that every time he meets with American Jews, there is only one subject they want to talk about—Israel. "Yet every time a strategic reevaluation concerning Israel is called for, the silencing voices are heard: Shoah, pogroms, self-hating Jews. Again anti-Semitism, swastikas, and Hitler decide the debate on Jewish identity and an opportunity for dialogue dies before it even begins." Burg believes that Israeli Jews will have security only when Palestinians have it, and vice versa—but Jews are too obsessed with something that happened sixty years ago to think about what would really be good for Israel. They cannot stop talking and obsessing about Nazis, swastikas and Hitler—for one thing, although Burg does not say as much, this material is too stimulating, too addictive, too exciting. And it's all been fully internalized in these American Jews who want to talk to him, and it's all just below the surface waiting to come out.

Indeed, it's hard to imagine American Jews using references to swastikas and Hitler to repress debate if they had not deeply internalized the Nazi phenomenon. To them, everything Jewish is irreducibly connected to—therefore defined by—the crime of the Holocaust. They're not even fantasizing about real Jews that died fighting real Nazis; instead they engage in fantasies of an imaginary Israel in which heroic commandos avenge the six million by killing Palestinian terrorists. But how can killing Palestinians redeem dead Jews? You can believe that only if you believe implicitly and explicitly in the moral ascendancy of redemptive violence. If ever there was one thing the Likudniks and Christian evangelicalism agree on, it's that.

But how much of that fantasy is unconscious Jewish imitation of the Nazi brutality, and how much is a fantasy about Palestinians *as* Nazis? It could be either, or both at the same time.

The Palestinian allows the settlers to play at being Nazis, but he can also be fantasized as the omnipresent Nazi that one symbolically punishes—both fantasies are opposite sides of the same coin, and both are equally pathological. "Hitler is no more," Burg writes. "But we still suffer his evil legacy, and refuse to be comforted. It was easy for Hitler to take our lives away from us, and it is difficult for us to get Hitler out of our lives."[43]

29

But how can one even claim that one is a victim, in 2012, of something that happened in the 1940s? Does victim status exist forever—does the statute of limitation *never* run out? When people internalize the aggression of the Shoah is it not, for the majority who were born after it happened, an *elective* trauma? Israel and its proxies insist that it is central to Jewish identity—one achieves authenticity as a Jew by standing with the six million that were murdered, just as identifying with the suffering of Jesus was once a way to experience one's place in the Christian elect. Indeed, when victim status is voluntarily adopted by Jews, one might legitimately wonder about the extent to which it is an internalized form of the Christian fantasy of inherited Jewish guilt. Israeli Zionists are, after all, increasingly borrowing the apocalyptic style from the Christian Zionists and the rightwing evangelicals.

What identification with the Holocaust greatly reduces, however, is a sense of one's own agency—those in the Israeli political class that talk about the Holocaust, like the operatives in Kafka's *The Trial*, reveal only those parts of the truth that generate anxiety, fear, guilt or anger. These negative emotions interfere with one's ability to make moral choices, and also tend to conceal the information necessary to make them. The constant reiteration of the Holocaust by Israel and its US proxies is unmistakably a product of propaganda, in this case reinforced by a world of artificially-created nightmare—exactly the world of Kafka and German Expressionist films of the 1920s. Indeed, the Holocaust feels, to a growing number of young Jews in Israel and America, more like the nightmarish denouement of *The Cabinet of Dr. Caligari*, than a reason for doing anything good with one's life. Dripping with the negative charisma of a Grimm Brothers folk tale, and therefore rife with emotion, it yet seems strangely unconnected to real historical events that can be understood or debated. Yet its emotional impact is still powerful—if only because of inter-generational trauma, or simply a matter of generalized angst about living in a dangerous world; either way, its emotional impact continues to grow, even as it becomes more unknowable cognitively and historically.

For many Jews—and not a few Germans—all of life's traumas, grievances, disappointments, fears and resentments tend to become subsumed into the larger, over-arching traumata of the Holocaust. Emotions cannot be compartmentalized in the same way that ideas are; and the outcome of such emotional homogenization is that victimization connected to the Holocaust becomes conflated with all other strong emotions felt by the individual, rather than a standard for the thoughtful development of a moral code. That's a sure and certain recipe for exacerbating victimology on a mass basis, or in ways that are unhealthy to the individual. But that is precisely what the Israeli state appears to want, not merely to create victim-aggressors, but also because it prefers for its citizens to believe (and believes itself) that anti-Semitism is to blame for all of Israel's problems. It is *much* easier to convince the people of Israel that they are right, and the entire world is wrong, if you can convince them that they are all victims.

Disappointments large and small—in fact every unresolved emotional conflict—are quickly subsumed into the larger tragedy of sixteen centuries of anti-Semitism, to be finally submerged into the Black Hole of the Shoah. This free-floating Holocaust trauma is represented by the rightwing government of Israel as being not only ever-present and thus eternal, but diabolically endowed with superhuman qualities, forever waiting to pop out from under the bed and burn the house down. The big problem with the idea of the Next Holocaust, however, is that anti-Semitism has greatly diminished in the West. It is growing in the Arab world, to be sure, but Arab anti-Semitism is to a great extent driven by the behavior of the government of Israel; and if anti-Israel feelings continue to grow, that is mainly because of daily footage of Israel murdering and beating Palestinians on Al Jazeera. Israel could quickly make progress toward resolving that situation—and make the world exponentially more safe for Jews—by giving the Palestinians their own state, or full citizenship in the existing one.

But the state of Israel doesn't want resolution, any more than the original Zionists wanted to make the world safe for Jews. It is still, as was Zionism in the beginning, about the heroic warrior ethic of organized victim-aggression, while at the same time maximizing aggression for future conflicts. The use of constant Holocaust reiteration by the Israeli state makes it increasing a phantasmagoric phenomenon, to the point where younger people may actually have difficulty imagining Hitler, Nazis, or Auschwitz as part of the real world. They know what they are supposed to feel and think about it, yet cannot help sensing something self-exculpatory and dishonest about the people and power centers that promote so much information about it.

The increasingly dreamlike feelings associated with the Holocaust sometimes produces intense pain in the individual, because such an individual often feels alienated from something that is supposed to be (because the state tells him so) an intimate part of his own identity. Far from being anybody's core identity, in 2012 the Holocaust seems more like a bad dream than a historical event—memory is not, after all, exactly the same thing as experience: in fact, memory is regularly transformed, edited and enhanced by the unconscious mind to circumvent experience *and* logic. The Israeli state (and Americans Jews that uncritically defend everything done by it) frantically try to compensate for this growing sense of unreality through daily reiteration of the Holocaust as the controlling metaphor for the entire spectrum of moral experiences inherent in modernism; but there comes a time when both mind and emotions simply refuse to take it anymore. In fact, the Holocaust is over, and anti-Semitism isn't as bad as it once was, and it becomes painfully clear that the powerful forces promoting victimology are doing it for their own pathological and political reasons. And those pathological and political reasons are both aggressive and self-destructive.

In any case, one cannot go back and live emotionally and cognitively in the 1930s and 1940s; and the fact that Israeli and Jewish leaders seem always to represent Holocaust victims as saints or superheroes, rather than humans who often made bad as well as good decisions, makes the Holocaust seem even more remote. Since it is always being brought up by people and institutions that wish to use it to get money or power, is it any wonder that some good people try not to *ever* talk or think about it, yet end up living with it as an ever-present ghost whose name they once knew but now cannot remember?

What is missing is a *moral framework* for this welter of history, memory, propaganda and rampant bad faith. What is needed is a sorting out of its meaning, because only when meaning is discovered—only when the ghosts are named—can people move on. But the Holocaust resists deconstruction; and like the entrepreneurs of guilt and violence that they are, the Israeli state and US politicians manufacture their own meaning, and that meaning is—surprise, surprise!—more power and money for themselves; and continuing uncritical support for everything the Israeli government does, including giving Israel more money than any other country in the world.

For many young Jews who see through this use of religious nationalism by rightwing Zionism, and likewise find the carnival-barker charlatanism of its representatives in the US distressing, the emotional alienation that results is quite painful. The Holocaust was real, but why are those promoting it and always talking about it such fourth-rate hucksters? *The truth is harsh*: The Holocaust has tended to corrupt almost everything in our world; and one reason people have such a hard time understanding the Holocaust is that most of the people and institutions talking about it are money-grubbing, power-hungry hustlers, heartless charlatans and exploitive knaves, or otherwise under the influence of the various pathologies generated by the Nazi madness.

The Israeli state deals with the increasingly dreamlike nature of the Holocaust by transforming whatever is left of its thematic memories directly into a warrior ethos. An obsession with the Nazi holocaust, thanks in part to all the institutions promoting detailed information about it, allows both perpetual victim status and systemic aggression to be internalized *at the same time,* in their purest forms. Holocaust museums, Holocaust studies, and the Holocaust narrative have all become invaluable cultural reference points for the quick and reliable education of the victim-aggressor. All offer spectacular and concrete advantages to those molding Israel into a permanent warrior-state.

In the meantime, the radical victimology of state Holocaust-worship simply produces more emotional disorientation. It also produces guilt, to be sure, for not having died in a gas chamber; and secondly, for not really caring one way or the other, because how can anyone ever care for six million people? It is simply impossible, statistically. Everything about the Holocaust seem to lead to an abiding sense of the uncanny—even fanatical Zionists often discover to their dismay that there are people who have been using Holocaust imagery all along solely to serve their private interests. All of these things create an odd and dreamlike mental environment when thinking and reading about the Holocaust, not to mention a fair amount of shame. The harsh and hyper-competitive societies of Israel and America can only exacerbate the resulting disorientation.

If it sometimes creates a sense of wanting to wake up from a dream ("History is a dream from which I am trying to awaken," as Bloom says in *Ulysses*), it also creates a genuine feeling of *not* wanting to wake up, because of an intense fear of what one might see and feel when one finally *does* regain consciousness. For the Israelis in particular, it is getting harder to keep the electrical charges of the Holocaust and the Naqba on alternating currents; and all the various traumas of the Israeli tragicomedy are increasingly conflated into one hallucinated bandwidth—so after awhile it is almost better to stay in the dream, than to venture back and forth between nightmare and daily life. The Holocaust has become near and far at the same time, completely familiar but at the same time difficult to remember even in dreams. This dreamlike status serves the interests of the Zionist state quite well. The Israeli political class and its proxies encourage just enough introspection about the Holocaust for people to think obsessively about it, while discouraging sufficient introspection that they might see how the Holocaust is changing their personalities.

30

Of course there is a historical basis for the Jewish preoccupation with victimization, one that predates the Holocaust and the state of Israel. It comes from sixteen hundred years of Christian anti-Semitism, of which the Holocaust was the culmination. Like the Serbs, the history of the Jews in Europe is to a great extent a story of persecution and difficulties. That doesn't mean that Jewish life was only about persecution—in fact, the Jewish communities of Europe were diverse, they were nuanced, and they contained a world of human aspiration and capability. Reading Nachum T. Gidal's excellent *Jews in Germany: From Roman Times to the Weimer Republic*, one gets a sense of the fantastic variety of Jewish life in German-speaking lands over a thousand years, and above all the extent to which Jews were often able to define their own lives, communities, and values despite the restrictions placed upon them. But the restrictions were always there, in the form of discriminatory laws and near-universal prejudice against Jews and Judaism; and so was the possibility of violent pogroms from Christians. And when the violence came, there was little Jewish leaders could do about it.

Even when Jewish communities flourished and lived in peace for long periods, the *possibility* of violence was always tangibly and inescapably there; and in certain ways that was worse than the violence itself. The attitudes created by this discomforting reality had a profound effect on both the victims (European Jews) and the victimizing majority (European Christians). Christendom became accustomed to repressing people whose religion was different than theirs; Jews, on the other hand, grew accustomed to the idea that there was little they could do about it. Both Christians and Jews internalized the toxic feelings that arose from their respective situations. Like anybody else, Jews didn't like being oppressed—they simply had no choice but to make a communal and psychological adjustment to Christian anti-Semitism. For the Jews (and also the Serbs), persecution and victimization was the social role that made the deepest impression, because it was always there, and because nobody could do anything about it except make some kind of adjustment to it; and because when repression occurred in the form of unjust laws and decrees (or outright violence), it left an indelible mark on the souls of its victims. The *possibility* of victimization was always there. The inevitable result was often a kind of forced sadomasochistic adjustment to something that couldn't be avoided or defeated.

Today, the recurrence of such overt oppression is unlikely to return. On the other hand, Jewish and Serbian nationalists don't want to see the consciousness of victim status go, because it's too useful to them—it's one of the main building blocks of nationalism, and often the key to the continuation of their careers. That's why they're always talking as though they're still being victimized. The sense of victim status is unhealthy, but Jewish and Serbian nationalists want people in their group to feel aggrieved, because un-redressed grievances are the emotional fuel for nationalism; and when it is there, they can play on it in their speeches for their own political advantage, although at this point the Serbs must take care not to overdo it. In other words, both are invested in encouraging a form of situational paranoia in their particular group.

Situational paranoia, as used here, means paranoia coming not from a biologically-based mental illness or personality disorder, but from memories of past social injustices that cause people to perceive the world illogically in the present. There are two problems here. One is that people continue to be paranoid even after the victimization has stopped, and continue to see injustice and persecution where it doesn't exist. The second problem is one that occurred in Serbia during the 1990s, and still occurs in the state of Israel, when a government deliberately keeps a sense of victimization alive even when it isn't actually occurring anymore. A government can do this by constantly invoking cultural reference points that arouse feeling of persecution and victim status. This *false consciousness* of victimization is often made more potent by the tendency of the unconscious mind to conflate one's personal resentments with the larger issues of society, so that a sense of victimization become a single emotional orientation in an individual's emotional life. Under those circumstances, paranoia quickly—and in some cases permanently—becomes the most powerful part of one's emotional make-up.

To a remarkable extent, nationalism is based on this false consciousness of victimization, and on the resentments of people who feel (often correctly) that they've failed in life, and who seek to identify with something that is stronger and better than they are. You might think that nationalism would be based on a sense of what is *good* in one's nation, but generally it isn't. Since people attracted to nationalism tend to have incomplete and emotionally unsatisfying lives, they are looking both for someone to blame for that condition, and also for something larger and more powerful than they are. Nationalism fulfills both needs. It is driven by resentment, by the desire to be part of something powerful without sacrifice or hard work, and a chance to hate some designated person or group who then becomes the scapegoat for everything bad in the world.

Nationalism is particularly dangerous because it is a form of mass narcissism, which in turn is based on the very low self-esteem mentioned above. The individual must create a larger, more heroic persona to replace the failed emotional life of the individual. Nationalism supplies a group folk process to create this exciting, heroic new narrative that is bigger than anything the individual could have imagined before. (And bigger than any one person in the group.) Since there is always the threat that the low self-esteem may re-assert itself, however, the heroic new group identity must attack some 'Other', a person or country that threatens to bring down the illusion. The most powerful representative of this new identity is the state—therefore what the state does is good, and what gets in its way is bad. In religious nationalism, this mass narcissism is strengthened by the idea that it is simultaneously the will of the group, and the will of God. The best and highest good in life, then, is to serve the theocratic state, if there is one.

The existence of a state makes religious nationalism particularly dangerous. Nationalism allows people to transform their private rage into mass aggression; the state gives the true believers permission to focus their rage at an approved target, because nationalism is always us against 'them,' against some other group or person. (Because without a target for the anger that is inevitably generated by a sense of victimization, the nationalist would turn on himself.) The 'Other'—the one who is different and who becomes the object of the nationalist's anger—is necessary for the release of built-up rage. Nationalism is the belief-system of choice most often chosen by demagogues and charlatans to gain power, but it is also the emotional orientation that usually underlies hate campaigns against a person, race or religion.

For that reason, Hitler played relentlessly on the German sense of national victimization and humiliation throughout his career. In his hands, the Treaty of Versailles became the controlling metaphor in a world saga in which he was a dark avenger of Germany's shame. And it worked well for him, because part of the narrative was reality-based—nobody could deny that Versailles hadn't happened, that it wasn't grossly unfair, and that it wasn't to some extent intended specifically to humiliate Germans. Visitors to Germany during the 1920s noticed one recurring theme, regardless of how people came down on the political spectrum: *everybody* was furious about the humiliation of Versailles. But Versailles gradually became a stand-in for everything else that was bad in the world, every resentment and injustice that every German had ever felt. And as the reality-based anger was gradually transformed into a dangerously irrational rage, it became easier to present the Jews as the bogeymen of this scenario, the monsters that administered the "stab in the back" that delivered the German nation to her enemies.

Hitler began with a legitimate victimization of Germany, which was Versailles, but then offered it up as a coat-rack on which Germans could hang every bad thing that had ever happened to them. And he provided them with a way to turn that scalding sense of inferiority and resentment into aggression, to act out their resentments in war and genocide. Israel, on the other hand, came into existence almost entirely because of a people's nationalism based on a much more extreme injustice—in fact the worst injustice in the history of the world. Early Zionists went out of their way to attach this grievance to Zionism, since the latter was mainly a response to the former. And it was not an imaginary or overdrawn grievance—it was all too real. But so, ultimately, was the aggression of the Israelis.

The problem is that the Israeli state and its proxies in the US keep that experience uppermost when dealing with every issue. The intent is to create a sense of victimization in the present moment, even when it doesn't exist. It is for this reason that the Holocaust is constantly referred to, and why it often seems more real and more painful as its actual historical memory grows dimmer. In Israel/Palestine, according to the Zionist scheme of things, the Bad Guys are the Palestinians, whose very existence was once denied, and who cannot even buy property inside Israel. But the real danger is that the prominence of victimology as a psychological system allows the Palestinian to become, in the mind of the Israeli Jew, a stand-in for the Nazi. For those who have internalized the aggression of the Holocaust, torturing a Palestinian is a chance to *punish* a Nazi while *acting* like a Nazi.

The Palestinian is the perfect 'Other' for the Jewish nationalist, who has embraced victim status as the core value of Jewish identity. The Zionist will never feel guilt for what is happening to the Palestinians, because the Palestinian has only a Naqba, whereas the Zionist has the Holocaust. In the patriarchal world of the victim-aggressor, size is everything.

Both forms of nationalism, Jewish and Serbian, encourage people to see slights and injustices where they do not exist. Serbian nationalists claimed repeatedly that Serbs were being persecuted in Yugoslavia, whereas in reality they were in a privileged position. (Almost the entire army, for example, was Serbian.) It is no wonder that certain American Jewish leaders see anti-Semitism hiding under ever bed, even when it isn't—but if they stopped playing the victim, they would have to start being a bit more accountable for their own behavior. The public role of victimology is to play on fears, resentments and trauma from the past, while using them to justify one's own crimes, misdemeanors and mistakes in the present.

31

The importance of victimology is that it facilitates—that is, it provides psychological momentum—to the transformation of a victim into a victim-aggressor. The victim-aggressor in power seeks to start wars, to legitimatize torture, to promote Islamophobia, racism and institutionalized oppression of one group by another. Only in a conflicted world are they able to feel even partially comfortable. And if people in their own group get hurt in the process, they really don't care, despite their protestations of love for them. The real goal of the victim-aggressor is conflict and death—that's what they really want, despite what they say, and despite what they think. Whether it's their people or somebody else's, it ultimately doesn't matter to them. All they really want is the body count.

The victim-aggressor now firmly ensconced in the political class in Israel—and those in the US that uncritically support them—strive mightily to convince themselves and the world that their problems are caused by everybody else; but in reality it is their own behavior that overwhelmingly arouses enmity against Israel, behavior that began in the ethnic cleansing of Palestinians in 1947-49 and which continues because of the construction of an apartheid society. Victim-aggressors are psychological archetypes in Israel; and under the influence of victimology will vehemently disclaim responsibility for any bad choices they make. They are always right, because they are always the victim. People who deal with Israel's proxies in domestic US politics would do well to remember this—but they should also remember that the victim ultimately becomes an aggressor. Under the tutelage of the neo-cons, the US Israel Lobby wants impunity for Israel, but it also wants war between Islam and the West.

32

Zoe Zenowich, the managing editor of the *Excelsior*, a student newspaper at Brooklyn College, has written about the extreme subjectivity of elective victim status—or, to put it another way, the way that victim status tends to compromise judgment. An audience at Brooklyn College was listening to a speech by David Horowitz, who Zenowich accurately describes as "the Glenn Beck of Zionists—a rambler of hate who continually contradicts himself and history." Horowitz is an extreme rightwing Zionist, and an enthusiastic promoter of hatred against Muslims. He is, in other words, a professional hate-monger.

Here is Zenowich's account:

"Horowitz, who admitted he had actually never even been to Israel, proceeded to give everyone a lesson in Middle East politics: according to him, Muslims in the Middle East are 'Islamic Nazis' who 'want to kill Jews, that's their agenda.' He added later, 'all Muslim associations are fronts for the Muslim Brotherhood.' Horowitz appeared to be too delusional to even be quoted, or taken seriously if it weren't for the audience members who so fervently agreed with what he was saying."

"The most revealing moment came when a young Arab-American woman directed a question to Horowitz and the audience: 'You talk about Muslims as if you know them—we have a Muslim American Society, we have a Palestine Club [on campus]. I want to raise the question to any of the Jews in this room, and students, have you guys ever been threatened by a Muslim on campus or an Arab?'

"To this, the crowd almost unanimously spun around in their seats to face the young woman and replied 'Yes.' Someone shouted, 'and we're scared when we see Muslims on buses and airplanes too.'"

"Horowitz encouraged anti-Muslim hate by telling the crowd,

'no other people have sunk so low as the Palestinians have and yet everybody is afraid to say this,' claiming that Muslims are a 'protected species in this country' and that he's 'wait[ing] for the day when the good Muslims step forward.'"

This exchange is interesting because it vividly suggests how desperate some people who support systemic evil are to be seen (and to see themselves) as victims. Given the fact that Horowitz is a rightwing extremist, and that the members of this audience came to hear him speak, we shouldn't assume that the Jewish members of the audience were typical of most American Jews. But the desperation to disguise aggression with victim status is utterly typical of the victim-aggressor. What the world sees as aggression, he or she sees as victim status. Thus the people who came to hear David Horowitz weren't bigots who hate Muslims, but simply people who can see how intrinsically evil Muslims are. They are not people who support torture and apartheid, but sensitive, misunderstood individuals who are constantly being tormented by an unfeeling world. They are not Jews who support religious bigotry, but victims of anti-Semitism.

33

In Christianity, it is the victim status of Jesus Christ on the cross that brings salvation. Jewish nationalism provides salvation in a shared Jewish identity based on victim status. Both send the message that violence is inevitable and redemptive; both encourage aggression, which victim status both generates and redeems. And the broad church of Judeo-Christian trauma receives all denominations, providing they accept—or at least refrain from seriously challenging—the central dogma of salvation through victim status.

The idea that a shared religious orientation can be based on mass trauma is incredibly useful to a warlike state, because it can quickly be translated into organized aggression. As Judeo-Zionism becomes ever more like evangelical Christianity, a huge Christian Zionist movement, funded by ecstatic neo-cons and narcissistic Christian billionaires, has arisen to welcome the lost tribes. Judeo-Christianity uses the thaumaturgy of real-time trauma bonding to transform victims into victim-aggressors through baptism by torture; and upon perfecting its method for doing so, becomes the consummate modern church of the patriarchal-warrior ethos.

Fox News reports:

> *"In a tearful ceremony in the White House rose garden, the long-antagonistic faith communities of Christianity and Judaism were happily united today under a New World Order. Lenny Bruce was invited, but could not attend because of his multiple addictions and the untimely occasion of his death forty-five years ago..."*

34

Study the statements of the Los Angeles police officers that beat Rodney King, and you will see a persuasive example of victim-aggression. The victim-aggressor often responds to an *imagined attack* by his perceived enemy, without being consciously aware of it. This kind of misperception is usually situational, almost always based on things that have happened in the past, and is driven by irrational fear. The police officers that beat Rodney King spoke vehemently about what a threat he was: he was tall, seemingly very strong, totally intoxicated and perhaps drug-deranged, and he had originally tried to flee arrest. He could easily wreak havoc on them if not restrained properly, the officers insisted. All this seems reasonable until one looks at the video of the beating. At the time of the beating, King was down on the ground, ensnared in a rope or cable, clearly semi-conscious, moaning and rolling slowly back and forth. Standing over him were several police officers beating him with batons. If the officers found him threatening, why weren't they taking advantage of his semi-conscious state to put handcuffs on him, and place him in the back seat of the radio car?

They didn't put handcuffs on him because he wasn't really threatening them, and their professionalism was sufficiently intact for them to be consciously aware of that. At the same time, the officers may have *felt* very threatened by King, despite the evidence of their eyes. This fear came from their own emotional backlog of fear, in the form of a long series of fear-responses built up over years of operating in very poor neighborhoods where crime rates are astronomical. It was all those males that resisted arrest in the past that the Los Angeles police officers were really battling as they beat up the hapless King. He probably looked like a great many people they had arrested before—King is an African-American male—and that fact alone, combined with the fact that he was clearly intoxicated, triggered a fear reaction that caused officers to believe that King threatened them even as he lay semi-conscious on the ground.

The problem here is that the police involved weren't able to act on what they saw, but instead acted on emotion, in this case a negative emotion—fear—that was conditioned by things that had happened to them in the past. For whatever reasons, the officers *felt* that King could hurt them, even though he clearly wasn't able to do so. This unrealistic but powerful fear caused this group of Los Angeles police officers needlessly to beat up a semi-conscious, subdued suspect who was already in custody. That in turn kicked off one of the worst riots in the history of Los Angeles.

In other words, people often perceive themselves as victims even as they engage in ferocious aggression. When Israeli commandos stormed the Turkish ship *Mavi Marmara* on the morning of May 31st, 2010, some of the activist passengers resisted with fists, knives and rods. The commandos proceeded to kill nine of them, including some who hadn't resisted, killing some execution-style by bullets to the back of the head. And they refused to give medical help to the people they'd wounded, callously allowing them to bleed to death. But the Israeli commandos did not grieve for the people they'd killed, nor did they express doubt about the way they'd planned and carried out the operation. Nor did the Israeli government. No, both government and commandos saw *themselves* as victims; to them, the dead Turks weren't even worth mentioning. That was the line taken by the Likudnik government of Israel, and it was quickly picked up by most people in Israel and almost all US Jewish leaders.

The reaction of the Israelis—to posture themselves as victims when their armed services had just killed nine people—was so lacking in compassion, remorse and coherence that it was just as shocking to people around the world as the actual killings themselves. But this is not unusual for the Israelis. They really *did* think of themselves as victims, even though they were the aggressors. The individual commandos involved gave several near-tearful interviews with Prime Minister Netanyahu in which they spoke about the unthinkable ignominy of people actually resisting their aggression. (The Israeli commandos boarded the Mavi Marmara in international waters, rather than waiting until it got inside Israeli waters, which makes it a war crime.) Netanyahu and his proxies in the US went ahead to give the usual speeches about how anti-Semitic it was for the world to criticize the Israelis. It was precisely that overwhelming sense of victim status, and the entitlement that usually accompanies it, that arguably drove the Israeli aggression in the first place—a dangerous emotional orientation that has been growing amongst Israelis since 1948.

35

Victimology is that pathological state in which victims refuse to move on to the next stage, of working with others to repair those things in the world that have hurt them. That's not too surprising, since victim status removes the responsibility for making moral choices; and it's also a perfect concealment for the victim's own aggression. So the person intoxicated by victimology won't go easily from being a *victim* to being a *survivor*, and therefore cannot become a *protagonist*. As a result, he is not even able to play the leading role in his own life-story. The resulting frustration drives him to hurt others; but he believes he is only protecting and defending himself, because he is the pitiful victim who never acts but only reacts. Victimology, like narcissism, obscures the victim-aggressor's ability to feel the pain of his victims, because it is only *his* pain that is important. Indeed, aggression is a sedative for such a person, to which the victim-aggressor mistakenly clings as the standard for recovery. But it is addictive, this sedative; and for that reason victim-aggressors often find themselves doing things that they know will hurt themselves—and their own people—in the long run. But they can't stop. Victim status is too attractive. Ultimately victim-hood, like misery, needs company.

36

In 1981, the Israel Lobby was mainly responsible for defeating Adlai Stevenson III during his run for governor of Illinois. The American Israel Public Affairs Committee (AIPAC), the flagship organization of the Israel Lobby in America, opposed Stevenson because he wanted to cut US aid to Israel until it slowed down illegal settlements in its occupied territories. Stevenson's position was a very good one, for three reasons: It was in line with American policy at that time; international law universally condemned Israeli settlements; and most importantly, Stevenson understood that someday Israel could increase its security by making a "land for peace" deal with Palestinians with Arab brokers. But AIPAC was already firmly on the side of the racist settlers. AIPAC, working in concert with local Jewish leaders in Illinois, succeeded in defeating Stevenson by one-seventh of a percent.

Stevenson told writer Michael Massing that because of his opposition to unlimited expansion of settlements "the Israel lobby lowered the boom. The money dried up." Many local Jewish groups and individuals were told by AIPAC not to support him. This astonished Democrats, who were blissfully unaware of the undemocratic nature of religious nationalism, and the extremes to which it was now influencing the organized Jewish community—they had chosen both to ignore how the Lobby was using money and peddling influence, and above all how ruthless religious nationalism could be when used as a political force. At the same time, politicians were learning that they could get money from AIPAC for simply voting the way AIPAC wanted them to, and all they had to do was put Israeli interests in the Middle East before US interests. Some convinced themselves that Israel's interests were exactly the same as American interests.

Manning wrote later how the Israel Lobby raises money. "A candidate will contact AIPAC and express strong sympathies with Israel. AIPAC will point out that it doesn't endorse candidates but will offer to introduce him to people who do. Someone affiliated with AIPAC will be assigned to the candidate to act as a contact person. Checks for $500 or $1,000 from pro-Israel donors will be bundled together and provided to the candidate with a clear indication of the donors' political views." All of this is perfectly legal, but immoral, because AIPAC uses donations to influence votes on American foreign policy. "In addition, meetings to raise funds will be organized in various cities. Often, the candidates are from states with negligible Jewish populations."

"The Center for Responsive Politics, a nonpartisan group that analyzes political contributions, lists a total of thirty-six pro-Israel PACs, which together contributed $3.14 million to candidates in the 2004 election cycle. Pro-Israel donors give many millions more." What politician could refuse that kind of help? But there is a very threatening dimension to the Israel Lobby's operations. If you don't agree with everything that Israel does, and you don't vote as the Lobby wants you to, your largest donors may stop taking your calls, even if they agree with you on all other domestic issues. This highly organized emphasis on the use of funding to serve Israel's rightwing government will almost always make the difference in a close race between defeat and victory. Furthermore, Israel has been moving to the right throughout its existence, and as part of that dynamic AIPAC supports the Israeli rightwing parties that currently dominate Israeli politics, including the neo-fascist parties.

Liberals were genuinely shocked by Stevenson's loss. They were in the habit of thinking of Israel as a kind of idyllic place where hard-working kibbutzim made the desert bloom, an inspiring place where nice American Jews—liberals all—sent money to plant trees. Furthermore, American progressives had come to regard American Jews as reliable supporters of diversity, civil rights and international peace. But Jewish organizations didn't vote for liberal values in Illinois in 1982, at least not like they had before—nor did they anywhere else where the Israel Lobby told them not to. In Illinois the Lobby (with the help of local Jews) had knowingly and deliberately defeated one of the country's best and most popular progressives. Non-Jewish liberals couldn't make heads or tails out of it, because they failed to see the growth of religious nationalism within the organized Jewish community. Nor did they understand the fanatical nature of religious nationalism.

The behavior of the organized Jewish community in 1982, and in the thirty years since, has been a hard school for all concerned, as increasing numbers of hard-line leaders with neo-con values have taken over the Jewish organization. The nature of Judaism in American has changed much more than most people are willing to admit. Jews may say—and may tell themselves—that they are liberals; but far too many of them will turn on liberalism to embrace the brutality of the settler movement in the West Bank when the Israel Lobby tells them to. Almost all Jewish organizations follow the same electoral strategy devised in Israel and promoted by AIPAC, even when some individuals know very well that it will hurt Israel in the long run. The toxic combination of religious nationalism and victimology is simply too powerful to resist.

37

The extreme aggressiveness of Zionism after the collapse of final-status negotiations in Israel in 2000 has completely reversed the moral trajectory of the organized Jewish community in the US. Jewish life in America was traditionally associated with liberalism, and Jewish public interest groups reflected that. Reform Judaism, for example, was so supportive of the civil rights movement in the 1960s that J. Edgar Hoover's FBI investigated its major organizations. But throughout the second half of the twentieth century, religious nationalism gradually became increasingly dominant, especially to Jewish leaders. This was to some extent an accommodation to American power in the world, facilitated by ambitious leaders with neo-conservative ideas; but even more it was about the Holocaust—or rather, the use of it—which became more important as time went on, at least partly because it became more organized. The only people who seemed to be absolutely certain about the meaning of the Holocaust were the more extreme rightwing Zionists and Jewish nationalists: *Jews can't trust the non-Jewish world, the world hates us, and it's just a matter of time until there is another Holocaust.*

Therefore everything depends on supporting Israel, no matter what. These people, and others of like mind, gradually took over the major organizations of American Jewry. By the end of the twentieth century, Jews were still liberal on some domestic issues, and still voted Democratic, but were much, much more passionate about the state of Israel, which they were expected to support unconditionally by Jewish leaders. And if Jewish liberalism collided with uncritical support for Israel's latest government, no matter how rightwing or racist, Jewish leaders were prepared to quickly abandon or oppose a liberal who refused to follow the AIPAC line, even if that liberal's positions were great on domestic issues. This should have surprised no one, since Jewish leaders defeated Adlai Stevenson III in 1981 solely because he expected Israel to follow the same international laws that everybody else follows. But nobody wanted to think about that, because its implications were too disturbing. Liberal Democrats—certainly the elected officials—simply began to vote as AIPAC told them to, because if they didn't, they wouldn't get money from AIPAC for their next election, and they were sure to get highly organized and often fanatical opposition.

The extent to which Jewish organizations had moved from liberal to extreme rightwing positions became painfully clear in 2010 with the decision of the three largest Jewish groups in America—the Simon Wiesenthal Center, the Anti-Defamation League, and the American Jewish Committee—to oppose the building of the Park51 center, a Muslim-operated community center in downtown New York City. This was in response to a public hate campaign led by two Zionist neo-fascists, Robert Spencer and Pamela Geller. In following their lead, the big Jewish organizations signaled that their leaders—the leaders of the largest organizations in the organized Jewish community—had turned consciously and decisively against the defense of religious liberty. Since freedom of religious conscience is the *sine qua non* of Judaism in America, the betrayal of it by Jewish leaders demonstrated clearly their growing recklessness, since opposition to religious liberty could be used in attacks against Jews in the future.

This betrayal of religious liberty happened because of rising Jewish bigotry against Muslims. Some Jewish leaders—often the older ones—believe that promoting bigotry against Muslims and Muslim organizations helps Israel, as well as supporting the settlers and the rightwing parties now in government in Israel. Typical of this generation is Malcolm Hoenlein, a major leader in the Conference of Presidents of Major American Jewish Organizations, who is an enthusiastic supporter of the thuggish settlers' movement in the West Bank and an opponent of peace in

Israel/Palestine. The current rightwing government in Israel is on the same page, even believing that supporting the settlers is part of a religious war of the West against Islam, and therefore a good thing. Progressive Jews are aware of this and are doing their best to counter it. For example, in a mailing to members in spring of 2011, the progressive organization 'A Jewish Voice for Peace' (JVP) wrote: "As Islamophobia rises in the US, we see it as part of our responsibility—as Jews and as Americans—to speak out against it. This is due especially to the unfortunate truth that Islamophobia is being fueled by a few large Jewish organizations to build support for Israel."

Sadly, JVP and its new rabbinical council has at present but a tiny fraction of the resources of the traditional Jewish organizations, whose leaders have almost without exception transformed themselves into stalwart members of the Israel Lobby. This means the larger Jewish organizations accept and faithfully promulgate the political line that emanates from the Israeli Foreign Office, and are all therefore virtually indistinguishable from each other and from the rightwing Israeli government. It is a disaster for American foreign policy that they have so much power, to be sure—but it is in some ways an even more pronounced disaster for Judaism in America that this highly nuanced, profoundly educated and hard-working faith community now sees itself as simply an extension of the Israeli state. That means that Judaism is in the process of being nationalized by Israel as a state religion.

The most powerful of the Israeli proxies is the American-Israeli Public Affairs Council (AIPAC), which was mainly responsible for the unfortunate defeat of Adlai Stevenson III in Illinois. In 2011, AIPAC completely dominates Congressional policy in the Middle East through money and the political influence money can buy. (An actual majority of elected politicians in Congress now receive money from AIPAC.) AIPAC actively discourages Congress from considering American interests in the Middle East, taking the position that Israeli interests are invariably the same as US interests. (How could *any* country have *exactly* the same interests as any other country?) During Cast Lead, the Israeli War against Hamas in Gaza, a statement was adopted by both Houses of the US Congress. And who wrote that statement? An objective American, one would think, an honorable person anxious to promote a balanced point of view regarding American interests in this and other conflicts. But the statement of uncritical support for Israel was actually written by AIPAC, the representative of a foreign nation, whose staffers are well-paid to write things representing Israeli interests. In the pathetic charade that has become American foreign policy in the Middle East, this Israeli document was adopted without comment by the assembled legislators—except that they pretended, as a group, that it was an American document representing American interests. The assembled legislators were handsomely paid by AIPAC for their services in the next electoral cycle.

And the fact that most important Jewish leaders now accept the idea of a war of the West against Islam demonstrates the pervasive—and detestable—influence of the neo-conservative moment on the organized Jewish community in the US, and on American foreign policy. Consider the famous letter sent by the neo-cons in 1996, pleading with Netanyahu not to make peace with the Palestinians. What is the current belief of a 'Clash of Civilizations' but an updated version of that idea, featuring Israel as a nuclear power in the vanguard of a religious war against Islam? Considering the role that American Jews once played in the various peace movements, the neo-con influence on American Judaism is beyond irony, and beneath contempt. And it increasingly involves not just an extreme intervention in American elections, but the creation of a thought police as well, to keep dissenters in the Jewish community in line. To understand fully why this is so dangerous one must look at individual cases in which the Israel Lobby has been involved.

38

In 2006, the Richard Rogers Partnership, an internationally-admired architectural firm headquartered in London, found out just how strong the American Israel Lobby can be. The Rogers Partnership allowed a group called Architects and Planners for Justice in Palestine (APJP) to meet in its London offices. This was a group of architects that believed that Israel needed to make peace with the Palestinians, and that the administration of occupied Palestinian territories had been bad for both Palestine and Israel. It probably accurately represented the feeling of a majority of secular British Jews at that time, especially those with social justice concerns.

The APJP was, in the group's own words, formed "to raise awareness in the planning, design and construction industries as to how those professions were central to the occupation of Palestinian land and to the erosion of human rights." The meeting space had been rather casually provided by Lord Richard Rogers, who in 1996 had been created Baron Rogers of Riverside, and who was the presiding creative and administrative force in the Partnership. Lord Rogers was also the architect of some relatively inventive modernist structures, probably the most notable being the Pompidou Centre in Paris (and the most ironic—given his imminent fate at the hands of the US Israel Lobby—being the building for the European Court of Human Rights in Strasbourg). Many of the architects present at the APJP meeting were Jewish, and many had ties to human rights organizations in Israel.

Lord Rogers spoke only for a few moments to the group before leaving, referring mainly to the connection between architecture and human rights. A distorted version of this meeting was dutiful leaked, and supporters of the Likud government in Israel quickly floated a false statement that Rogers opposed Israel's right to build a separation wall. Others in that camp then initiated a sensational series of articles in the London press incorrectly alleging that the purpose of the meeting was to "boycott Israel"—which was false, since Rogers has always opposed a boycott—and operatives in the US Israel Lobby were notified. It turned out that Roger's economic and architectural interests in the US made him vulnerable to political and economic extortion; one really can't blame Rogers for not knowing that, because there is nothing in Britain as rich, powerful or ruthless as the Israel Lobby in the States.

Rogers had recently been chosen to design the Jacob Javits Conference Centre in New York, which was estimated to cost $1.7 billion. Architect Abe Hayeem tells what happened next: "Without waiting to ascertain the facts, Tony Gargano, the state's chief development official, summoned Lord Rogers to New York, like a suspected criminal, to face a tribunal of city councilors, heads of certain prominent mainstream Jewish organizations and elected officials. These included New York State Assembly Speaker Sheldon Silver and congressman Anthony Weiner, who demanded Rogers be dropped from the Javits project. Another major project that Rogers was working on, the Silvercup Studios in Long Island City in Queens, also seemed to be under threat."

David Harris, of the American Jewish Committee, did not wait long to also plunge his little knife into Rogers, reaping whatever ensuing publicity benefits might be available. He wrote a letter to the agency responsible for commissioning the Javits Center containing the following fraudulent claims:

> "Clearly, the agenda of this group [the APJP] reflects very deep seated anti-Israel and anti-Semitic views. We remain very concerned about the possibility of illegal or improper actions by Lord Roger's company while working on such an important and publicly funded project, especially one which memorializes Jacob Javits, a strong opponent of bigotry and

steadfast supporter of Israel."[44]

Whether Lord Rogers might be the best architect for the job never seemed to cross anybody's mind. But the Lobby operatives did threaten him with federal and New York state anti-boycott laws, despite the fact Lord Rogers opposed boycotting Israel. What Lord Rogers should have done, had he stopped to think about his integrity instead of his bank account, was to hire a good attorney and start talking breach of contract. Instead he evidently followed the conventional advice and hired PR consultant Howard Rubinstein, a crisis consultant and a slippery character who knew exactly what the Lobby wanted, and quickly advised Rogers to give it up.

To begin with, Rogers had to publicly denounce boycotts of any kind (despite the fact that he'd never advocated one) and disassociate himself from the Architects and Planners for Justice in Palestine. Then he had to make a statement written by Rubinstein stressing his Jewish roots. (Why did he have to discuss his Jewish roots publicly? This seems like a little strategically-applied *schadenfreude* by the egregious Rubinstein, who appears to have been just as invested in bringing Lord Rogers down a peg or two as helping him out of his dilemma.) Rogers was forced to make the following vacuous and completely pressured statement, obviously coerced and probably written by his tormenters:

> "Hamas must renounce terrorism, Hamas must recognize Israel's right to exist. Just making a statement is not enough. They have to back it up. The wall between Israel and the Palestinians has proven to prevent many suicide bomber attempts and deaths. And I am in favor of it to thwart terror attacks on Israel."

A year later the APJP, without Lord Richard Rogers, circulated a petition criticizing architects illegally building settlements in the Israeli Occupied Territories, appearing in the May 2007 issue of *The Times* in London. A great many architects and academics supported it, including four former and one future president of the Royal Institute of British Architects (RIBA), not to mention a great many Israeli architects and human rights organizations. The Simon Wiesenthal Center of Los Angeles, California, predictably came up with an unknown British group called British Architect Friends of Israel, and together they called for the expulsion of RIBA from the international organization of architects, and ritually accused the petition-signers of being anti-Semites.

But Lord Richard Rogers, Baron Rogers of Riverside, did not need to concern himself with this, since he had publicly disassociated himself from the signers.

No less than Abraham Foxman of the Anti-Defamation League gave Roger his gracious imprimatur to continue with his profitable architectural activities in the US. ("If we didn't believe that people could change hearts and minds, we wouldn't be in business.") One has to wonder, however, if Rogers will ever equal or exceed his former triumphs such as the Pompidou Centre. Once you have been coerced into publicly denouncing those values that you have spent a lifetime developing—those beliefs that make you what you are—your creative faculties have a way of dissipating. When Lord Richard Rogers caved to the Lobby and stepped up to renounce his most intimate beliefs at the behest of his tormenters, he damaged, perhaps irreparably, his identity as an artist; and also, most likely, as a Jew.[45]

39

This highly unpleasant incident is related because it demonstrates, in a single case, the incredible political clout of the Israel Lobby in America, not to mention certain (although not all) of its mostly undemocratic tactics. The Lobby engages in the blanket denunciation of critics of Israel as anti-Semites or self-hating Jews, utterly trivializing the issue of real anti-Jewish bigotry and insulting the memory of every Jew who ever died because of it. Featured also is the use of outright deceit and distortions, not to mention the easy access of Lobby players to the media, and their skill in manipulating media by floating successive, highly calibrated and gradually escalating lies to deceive the public. The Rogers case also involved the three largest US Jewish organizations (Abraham Foxman's Anti-Defamation League, the American Jewish Committee and the Simon Wiesenthal Center) which under current leadership operate as components of the Israel Lobby in the US. The Rogers case is an example of attempted extortion. This involved a sum of almost two billion dollars, the threatened loss of which was raised exclusively to intimidate and publicly humiliate those who would advocate human rights in Israel/Palestine. As in almost all similar cases, this example also illustrates the flagrantly self-destructive nature of the Lobby, since Israel's future security can be guaranteed only if the Palestinians have the same security and human rights as Jews. But peace and security is not what the Israel Lobby wants.

The Rogers case also illustrates rather well a tactic adopted over the last two decades by the ADL's Abraham Foxman, and developed by him into something resembling an authoritarian art form—that is to say, the habit of coercing public apologies from people, usually by requiring them to engage in the recitation of a carefully-composed public apology, the entire process of which is solely intended to humiliate the targeted individual in full view of the American public. And why must any supposedly free person apologize to Abraham Foxman? Almost always because they said something about Israel that Foxman didn't like, however true it may have been, for which they must therefore be publicly humiliated. The remarkable thing is that so many people are willing to comply with such a destructive process.

This ritual of public apologia, which many people think of as practically an invention of Foxman, uses some of the dynamics of a Stalinist show trial, although in a much more compact way. (Of course the fate of the victim is different—in Soviet show trials, disgraced individuals were shot; Foxman's victims are merely rendered unemployable.) One also notices that Foxman's gambit is perfectly adapted to the dynamics of a celebrity culture addicted to sound-bites. The methodology revolves around gradually skewering the victim in the most public way possible. The victim is at first denounced as an anti-Semite or self-hating Jew, or simply a bigot, by the omnipresent Foxman. He adduces no evidence, nor does he make any argument, because he doesn't have to—he simply makes the accusation in his usual in-your-face manner. (Foxman knows American media would never examine his charges on their merits, because the media is interested in the drama of public humiliation.)

The targeted person tries haltingly to explain himself, but is repeatedly denounced, each time in stronger language. With each renewed plea that he *really* isn't an anti-Semite, that he really wants to *help* Israel, he manages to sound increasingly guilty, if not of anti-Semitism, of something spectacularly bad. (A discomforting reality of celebrity culture is that when one is publicly accused of something, denial makes one sound guiltier.) In the case of Foxman, the accusations are made on network TV and in widely-circulated press releases that appear in the *New York Times*. A particularly galling aspect of electronic media is that when one is charged with a supposed thought crime inherent to criticism of some Israeli policy—and the accuser is given a media pulpit to do so—some perception of guilt exists for the lifetime of the person accused. Once his guilt is fixed in the public imagination, the real question that arises about the accused is what other horrible things he may think or say in addition to his present heresy. Most of Foxman's victims therefore conclude that resistance is futile.

There is only one way out for the person accused of anti-Semitism by Foxman. The heretic must acknowledge his essential wretchedness, throw himself on the dubious mercy of the public, and plead for forgiveness and redemption from his powerful accuser.

During the process of denunciation, Foxman will typically make references to the Holocaust, indicating the seriousness of the accusation and establishing Foxman's, and Israel's, victim status preparatory to attacking the targeted individual. (The Holocaust references, although they have nothing to do with the matter at hand, also demonstrate through a crude guilt by association the nearly irredeemable loathsomeness of the victim.) The Accused One is finally allowed—or encouraged—to haltingly make his apology, sometimes wiping away a tear or two, and in so doing pledges his unqualified love for the Holy State.

To punch up the inherent drama of this public burning—and again to signal the victim's bottomless capacity for perfidy—the indefatigable Foxman often demands a *second* public apology or statement from the accused, if he decides that the first one isn't sufficient. That puts Foxman in the position of being able to organize the culprit's social rehabilitation under the watchful eyes of the American media. That aspect of the interaction—that people must personally apologize to Foxman, and to his Anti-Defamation League—makes him the main power center capable of redeeming those that have thought, said or done something insulting to Israel's current rightwing government.

It also reinforces Foxman as the proper arbiter of moral certainty regarding everything having to do with Jews, Nazis,

Israelis and the "special relationship" between America and Israel—to which everything else is merely prelude. In a celebrity culture, that makes Foxman a little like a religious figure, but also the focus of one of the most vulgar interactions imaginable in a supposedly free society. The actual function of Foxman's gambit is always about power—beginning with his own power—but it is also about the power of the Holocaust as it is used to intimidate people, and the power of the Israel Lobby to make people back down if they wander too far away from the Lobby's political line. Under Foxman, the ADL is unmistakably a thought police, a theater for public punishment, and an address for redemption, all in one agency. But it is also demeaning, disgusting, and on aesthetic and ideological grounds a disaster for American civilization.

The fact that people are so often persuaded to publicly apologize for things that are no more than the truth as they see it; to weep and grovel for having uttered opinions they really believe; to read statements denouncing their own beliefs, and in that manner to engage in carefully-orchestrated rituals of self-abnegation such as the unlucky Lord Rogers was forced to do; has enabled Foxman, the ADL and the rest of the Israel Lobby to establish themselves in America as representatives of a state thought police. Not the US state, to be sure, but a foreign state—the state of Israel as it is represented by its well-connected proxies in American political life.

In short, defending Israel isn't enough—Israel's critics must be silenced precisely because so much of what Israel does is indefensible. The following short vignette is by way of documenting something that happens rather regularly to Palestinian boys in East Jerusalem since the government is trying to ethnically cleanse the neighborhood of Palestinians and replace them with Jewish settlers.

40

Fifteen-year-old Luai from Silwan [an East Jerusalem neighborhood] walked to the Al Mascobiyya Interrogation Centre after his mother told him that the [Israeli] police had come to their house looking for him. Luai reported arriving at the interrogation centre at around 1 PM and waiting for his mother to arrive. "I had barely waited two minutes when I saw an interrogator named 'Shadi,' recalls Luai. "I know him because he interrogated me several times in the past. Once he spotted me, he rushed towards me with another man in civilian clothes…and dragged me to another building across the street."

"'What's going on?' I asked, but they didn't respond. I was scared and didn't know where they were taking me."

Loai reports being taken to another building and placed inside a large room. "Shadi forced me to kneel down and face the wall with hands behind the back of my head. 'Don't say a single word or I'll beat the hell out of you,' he said to me." Luai reports being kept in this position for about three hours whilst Shadi and the other man remained in the room smoking and talking to each other.

"Whenever I moved my head, they would slap me on the neck," recalls Luai.

About three hours later, the two men started to interrogate Luai, and accused him of throwing stones and Molotov cocktails. The only evidence the interrogators referred to was that of 'our informers in the neighborhoods.'

Luai denied the accusations against him. "I wasn't scared," says Luai, "as I have got used to this, as this is the fifth time they have arrested me."

Contrary to Israeli law, Luai was interrogated in the absence of a family member, and at the conclusion of the interrogation, was made to place his fingerprints on a blank piece of paper. Luai was then handcuffed and taken to a cell where he was detained with five other detainees, including adults and children. The following day, Luai was taken to court but says he did not understand what the judge was saying as he was speaking in Hebrew.

Following his court appearance, Luai was taken back to Al Mascobiyya for a second night, before being released on 14 January 2011, on NIS 500 (US $140) bail and a bond of 3,000 NIS (US $840). Luai was also given a five-day home detention order.

"My father has decided to leave Silwan," Luai says, "and take us to Anata refugee camp because he's tired of soldiers and settlers harassing us. Settlers who live in our neighborhood keep insulting us and soldiers arrest us whenever something happens. My brother, Feras, was released yesterday and is now under home arrest for six months, and my father is summoned from time to time. Our house is also under threat of demolition."

"Therefore, my father had decided to leave Silwan and spare us the suffering. That means we're going to start a new life in Anata and go to new schools. We will leave our relatives and friends behind because my father doesn't want us to get arrested and beaten by soldiers."

This report was compiled from testimony given by the boy named Luai to an organization called "Defense of Children International—Palestine Section," received on 12 February 2011. (The same organization reports 13 similar narratives from East Jerusalem.) What is so striking about this is that it isn't a horror story, but on the contrary feels utterly normal—this is simply life for Palestinians in East Jerusalem. One is impressed by the sense of being completely helpless from aggression by the oppressor, especially from the point of view of a parent who wishes to protect his children. For that reason Luai's father would rather take his family to a refugee camp rather than live in his own home in East Jerusalem. This is called slow ethnic cleansing.

41

Various high-profile public spokespersons for the Israel Lobby insist that there *is* no Lobby, that it simply doesn't exist, and that any suggestion that it *does* exist is anti-Semitic. (Abraham Foxman makes this claim in his book *The Deadliest Lie*, despite the fact that he is himself one of the Lobby's main spokespersons.) This creates a dilemma both for Foxman and for others engaged in the lobbying effort for the Israeli cause. On the one hand, they expect the Israel Lobby's ideas to be taken seriously—but at the same time, they insist that the Lobby doesn't exist. They can't have it both ways, but that's evidently what they want.

Got it? There's no Israel Lobby, but you'd better not contradict its political line, or there'll be swift and certain retaliation. You're anti-Semitic if you oppose the Lobby's ideas, but equally anti-Semitic if you acknowledge that it exists. To help readers with this Orwellian dilemma, the following 12-step program is offered for people addicted to telling the truth about American public discourse. These "12 Steps of the Israel Lobby" are to be memorized, and read if possible in a venue featuring the theme song of "The Twilight Zone" in the background. (At the end, the supplicant might consider murmuring softly "I *love* the Lobby" several times.)

1. The Israel Lobby does not exist. In those cases where it does exist, its conclusions cannot be questioned.

2. All criticisms of Israel are false. They are invented by anti-Semites, self-hating Jews, and terrorists. Also by crypto-Nazis, apostates and liars.

3. All critics of Israel must be punished by extracting a public apology. Some offenders may be required to

apologize more than once.

4. Those who criticize Israel and do not apologize must be endlessly harassed, and fired from their jobs if possible. In academia they must be denied tenure.

5. Any Arab or Muslim that criticizes Israel is a terrorist, and deserves to die.

6. To praise anybody who ever criticized Israel is the same thing as criticizing Israel itself. Just as all things Israeli are good, anybody that criticizes Israel is bad.

7. In any conflict involving Israelis and Palestinians, the Israelis are always the victims. If an Israeli kills a Palestinian, the Israeli is still the victim because the Palestinians are trying to make the Israeli feel bad.

8. Israel/Palestine is never debated. That implies another side to the issue, and there is only one side. Therefore debate is suppressed or disrupted.

9. The United Nations, the World Court, the various UN agencies, every human rights organization and Non-Governmental Organization not approved of by the NGO Monitor [an Israeli screening operation] is anti-Semitic. This is because any of these organizations are likely to criticize Israel's human rights abuses of Palestinians—and as any fool knows, that means that they hate Jews.

10. The interests of the United States are exactly the same as the interests of Israel. If they aren't, the interests of Israel take precedence.

11. Any war that the US is likely to be involved in must be evaluated from the point of view of its helpfulness to the current government of Israel.

12. Anybody who threatens to make sense while criticizing Israel must be immediately shouted down. If shouting doesn't work, screaming and crying are recommended. As a last resort, one must declare that criticisms of Israel are making one feel "unsafe."

The above is satire, but is a satirical treatment of a reality that is petty, tiresome and undemocratic. The Israel Lobby operates as a thought police, spending millions of dollars to prevent Americans from having a candid discussion of American interests in the Middle East. It will continue to do so until we are courageous (and patriotic) enough to restore free speech and freedom of association to American discourse about the Middle East.

42

The American Israeli Public Affairs Council (AIPAC) doesn't just control opinion about Israel in the House of Representatives and the Senate. They and the other organizations that constitute the Israel Lobby have gradually come to have enormous influence over any issue that they define as *concerning* Israel. Over a period of years that has gradually come to mean the entire Middle East and those fifty or so Muslim-majority countries that we call the Muslim world. Thus AIPAC, the neo-cons, and the other organizations in the Israel Lobby have, through the default and cowardice of our elected officials (and their desperation for campaign funds), gradually come to have a disproportionate influence on American policy relating to those huge sections of the earth where the majority practices Islam. This is bad for the world, for America and ultimately bad for Israel. It is also bad for American Judaism, which the Israel Lobby has high-jacked to serve its geo-political agenda.

Finally, the power of the Israel Lobby doesn't just happen because of a small minority of billionaire Zionists, neo-con foundations and high-profile character assassins. The real power comes from the people who are too cowardly to stand up to them—that is, the majority of the people that are overwhelmingly of Christian origins. But the dirty little secret about Christians in public life is that they are terrified of being called anti-Semites by the Israel Lobby, and will do or say anything to avoid it—and if they receive money for keeping their mouths shut, so much the better.

Let us take the famous mainstream media, or MSM, as an example. Most of the people who own and work in media come from a nominally Christian background. And yet they are so terrified of the Israel Lobby and so willing to do its bidding that they knowingly suppress the free exchange of information, even information that would be interesting and helpful to most Americans. Let's be clear about this: what this really means is that the power of the Israel Lobby doesn't come from a minority of neo-cons and rightwing Zionists and AIPAC staffers. They're just the fanatical ones with money and power who initiate the self-destructive policies and the censorship. The ones who make those destructive policies work are the people in the trenches who say nothing, yet participate in the suppression of ideas, stories and opinions that aren't approved by the Israeli state. The real power of the Israel Lobby, in other words, comes not from aggressive Jewish Zionists but from gutless Christians.

43

"Few people think of Judaism as a political movement the way they might consider Islam or Christianity. When I think of Judaism, I think of latkes, challah, Woody Allen and Passover Seders. I think of my mother yelling 'Oy vey' when I did badly on a quiz or when she burned the Rosh Hashanah brisket. If you're an American of any religion, this is probably the image you have of Jewish people as well."

"But there's a whole other section of the world that has a very different perception of Jewish people. To them, Judaism is nothing but a political movement. They think of Jewish people—Israelis—who rode in on military jeeps and evicted them from their homes. They think of Jewish people who have blocked them off from the rest of the world, by physical wall or economic blockade. They think of Jewish people who have stolen their land and denied their history."

"I agree that it would be wrong to draw conclusions about Israelis or Jews in general because of some Israeli policies and military actions — just as it would be wrong to judge any community by the actions of its worst representatives. But how do we deal with Judaism when almost all American Jewish organizations unconditionally support Israeli policies?"

"In the secular, post-religion age in which many of us live, Judaism has been preserved by another faith: nationalism. Allegiance to Israel is integral to the American Jewish experience, perhaps even more so than the religious and cultural tradition born out of the Diaspora. And organized Judaism's political leanings are nearly monolithic.

Questioning this allegiance is the worst taboo within the organized Jewish community. Academics like Noam Chomsky and Norman Finkelstein who criticize Israel are dubbed 'self-hating Jews' by the American Jewish mainstream. Jewish pro-

Palestinian groups like 'Jews Say No' or 'Jewish Voices for Peace' are on the ultimate fringe. There are a few semi-mainstream Jewish groups that do criticize Israel, but there are none that will even entertain the idea of a non-Jewish Israeli-Palestinian state."

"The result is a near-total politicization of Judaism, analogous to Islamism in the Middle East or Sarah Palin's brand of political Christianity here. While, unlike these ideologies, American Jews do not advocate for our government to be founded on Jewish values, we do advocate specific policies in the Middle East. Like the Sabbath prayers and the stories of the Torah, the history of modern Israel – often stripped of its unsavory bits – is an integral part of Jewish education. The Israeli independence fighters are heroes for American Jews, just like George Washington or Paul Revere. Millions of dollars are spent to teach young Jews to love Israel and to defend Israel from its critics. The proof is overwhelming and undeniable: Maintaining a Jewish nation-state in Palestine has become one of organized Judaism's core goals."

"And just as it is fair to criticize Israeli policies, it is fair to criticize its apologists – groups that claim to represent the entire American Jewish community. American Jews have traditionally been at the forefront of progressive movements. But in recent years, American Jewish institutions have trended toward the ugly side of Zionism, defending – or at least apologizing for – the Israeli hard right in its continuation of the occupation of the West Bank and repression of Palestinian identity. The undeniable injustices of the Israeli government and military warrant criticism; silence in the face of these injustices warrants criticism as well."

"It is time for American Jews to stand up against oppression, violence and religious fundamentalism. The tribalism that has persuaded the Jewish people to stand up categorically for Israel for so many years is foolish and outdated. The occupation of the West Bank is wrong. The blockade of Gaza is wrong. The displacement of Palestinian villages is wrong. The continued construction of settlements is wrong. And American Jews have enabled all of it. It's about time a Jew stood up and said so."[46]

47

The above was written by an extraordinarily courageous young sophomore at Princeton named Brandon Davis, and published in *The Daily Princetonian* in October 2011. (About half of the student comments were positive; the negative ones were full of personal invective calling Davis a self-hating Jew.) The full-frontal campaign to transform Judaism into something completely different from what it was before is a reality, but not one people feel comfortable acknowledging. Uri Avnery, the Israeli peace campaigner, has pointed out that religion in Israel is no longer real Judaism but has become a profoundly unattractive "religious mutation," as unlike early twentieth-century Judaism as Pentecostal snake-handling is of High-Church Anglicanism. Avnery points out that Orthodox Judaism in Israel is not only the remnant of Ashkenazi Jewish practices but also of the Sephardim, a shotgun wedding that has often brought out the worst and most rightwing aspects of both Orthodox traditions. And the government-supported "national-religious" Jews, an even more conservative third group, have become the storm troops of the racist settler movement in the West Bank.

Both Orthodox and "national-religious" Judaism is the remnant of what was once a great world religion—now both compete with each other to brutalize the Palestinians and steal their land. Both, to put it another way, are the foot soldiers of the slow ethnic cleansing that is currently going on in the West Bank; religion as taught by their rabbis and teachers emphasize their obligation to redeem Jewish suffering by taking Palestinian land away by force from the people that own it. This is nothing less than the Christian obsession with redemptive violence, enhanced and focused by internalized Holocaust aggression.

Uri Avnery writes of the way that that "national-religious" Judaism was consciously brought into being by the Israeli leaders: "Thanks to the massive support of the Zionist leadership, the 'national-religious' camp grew in Israel at a dizzying pace. Ben-Gurion set up a special branch of the educational system for them, which grew more extremist by the year, as did the national-religious youth movement, Bnei Akiva. Members of one generation of the national-religious community became the teachers of the next, which guaranteed an inbuilt process of radicalization. With the beginning of the occupation, they created Gush Emunim ("the Bloc of the Faithful"), the ideological core of the settlement movement. Nowadays this camp is directed by Rabbis whose teachings emit a strong odor of Fascism." Both "national-religious" and Orthodox basically the same thing, Avnery believes, and "together constitute an Orthodox-national-religious bloc."

This new religion "does not resemble the Judaism which existed in the Diaspora, neither the Orthodox nor the Reform model. It must be said: the Jewish religion in Israel is a mutation of Judaism, a tribal, racist, extreme nationalist and anti-democratic creed." Avnery also writes that they "teach their pupils the history of the Jewish people only (based, of course, on the religious myths), nothing about the history of the world, of other peoples, not to mention other religions. The Koran and the New Testament are the kernel of evil and not to be touched."

"The typical alumni of these systems know that the Jews are the chosen (and vastly superior) people, that all Goyim are vicious anti-Semites, that God promised us this country and that no one else has a right to one square inch of its land. The natural conclusion is that the 'foreigners' (meaning the Arabs, who have been living here for 13 centuries at least) must be expelled—unless this would harm the Jews."

"From this point of view, there is no longer any difference between the Orthodox and the national-religious, between Ashkenazim and Sephardim. Seeing the 'youth of the hills' who terrorize Arabs in the occupied territories, one cannot distinguish among them anymore—not by their dress, not by their body language, not by their slogans."

"The source of all this evil is, of course, the original sin of the State of Israel: *the non-separation between state and religion, based on the non-separation between nation and religion.* Nothing but a complete separation between the two will save Israel from total domination by the religious mutation." (Italics added.) Which mutation can only further degrade American religion, one might add, which has already been degraded by Jewish and Christian leaders themselves in their celebration of Judeo-Christianity, which now stands revealed as the glib bastard child of Christian and Jewish degradation.

48

The most important aspect of the rise of Judeo-Christianity is not its vulgarity, because vulgarity can be endured—indeed, both the vulgar and the obscene are the staple of much satire in America, not to mention the political comedy of such geniuses as Jon Steward and Stephen Colbert. Far more dangerous is what is happening in the Middle East—but that, too, is partly driven by a madness that is also, paradoxically, now reaching critical mass in America. The Israel Lobby in the US and the rightwing government in Israel are increasingly irrational; and rightwing Jewish cults such as Aish HaTorah play an increasingly important role in Israel, and have a distinct apocalyptic subtext. Certain violent events will bring about the end of human history as we know it, according to almost all of the ultra-conservative Christian and Jewish cults (and they can hardly wait for that to happen). The Israeli cultists, the Christian Zionists of the US, and the rightwing Christian evangelicals are all tuned into this central idea. The mainline Protestants and US Council of Catholic Bishops do their part by saying almost nothing about the Middle East, and secular liberals are silent as the grave. Everybody knows that something is afoot, but nobody wants to be kicked around by the Israel Lobby, and even those few who aren't afraid don't know what to do.

To Jewish victimology add the Christian addiction to redemptive violence, melded together in an obsessive, total internalization of the Holocaust; and then top it off with Zionist worship of the Israeli state. What you will shortly have is something darker than nihilism, and more pathological than mere mental illness. What you are starting to get, quite simply, is a number of people who are intent on resolving the problem of good and evil by destroying the world, and themselves along with it. A fair number of them are people who feel that a world in which the Holocaust can happen is not a world that should be allowed to exist. Some of them have even admitted as much. They do not believe that humanity can change, because they are not willing to change themselves, nor will they reconsider their own their fondest beliefs; worst of all, they are not even willing to try.

Increasingly the Ivy League-educated, intensely literate Jewish neo-cons in America have adopted the same desperate attitude of the evangelicals and the extreme rightwing Jewish settlers on the West Bank. The difference is that they do not seem to be conscious of it—perhaps they cannot allow themselves to become conscious of it—nor of the self-defeating undercurrents of their support for the Likudniks and neo-fascists currently in government in Israel. The older Jewish leaders in the US have likewise signed up for the same apocalyptic solution, which means not just more ethnic cleansing of Palestinians but also sure and certain war in the Middle East. And then there is the rise of Israeli fascism, not just against Palestinians but against dissenting Jews who dare to define themselves as 'post-Zionist.'

For neo-cons, the irrational and tribal side of the evangelical/neo-con deal has far out-stripped every other aspect of their original collaboration; and that is what increasingly makes neo-conservatism itself a kind of cult for authoritarian intellectuals, rather than a considered geo-political worldview. The most striking aspect of the political class in Israel *and* most of the institutional Jewish leadership in the US is their self-destructiveness: the permanent war that the neo-cons advocate will create many, many more problems for Israel than it could possibly resolve. This irrationality has alarmed the WASP paleo-conservatives, first because there are now almost as many Jewish multi-billionaires as Protestant ones, but also because the old-boy Prods can no longer control the volatile Zionists they had originally hired on as errand boys and mercenaries.

The paleos are alarmed for reasons that should also alarm us, but not because it inconveniences a few rich Protestants. The neo-con approach to problem-solving no longer makes sense, nor is it based on enlightened or even informed self-interest, but has instead become an apocalyptic movement based on identification with the Holocaust, driven by an almost complete internalization of its trauma and an ever-present and semi-hysterical death worship of the six million. This fixation on Holocaust trauma, invoked regularly by the powerful in both Israel and the US, is used to repress all consciousness of Palestinian suffering or even the existence of Palestinians. But the emotional effect of such a strategy is ultimately a kind of madness.

The basic neo-conservative idea is that both America and Israel must exist in a state of permanent war against much of the rest of the world, an idea that neo-cons first expressed in their public letter to Netanyahu in 1996 warning against a peace deal with the Palestinians. Eventually the neo-cons want Israel's war against the Arabs to become America's war against the Muslim world, against those fifty or so countries in which Islam is the majority religion; and they believe that it should be ongoing. But what country can remain in a state of permanent war for long? Why is religious war better than peace? Permanent war is an abomination, and people who believe in it are insane.

The apocalyptic, victimology-driven Jewish neo-cons who long for permanent war do not flinch for a moment at the potential loss of Jewish lives; indeed, they have lived for years in an unbalanced moral and emotional universe in which it is assumed as self-evident that the world hates Jews, that everybody is against them, and a new Holocaust is on the way. In fact this is so self-evident and so necessary to their *weltanschauung* that the neo-cons will do almost anything to *make* it happen, to *prove* for all time that everybody hates Jews.

The more Jews that die: the more children murdered: the more the neo-cons can trumpet to the world that everybody really *does* hate them. Their solution is an apocalyptic one, borrowed from the most hysterical and blood-obsessed form of Christianity, but going the Christians one step better—to the neo-cons the objective is not to *win* the Final Battle, but to *lose* it, thereby acting out to ecstatic completion the total authenticity of their victim status. The apocalyptic Judeo-Christian solution is, at bottom, a dangerous, narcissistic form of public suicide that seeks the destruction of the world as its answer to the paradoxes of the human dilemma.

Afterword

Institutional religions in the West are unable to bring peace to Israel/Palestine, because they're part of the problem. Meanwhile international social and economic difficulties multiply, as the power centers of the world are driven by aggression, exploitation and other forms of systemic evil. Religion in the West is unable to help us overcome the destructive forces of empire, war and oppression.

What is needed is a secular theory of how aggression, violence and evil work, why they are so compelling to so many people, and why they are able to influence otherwise normal men and women. That is the subject of my next book, *Trauma Bond: An Inquiry into the Nature of Evil,* the second book in the **Genesis Trilogy.** *Trauma Bond* deals with how aggression is internalized, the central role of deceit in systemic evil, and how both are enhanced by key cultural factors.

Religious establishments may someday reconstitute themselves as a source of moral instruction and inspiration in the West. Until then, secular people have to figure out on their own the underlying psychological realities that drive destructive social behavior. If you found *The Death of Judeo-Christianity* challenging, read the next book in the **Genesis Trilogy**. Watch for *Trauma Bond: An Inquiry into the Nature of Evil.* It's a book that will change the way you see the world.

Lawrence Swaim
Napa Valley

Notes/References

1. Carroll, James, *Constantine's Sword: The Church and the Jews* (New York: Houghton Mifflin Company, 2001), 150. Carroll encountered this story in the introduction to Cynthia Ozick's *Rescuers*, xi.
2. Ibid., 171.
3. Ibid., 202.
4. Ibid., 204.
5. Ibid., 203.
6. Ibid, 204.
7. Ibid., 171.
8. Ibid., 193.
9. Francis James Child, *English and Scottish Popular Ballads: Student's Cambridge Edition* (Boston: Houghton Mifflin Company, 1932), 368-369.
10. Jack Miles, "The Art of The Passion." In *Mel Gibson's Bible*, eds. Timothy K. Beal and Tod Linafelt, Chicago and London Univ. of Chicago Press, 13.
11. David Edelstein, Slate's Film critic http://www.slate.com/id /2096025
12. Jean Cohen, Jerusalem Post, 12 March 2004. First encountered in Timothy Kandler Bell and Tod Linafelt, *Mel Gibson's Bible: Religion, Popular Culture and The Passion of the Christ* (Chicago University of Chicago Press, 2006), 113.
13. Ibid., 113-114.
14. Leo Tolstoy would later do the same thing in "The Gospels in Brief," cutting out the miracles, crucifixions and resurrection to concentrate on Jesus' teachings. This resulted briefly in a small but energetic Christian movement called "Tolstoyism" in Russia, which the Bolsheviks crushed when they seized power.
15. Sunday Times of London, "The head Nazi-hunter's trail of lies," by Guy Walters (July eighteenth, 2009).

16. *Jewish Chronicle*, "It is right to expose Wiesenthal," by Daniel Finkelstein (August twentieth, 2009).
17. A handful of scholars mentioned Wiesenthal's tendency to confabulate in the early 1990s, but most did not, and this writer cannot remember a single instance in which a popular writer mentioned it.
18. Wiesenthal Center (2006), "SWC Condemns anti-Semitic statements by Venezuelan President Hugo Chavez, Demands Public Apology". Wiesenthal Center (2006), http.//Wiesenthal.com/site/pps/nl/content.asp?c=fwLYKnN8LzH&b=312458&content_id={17D5A467-8F24-4ADA-BCD3-DE4476D7F462}¬oc=1.
19. Obituary, "Justin Finger, 69, Dies; Lawyer Aided Causes," by Robert Mcg. Thomas Jr. (May eleventh, 1996).
20. Ben Harris, "Rabbi Noah Wienberg, Founder of Aish HaTorah, Died," *Jewish Telegraphic Agency*, 6 Feb. 2009.
21. Center for Constitutional Rights website, Mamilla Campaign, Appendix Two, Affidavit of Gideon Suleimani, Chief Excavator for the Israeli Antiquities Authority on the "Center of Human Dignity—Museum of Tolerance" site in Mamilla Cemetery. Submitted to the Israel High Court in 2009 (Unofficial Translation). Interestingly, Mr. Suleimani includes his Israeli ID number, 53599999. http://www.Mamillacampaign.org/photos/pdfs/Appendix2.pdf.
22. Raul Hilberg, *The Times*, (London), August 8, 2007.
23. http://www.logosjournal.com/issue_6.1-2/hilberg.htm
24. It was often said that eleven million in all perished in the gas chambers, but this often-quoted figure came from none other than Simon Wiesenthal, and is therefore not reliable. But many non-Jews did perish in gas chambers and in other ways, something Wiesenthal himself always insisted on. About that, he was right. The Nazi use of the industrial method of mass murder was not used on Jews alone, but on anybody who opposed them, along with all the Nazis

thought racially inferior (like Poles and Roma).

25. Kael's quote is referred to by David Denby as best evidence of her "almost comically obtuse negative review of the movie" in his January 10, 2011, review in the *The New Yorker* of Tomothy Snyder's Bloodlands, and the re-release of Shoah. Kael's original remarks appeared in *The New Yorker* in 1985, when Lanzmann's overblown snoozer first came out.
26. Godwin, Mike (January 12, 1995). *"Godwin's law of Nazi Analogies (and Corollaries)".* EFF.org. *Electronic Frontier Foundation.* Pp. "Net Culture—Humor" archive section. http.///www.eff.org/Net_culture/Folklore/Humor'godwins.law.Retrieved from a Wikipedia item May 18, 2010.
27. November 2007, STREIT UM SCHMIDT & POCHER Rettet das Nazometer! Henryk M. Broder, in *Der Spiegel* ("Conflict about Schmidt & Pocher: Save the Nazometer"). Retrieved from a Wikipedia item May 18, 2010.
28 Avraham Burg, *The Holocaust is Over, We Must Rise From its Ashes* (New York: Palgrave Macmillan, 2008), xiii.
29. Ibid., 4, 5 and 6.
30. Ibid., 8 and 9.
31. Ibid., 14.
32. Ibid., 14 and 15.
33. Ibid., 15 and 16.
34. Ibid., 23 and 24.
35. Hajo G. Meter, *The End of Judaism* (The Netherlands: Oscar van Gelderen, 2010), 122.
36. Ibid., 40.
37. The lives of the New Historians were changed forever after their work was published. Ilan Pappe left Israel, scorned by academics and regular citizens alike, who did not question his facts but were angry that he exposed things that most Israelis wanted to hide. Benny Morris quickly moved to the extreme political right, maintaining that the early Zionists did not dispossess enough Palestinians, and that many

more—perhaps millions—would have to be dispossessed in the future. He generally take positions similar to that of the Likud party, whose leaders probably wish he did not speak so openly and so publicly about the necessity for future ethnic cleansing of Palestinians if Israel is to remain a Jewish-majority state.

38. Philip Weiss, "Teaneck Harassment Trial Involves Pro-Palestinian Bumper Stickers," at *Mondoweiss, The War of Ideas in the Middle East*, posted May 25 2010, accessed May 27, 2010. www.Mondoweiss.net.
39. Peter Novick, The Holocaust in American Life (Boston, New York: Houghton Mifflin Company, A Mariner Book, 1999), 143-45.
40. Hajo G. Meyer, *The End of Judaism* (The Netherlands: Oscar van Gelderen, 2010), 187-88.
41. Avraham Burg, *The Holocaust is Over, We Must Rise From its Ashes* (New York: Palgrave Macmillan, 2008), 34-35.
42. Hajo G. Meter, *The End of Judaism* (The Netherlands: Oscar van Gelderen, 2010), 122.
43. Ibid., 40, 41 and 42.
44. 'Javits Center Architect Ties to Anti-Israel Group Merit Scrutiny', AJC Press Release, 2 March 2006. available http. //www.ajc.org/apps/ninet/content2.aspx?ITI2PHKoG&b=849241&ct=2020961. This press release in included in Abe Hayeem, "A Cautionary Tale," *A Time to Speak Out*, eds. Anne Karpf, Bring Klug, Jacqueline Rose, Barbara Rosenbaum (New York: Versobooks, 2008), 129.
45. Ibid., 125.
46. Brandon Davis, "The Politicalization of Judaism," *The Daily Princetonian*, October 10, 2010. C1

Circle is a symbol of infinity and unity. It's part of a growing list of imprints, including o-books.net and zero-books.net.

Circle Books aims to publish books in Christian spirituality that are fresh, accessible, and stimulating.

Our books are available in all good English language bookstores worldwide. If you can't find the book on the shelves, then ask your bookstore to order it for you, quoting the ISBN and title. Or, you can order online—all major online retail sites carry our titles.

To see our list of titles, please view www.Circle-Books.com, growing by 80 titles per year.

Authors can learn more about our proposal process by going to our website and clicking on Your Company > Submissions.

We define Christian spirituality as the relationship between the self and its sense of the transcendent or sacred, which issues in literary and artistic expression, community, social activism, and practices. A wide range of disciplines within the field of religious studies can be called upon, including history, narrative studies, philosophy, theology, sociology, and psychology. Interfaith in approach, Circle Books fosters creative dialogue with non-Christian traditions.

And tune into MySpiritRadio.com for our book review radio show, hosted by June-Elleni Laine, where you can listen to authors discussing their books.